Introduction to Data Mining

Introduction to Data Mining

Camila Thompson

CLANRYE
INTERNATIONAL
www.clanryeinternational.com

Clanrye International,
750 Third Avenue, 9ᵗʰ Floor,
New York, NY 10017, USA

ISBN: 978-1-64726-097-2

Cataloging-in-Publication Data

Introduction to data mining / Camila Thompson.
   p. cm.
Includes bibliographical references and index.
ISBN: 978-1-64726-097-2
1. Data mining. 2. Database searching. I. Thompson, Camila.
QA76.9.D343 I58 2022
006.312--dc23

For information on all Clanrye International publications
visit our website at www.clanryeinternational.com

Table of Contents

Preface

The purpose of this book is to help students understand the fundamental concepts of this discipline. It is designed to motivate students to learn and prosper. I am grateful for the support of my colleagues. I would also like to acknowledge the encouragement of my family.

Data mining is a process which deals with the discovery of patterns in large data sets. It applies methods from the fields of statistics, database systems and machine learning. Data mining aims to transform the information derived from a data set into a comprehensible structure for further use. Data mining also includes the data management aspects, complexity considerations, visualization, online updating, data pre-processing, model and inference considerations, and post-processing of discovered structures. It uses statistical models and machine-learning to uncover hidden patterns in a large volume of data. There are numerous fields where it is applied such as business, medicine, surveillance and science. This book aims to shed light on some of the unexplored aspects of data mining. Such selected concepts that redefine data mining have been presented herein. For someone with an interest and eye for detail, this book covers the most significant topics in this field.

A foreword for all the chapters is provided below:

Chapter – What is Data Mining?

The process of discovering patterns in large data sets using methods of machine learning, statistics, and database systems is called data mining. Some of the important tasks of data mining include data normalization and data integration. This is an introductory chapter which will introduce briefly all these significant aspects of data mining.

Chapter – Concepts of Data Mining

Many concepts and techniques are used for processing gathered data and information. Some of these include association rule learning, regression analysis, anomaly detection and binning. The topics elaborated in this chapter will help in gaining a better perspective about these concepts of data mining.

Chapter – Data Mining Algorithms

Data mining algorithm is a set of heuristics and calculations that creates a model from gathered data. A few of its algorithms are C4.5 algorithm, Apriori algorithm, k-nearest neighbors algorithm, etc. All these types of data mining algorithms have been carefully analyzed in this chapter.

Chapter – Cluster Analysis Method

Cluster analysis is a multivariate method to classify objects into different groups such that similar objects are placed in the same group. There are numerous methods that can be used to carry out cluster analysis such as consensus clustering, data stream clustering, hierarchical clustering, etc. This chapter discusses in detail these methods related to cluster analysis.

Chapter – Applications of Data Mining

Data Mining is widely used in various areas such as agriculture, fraud detection, healthcare sector, marketing intelligence and bioinformatics. This chapter has been carefully written to provide an easy understanding of these applications of data mining.

Chapter – Data Mining Softwares

There are many popular data mining tools and software which assist in data preparation, modeling, evaluation and deployment. A few such software are rapid miner, KNIME, SPSS Modeler, etc. The topics elaborated in this chapter will help in gaining a better perspective about these data mining software.

Camila Thompson

1
What is Data Mining?

The process of discovering patterns in large data sets using methods of machine learning, statistics, and database systems is called data mining. Some of the important tasks of data mining include data normalization and data integration. This is an introductory chapter which will introduce briefly all these significant aspects of data mining.

Data

A data set is a collection of information organized as a stream of bytes in logical record and block structures for use by IBM mainframe operating systems. The record format is determined by data set organization, record format and other parameters.

The physical structure of each record is nearly the same, and uniform throughout a data set. This is specified in the data control block record format parameter. The fixed-length records eliminate the need for any delimiter byte value for separate records. This means the data may be of any type (binary, floating point or characters) without using a false end-of-record condition.

The alternative to a data set is files, which are an unstructured stream of bytes that are favored by Unix, Windows and Mac OS. A data set typically contains a specific type of data such as names, salaries and sales data that are all numerical and fixed-format. In contrast, files may contain a wide variety of data types, such as text, graphics, audio data and video data which will be of variable format.

Data sets can be organized into a partitioned data set which may hold multiple members that each contain a separate sub-data set. This style of organization is similar to files being organized into directories or folders. PDSs are often used for executable programs and source program libraries. A PDS is analogous to a zip file in a file system, but the data is not compressed.

Types of Sources of Data

The data from multiple sources are integrated into a common source known as Data Warehouse.

- Flat Files:
    - Flat files is defined as data files in text form or binary form with a structure that can be easily extracted by data mining algorithms.

- ○ Data stored in flat files have no relationship or path among themselves, like if a relational database is stored on flat file, then there will be no relations between the tables.

- ○ Flat files are represented by data dictionary. Eg: CSV file.

- ○ Application: Used in Data warehousing to store data, Used in carrying data to and from server, etc.

- Relational Databases:

  - ○ A Relational database is defined as the collection of data organized in tables with rows and columns.

  - ○ Physical schema in Relational databases is a schema which defines the structure of tables.

  - ○ Logical schema in Relational databases is a schema which defines the relationship among tables.

  - ○ Standard API of relational database is SQL.

  - ○ Application: Data Mining, ROLAP model, etc.

- Data warehouse:

  - ○ A Data warehouse is defined as the collection of data integrated from multiple sources that will queries and decision making.

  - ○ There are three types of Data warehouse: Enterprise Data warehouse, Data Mart and Virtual Warehouse.

  - ○ Two approaches can be used to update data in Data warehouse: Query-driven Approach and Update-driven Approach.

  - ○ Application: Business decision making, Data mining, etc.

- Transactional Databases:

  - ○ Transactional databases is a collection of data organized by time stamps, date, etc to represent transaction in databases.

  - ○ This type of database has the capability to roll back or undo its operation when a transaction is not completed or committed.

  - ○ Highly flexible system where users can modify information without changing any sensitive information.

  - ○ Follows ACID property of DBMS.

  - ○ Application: Banking, Distributed systems, Object databases, etc.

- Multimedia Databases:

  - ○ Multimedia databases consists audio, video, images and text media.

  - ○ They can be stored on Object-oriented Databases.

  - ○ They are used to store complex information in a pre-specified formats.

- ◦ Application: Digital libraries, video-on demand news-on demand musical database, etc.
- Spatial Database:
  - ◦ Store geographical information.
  - ◦ Stores data in the form of coordinates, topology, lines, polygons, etc.
  - ◦ Application: Maps, Global positioning, etc.
- Time-series Databases:
  - ◦ Time series databases contains stock exchange data and user logged activities.
  - ◦ Handles array of numbers indexed by time, date, etc.
  - ◦ It requires real-time analysis.
  - ◦ Application: eXtremeDB, Graphite, InfluxDB, etc.
- WWW:
  - ◦ WWW refers to World wide web is a collection of documents and resources like audio, video, text, etc which are identified by Uniform Resource Locators (URLs) through web browsers, linked by HTML pages, and accessible via the Internet network.
  - ◦ It is the most heterogeneous repository as it collects data from multiple resources.
  - ◦ It is dynamic in nature as Volume of data is continuously increasing and changing.
  - ◦ Application: Online shopping, Job search, Research, studying, etc.

Data Mining

Data mining is looking for hidden, valid, and potentially useful patterns in huge data sets. Data Mining is all about discovering unsuspected/ previously unknown relationships amongst the data. It is a multi-disciplinary skill that uses machine learning, statistics, AI and database technology.

The insights derived via Data Mining can be used for marketing, fraud detection, and scientific discovery, etc.

Data mining is also called as Knowledge discovery, Knowledge extraction, data/pattern analysis, information harvesting, etc.

Types of Data

Data mining can be performed on following types of data:

- Relational databases.
- Data warehouses.
- Advanced DB and information repositories.

- Object-oriented and object-relational databases.

- Transactional and Spatial databases.

- Heterogeneous and legacy databases.

- Multimedia and streaming database.

- Text databases.

- Text mining and Web mining.

Data Mining Implementation Process

Business Understanding

In this phase, business and data-mining goals are established.

- First, you need to understand business and client objectives. You need to define what your client wants (which many times even they do not know themselves).

- Take stock of the current data mining scenario. Factor in resources, assumption, constraints, and other significant factors into your assessment.

- Using business objectives and current scenario, define your data mining goals.

- A good data mining plan is very detailed and should be developed to accomplish both business and data mining goals.

Data Understanding

In this phase, sanity check on data is performed to check whether its appropriate for the data mining goals.

- First, data is collected from multiple data sources available in the organization.

- These data sources may include multiple databases, flat filer or data cubes. There are issues like object matching and schema integration which can arise during Data Integration process. It is a quite complex and tricky process as data from various sources unlikely to match easily. For example, table A contains an entity named cust-no whereas another table B contains an entity named cust-id.

- Therefore, it is quite difficult to ensure that both of these given objects refer to the same value or not. Here, Metadata should be used to reduce errors in the data integration process.

- Next, the step is to search for properties of acquired data. A good way to explore the data is to answer the data mining questions (decided in business phase) using the query, reporting, and visualization tools.

- Based on the results of query, the data quality should be ascertained. Missing data if any should be acquired.

Data Preparation

In this phase, data is made production ready. The data preparation process consumes about 90% of the time of the project.

The data from different sources should be selected, cleaned, transformed, formatted, anonymized, and constructed (if required). Data cleaning is a process to "clean" the data by smoothing noisy data and filling in missing values.

For example, for a customer demographics profile, age data is missing. The data is incomplete and should be filled. In some cases, there could be data outliers. For instance, age has a value 300. Data could be inconsistent. For instance, name of the customer is different in different tables.

Data transformation operations change the data to make it useful in data mining. Following transformation can be applied:

Data Transformation

Data transformation operations would contribute toward the success of the mining process:

- Smoothing: It helps to remove noise from the data.

- Aggregation: Aggregation operations are applied to the data, i.e., the weekly sales data is aggregated to calculate the monthly and yearly total.

- Generalization: In this step, Low-level data is replaced by higher-level concepts with the help of concept hierarchies. For example, the city is replaced by the county.

- Normalization: Normalization performed when the attribute data are scaled up o scaled down. Example: Data should fall in the range -2.0 to 2.0 post-normalization.

- Attribute construction: these attributes are constructed and included the given set of attributes helpful for data mining.

The result of this process is a final data set that can be used in modeling.

Modeling

In this phase, mathematical models are used to determine data patterns.

- Based on the business objectives, suitable modeling techniques should be selected for the prepared dataset.

- Create a scenario to test check the quality and validity of the model.

- Run the model on the prepared dataset.

- Results should be assessed by all stakeholders to make sure that model can meet data mining objectives.

Evaluation

In this phase, patterns identified are evaluated against the business objectives.

- Results generated by the data mining model should be evaluated against the business objectives.

- Gaining business understanding is an iterative process. In fact, while understanding, new business requirements may be raised because of data mining.

- A go or no-go decision is taken to move the model in the deployment phase.

Deployment

In the deployment phase, you ship your data mining discoveries to everyday business operations.

- The knowledge or information discovered during data mining process should be made easy to understand for non-technical stakeholders.

- A detailed deployment plan, for shipping, maintenance, and monitoring of data mining discoveries is created.

- A final project report is created with lessons learned and key experiences during the project. This helps to improve the organization's business policy.

Data Mining Techniques

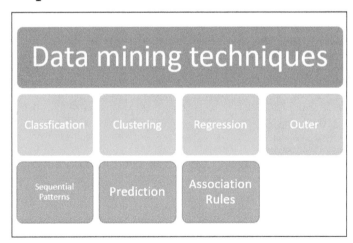

Classification

This analysis is used to retrieve important and relevant information about data, and metadata. This data mining method helps to classify data in different classes.

Clustering

Clustering analysis is a data mining technique to identify data that are like each other. This process helps to understand the differences and similarities between the data.

Regression

Regression analysis is the data mining method of identifying and analyzing the relationship between variables. It is used to identify the likelihood of a specific variable, given the presence of other variables.

Association Rules

This data mining technique helps to find the association between two or more Items. It discovers a hidden pattern in the data set.

Outer Detection

This type of data mining technique refers to observation of data items in the dataset which do not match an expected pattern or expected behavior. This technique can be used in a variety of domains, such as intrusion, detection, fraud or fault detection, etc. Outer detection is also called Outlier Analysis or Outlier mining.

Sequential Patterns

This data mining technique helps to discover or identify similar patterns or trends in transaction data for certain period.

Prediction

Prediction has used a combination of the other data mining techniques like trends, sequential patterns, clustering, classification, etc. It analyzes past events or instances in a right sequence for predicting a future event.

Challenges of Implementation of Data Mine

- Skilled Experts are needed to formulate the data mining queries.
- Overfitting: Due to small size training database, a model may not fit future states.
- Data mining needs large databases which sometimes are difficult to manage
- Business practices may need to be modified to determine to use the information uncovered.
- If the data set is not diverse, data mining results may not be accurate.
- Integration information needed from heterogeneous databases and global information systems could be complex.

Data Mining Examples

Example: Consider a marketing head of telecom service provides who wants to increase revenues of long distance services. For high ROI on his sales and marketing efforts customer profiling is important. He has a vast data pool of customer information like age, gender, income, credit history, etc. But its impossible to determine characteristics of people who prefer long distance calls with manual analysis. Using data mining techniques, he may uncover patterns between high long distance call users and their characteristics.

For example, he might learn that his best customers are married females between the age of 45 and 54 who make more than $80,000 per year. Marketing efforts can be targeted to such demographic.

Example: A bank wants to search new ways to increase revenues from its credit card operations. They want to check whether usage would double if fees were halved.

Bank has multiple years of record on average credit card balances, payment amounts, credit limit usage, and other key parameters. They create a model to check the impact of the proposed new business policy. The data results show that cutting fees in half for a targetted customer base could increase revenues by $10 million.

Data Mining Tools

Following are 2 popular data mining tools widely used in industry:

- R-language: R language is an open source tool for statistical computing and graphics. R has a wide variety of statistical, classical statistical tests, time-series analysis, classification and graphical techniques. It offers effective data handing and storage facility.

- Oracle Data Mining: Oracle Data Mining popularly knowns as ODM is a module of the Oracle Advanced Analytics Database. This Data mining tool allows data analysts to generate detailed insights and makes predictions. It helps predict customer behavior, develops customer profiles, identifies cross-selling opportunities.

Benefits of Data Mining

- Data mining technique helps companies to get knowledge-based information.

- Data mining helps organizations to make the profitable adjustments in operation and production.

- The data mining is a cost-effective and efficient solution compared to other statistical data applications.

- Data mining helps with the decision-making process.

- Facilitates automated prediction of trends and behaviors as well as automated discovery of hidden patterns.

- It can be implemented in new systems as well as existing platforms.

- It is the speedy process which makes it easy for the users to analyze huge amount of data in less time.

Disadvantages of Data Mining

- There are chances of companies may sell useful information of their customers to other companies for money.

- Many data mining analytics software is difficult to operate and requires advance training to work on.

- Different data mining tools work in different manners due to different algorithms employed in their design. Therefore, the selection of correct data mining tool is a very difficult task.

- The data mining techniques are not accurate, and so it can cause serious consequences in certain conditions.

Data Mining Applications

Here is the list of areas where data mining is widely used:

- Financial Data Analysis.

- Retail Industry.

- Telecommunication Industry.

- Biological Data Analysis.

- Other Scientific Applications.

- Intrusion Detection.

Financial Data Analysis

The financial data in banking and financial industry is generally reliable and of high quality which facilitates systematic data analysis and data mining. Some of the typical cases are as follows:

- Design and construction of data warehouses for multidimensional data analysis and data mining.

- Loan payment prediction and customer credit policy analysis.

- Classification and clustering of customers for targeted marketing.

- Detection of money laundering and other financial crimes.

Retail Industry

Data Mining has its great application in Retail Industry because it collects large amount of data from on sales, customer purchasing history, goods transportation, consumption and services. It is natural that the quantity of data collected will continue to expand rapidly because of the increasing ease, availability and popularity of the web.

Data mining in retail industry helps in identifying customer buying patterns and trends that lead to improved quality of customer service and good customer retention and satisfaction. Here is the list of examples of data mining in the retail industry:

- Design and Construction of data warehouses based on the benefits of data mining.

- Multidimensional analysis of sales, customers, products, time and region.

- Analysis of effectiveness of sales campaigns.

- Customer Retention.

- Product recommendation and cross-referencing of items.

Telecommunication Industry

Today the telecommunication industry is one of the most emerging industries providing various services such as fax, pager, cellular phone, internet messenger, images, e-mail, web data transmission, etc. Due to the development of new computer and communication technologies, the telecommunication industry is rapidly expanding. This is the reason why data mining is become very important to help and understand the business.

Data mining in telecommunication industry helps in identifying the telecommunication patterns, catch fraudulent activities, make better use of resource, and improve quality of service. Here is the list of examples for which data mining improves telecommunication services:

- Multidimensional analysis of telecommunication data.

- Fraudulent pattern analysis.

- Identification of unusual patterns.

- Multidimensional association and sequential patterns analysis.

- Mobile telecommunication services.

- Use of visualization tools in telecommunication data analysis.

Biological Data Analysis

In recent times, we have seen a tremendous growth in the field of biology such as genomics, proteomics, functional genomics and biomedical research. Biological data mining is a very important part of Bioinformatics. Following are the aspects in which data mining contributes for biological data analysis:

- Semantic integration of heterogeneous, distributed genomic and proteomic databases.

- Alignment, indexing, similarity search and comparative analysis multiple nucleotide sequences.

- Discovery of structural patterns and analysis of genetic networks and protein pathways.

- Association and path analysis.

- Visualization tools in genetic data analysis.

Other Scientific Applications

The applications tend to handle relatively small and homogeneous data sets for which the statistical techniques are appropriate. Huge amount of data have been collected from scientific domains such as geosciences, astronomy, etc. A large amount of data sets is being generated because of the fast numerical simulations in various fields such as climate and ecosystem modeling, chemical engineering, fluid dynamics, etc. Following are the applications of data mining in the field of Scientific Applications:

- Data warehouses and data preprocessing.

- Graph-based mining.

- Visualization and domain specific knowledge.

Intrusion Detection

Intrusion refers to any kind of action that threatens integrity, confidentiality, or the availability of network resources. In this world of connectivity, security has become the major issue. With increased usage of internet and availability of the tools and tricks for intruding and attacking network prompted intrusion detection to become a critical component of network administration. Here is the list of areas in which data mining technology may be applied for intrusion detection:

- Development of data mining algorithm for intrusion detection.

- Association and correlation analysis, aggregation to help select and build discriminating attributes.

- Analysis of stream data.

- Distributed data mining.

- Visualization and query tools.

Data Mining System Products

There are many data mining system products and domain specific data mining applications. The new data mining systems and applications are being added to the previous systems. Also, efforts are being made to standardize data mining languages.

Choosing a Data Mining System

The selection of a data mining system depends on the following features:

- Data Types: The data mining system may handle formatted text, record-based data, and relational data. The data could also be in ASCII text, relational database data or data warehouse data. Therefore, we should check what exact format the data mining system can handle.

- System Issues: We must consider the compatibility of a data mining system with different operating systems. One data mining system may run on only one operating system or on several. There are also data mining systems that provide web-based user interfaces and allow XML data as input.

- Data Sources: Data sources refer to the data formats in which data mining system will operate. Some data mining system may work only on ASCII text files while others on multiple relational sources. Data mining system should also support ODBC connections or OLE DB for ODBC connections.

- Data Mining functions and methodologies: There are some data mining systems that provide only one data mining function such as classification while some provides multiple data mining functions such as concept description, discovery-driven OLAP analysis, association mining, linkage analysis, statistical analysis, classification, prediction, clustering, outlier analysis, similarity search, etc.

- Coupling data mining with databases or data warehouse systems: Data mining systems need to be coupled with a database or a data warehouse system. The coupled components are integrated into a uniform information processing environment. Here are the types of coupling listed below:

  ◦ No coupling,

  ◦ Loose Coupling,

  ◦ Semi tight Coupling,

  ◦ Tight Coupling.

- Scalability – There are two scalability issues in data mining:

  ◦ Row (Database size) Scalability: A data mining system is considered as row scalable when the number or rows are enlarged 10 times. It takes no more than 10 times to execute a query.

  ◦ Column (Dimension) Scalability: A data mining system is considered as column scalable if the mining query execution time increases linearly with the number of columns.

- Visualization Tools – Visualization in data mining can be categorized as follows:

  ◦ Data Visualization,

  ◦ Mining Results Visualization,

  ◦ Mining process visualization,

  ◦ Visual data mining.

- Data Mining query language and graphical user interface – An easy-to-use graphical user interface is important to promote user-guided, interactive data mining. Unlike relational database systems, data mining systems do not share underlying data mining query language.

Trends in Data Mining

Data mining concepts are still evolving and here are the latest trends that we get to see in this field:

- Application exploration.

- Scalable and interactive data mining methods.

- Integration of data mining with database systems, data warehouse systems and web database systems.

- Standardization of data mining query language.

- Visual data mining.

- New methods for mining complex types of data.

- Biological data mining.

- Data mining and software engineering.

- Web mining.

- Distributed data mining.

- Real time data mining.

- Multi database data mining.

- Privacy protection and information security in data mining.

Tasks of Data Mining

Data mining deals with the kind of patterns that can be mined. On the basis of the kind of data to be mined, there are two categories of functions involved in Data Mining:

- Descriptive.

- Classification and Prediction.

Descriptive Function

The descriptive function deals with the general properties of data in the database. Here is the list of descriptive functions:

- Class/Concept Description,

- Mining of Frequent Patterns,

- Mining of Associations,

- Mining of Correlations,

- Mining of Clusters.

Class or Concept Description

Class/Concept refers to the data to be associated with the classes or concepts. For example, in a company, the classes of items for sales include computer and printers, and concepts of customers include big spenders and budget spenders. Such descriptions of a class or a concept are called class/concept descriptions. These descriptions can be derived by the following two ways:

- Data Characterization – This refers to summarizing data of class under study. This class under study is called as Target Class.

- Data Discrimination – It refers to the mapping or classification of a class with some predefined group or class.

Mining of Frequent Patterns

Frequent patterns are those patterns that occur frequently in transactional data. Here is the list of kind of frequent patterns:

- Frequent Item Set – It refers to a set of items that frequently appear together, for example, milk and bread.

- Frequent Subsequence – A sequence of patterns that occur frequently such as purchasing a camera is followed by memory card.

- Frequent Sub Structure – Substructure refers to different structural forms, such as graphs, trees, or lattices, which may be combined with item-sets or subsequences.

Mining of Association

Associations are used in retail sales to identify patterns that are frequently purchased together. This process refers to the process of uncovering the relationship among data and determining association rules.

For example, a retailer generates an association rule that shows that 70% of time milk is sold with bread and only 30% of times biscuits are sold with bread.

Mining of Correlations

It is a kind of additional analysis performed to uncover interesting statistical correlations between associated-attribute-value pairs or between two item sets to analyze that if they have positive, negative or no effect on each other.

Mining of Clusters

Cluster refers to a group of similar kind of objects. Cluster analysis refers to forming group of objects that are very similar to each other but are highly different from the objects in other clusters.

Classification and Prediction

Classification is the process of finding a model that describes the data classes or concepts. The purpose is to be able to use this model to predict the class of objects whose class label is unknown. This derived model is based on the analysis of sets of training data. The derived model can be presented in the following forms:

- Classification (IF-THEN) Rules.

- Decision Trees.

- Mathematical Formulae.

- Neural Networks.

The list of functions involved in these processes are as follows:

- Classification – It predicts the class of objects whose class label is unknown. Its objective is to find a derived model that describes and distinguishes data classes or concepts. The Derived Model is based on the analysis set of training data i.e. the data object whose class label is well known.

- Prediction – It is used to predict missing or unavailable numerical data values rather than class labels. Regression Analysis is generally used for prediction. Prediction can also be used for identification of distribution trends based on available data.

- Outlier Analysis – Outliers may be defined as the data objects that do not comply with the general behavior or model of the data available.

- Evolution Analysis – Evolution analysis refers to the description and model regularities or trends for objects whose behavior changes over time.

Data Mining Task Primitives

- We can specify a data mining task in the form of a data mining query.

- This query is input to the system.

- A data mining query is defined in terms of data mining task primitives.

These primitives allow us to communicate in an interactive manner with the data mining system. Here is the list of data mining task primitives:

- Set of task relevant data to be mined.

- Kind of knowledge to be mined.

- Background knowledge to be used in discovery process.

- Interestingness measures and thresholds for pattern evaluation.

- Representation for visualizing the discovered patterns.

Set of Task Relevant Data to be Mined

This is the portion of database in which the user is interested. This portion includes the following –

- Database Attributes.

- Data Warehouse dimensions of interest.

Kind of Knowledge to be Mined

It refers to the kind of functions to be performed. These functions are:

- Characterization,
- Discrimination,
- Association and Correlation Analysis,
- Classification,
- Prediction,
- Clustering,
- Outlier Analysis,
- Evolution Analysis.

Background Knowledge

The background knowledge allows data to be mined at multiple levels of abstraction. For example, the concept hierarchies are one of the background knowledge that allows data to be mined at multiple levels of abstraction.

Interestingness Measures and Thresholds for Pattern Evaluation

This is used to evaluate the patterns that are discovered by the process of knowledge discovery. There are different interesting measures for different kind of knowledge.

Representation for Visualizing the Discovered Patterns

This refers to the form in which discovered patterns are to be displayed. These representations may include the following:

- Rules,
- Tables,
- Charts,
- Graphs,
- Decision Trees,
- Cubes.

Data Normalization in Data Mining

Normalization is used to scale the data of an attribute so that it falls in a smaller range, such as -1.0 to 1.0 or 0.0 to 1.0. It is generally useful for classification algorithms.

Need of Normalization

Normalization is generally required when we are dealing with attributes on a different scale, otherwise, it may lead to a dilution in effectiveness of an important equally important attribute (on lower scale) because of other attribute having values on larger scale.

In simple words, when multiple attributes are there but attributes have values on different scales, this may lead to poor data models while performing data mining operations. So they are normalized to bring all the attributes on the same scale.

Person Name	Salary	Year of Experience	Expected Position Level
Aman	100000	10	2
Abhinav	78000	7	4
Ashutosh	32000	5	8
Dishi	55000	6	7
Abhishek	92000	8	3
Avantlka	120000	15	1
Ayushi	65750	7	5

The attributes salary and year of experience are on different scale and hence attribute salary can take high priority over attribute year of experience in the model.

Methods of Data Normalization

- Decimal Scaling,

- Min-max normalization,

- Z-score normalization (zero-mean normalization).

Decimal Scaling Method for Normalization

It normalizes by moving the decimal point of values of the data. To normalize the data by this technique, we divide each value of the data by the maximum absolute value of data. The data value, v_i, of data is normalized to v_i' by using the formula below,

$$v_i' = \frac{v_i}{10^j}$$

where j is the smallest integer such that max $(|v_i'|)<1$.

Example:

Let the input data is: -10, 201, 301, -401, 501, 601, 701.

To normalize the above data,

Step 1: Maximum absolute value in given data(m): 701.

Step 2: Divide the given data by 1000 (j = 3).

Result: The normalized data is: -0.01, 0.201, 0.301, -0.401, 0.501, 0.601, 0.701.

Min-max Normalization

In this technique of data normalization, linear transformation is performed on the original data. Minimum and maximum value from data is fetched and each value is replaced according to the following formula,

$$v' = \frac{v - \min(A)}{\max(A) - \min(A)}(\text{new\_max}(A) - \text{new\_min}(A)) + \text{new\_min}(A)$$

where A is the attribute data,

Min(A), Max(A) are the minimum and maximum absolute value of A respectively.

v' is the new value of each entry in data.

v is the old value of each entry in data.

new_max(A), new_min(A) is the max and min value of the range(i.e boundary value of range required) respectively.

Z-score Normalization

In this technique, values are normalized based on mean and standard deviation of the data A. The formula used is:

$$v' = \frac{v - \bar{A}}{\sigma_A}$$

v', v is the new and old of each entry in data respectively. σ_A, A is the standard deviation and mean of A respectively.

Data Integration in Data Mining

Data Integration is a data preprocessing technique that involves combining data from multiple heterogeneous data sources into a coherent data store and provide a unified view of the data. These sources may include multiple data cubes, databases or flat files.

The data integration approach are formally defined as triple <G, S, M>. Where,

- G stand for the global schema,
- S stand for heterogenous source of schema,
- M stand for mapping between the queries of source and global schema.

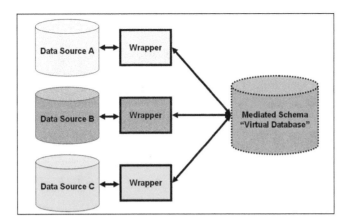

There are mainly 2 major approaches for data integration – one is "tight coupling approach" and another is "loose coupling approach".

Tight Coupling

- Here, a data warehouse is treated as an information retrieval component.

- In this coupling, data is combined from different sources into a single physical location through the process of ETL – Extraction, Transformation and Loading.

Loose Coupling

- Here, an interface is provided that takes the query from the user, transforms it in a way the source database can understand and then sends the query directly to the source databases to obtain the result.

- And the data only remains in the actual source databases.

Issues in Data Integration

There are no of issues to consider during data integration: Schema Integration, Redundancy, Detection and resolution of data value conflicts.

Schema Integration

- Integrate metadata from different sources.

- The real world entities from multiple source be matched referred to as the entity identification problem.

For example, how can the data analyst and computer be sure that customer id in one data base and customer number in another reference to the same attribute.

Redundancy

- An attribute may be redundant if it can be derived or obtaining from another attribute or set of attribute.

- Inconsistencies in attribute can also cause redundanciesin the resulting data set.

- Some redundancies can be detected by correlation analysis.

Detection and Resolution of Data value Conflicts

- This is the third important issues in data integration.

- Attribute values from another different sources may differ for the same real world entity.

- An attribute in one system may be recorded at a lower level abstraction then the "same" attribute in another.

Sequential Pattern Mining

Data mining consists of extracting information from data stored in databases to understand the data and take decisions. Some of the most fundamental data mining tasks are clustering, classification, outlier analysis, and pattern mining. Pattern mining consists of discovering interesting, useful, and unexpected patterns in databases. Various types of patterns can be discovered in databases such as frequent itemsets, associations, subgraphs, sequential rules, and periodic patterns.

The task of sequential pattern mining is a data mining task specialized for analyzing sequential data, to discover sequential patterns. More precisely, it consists of discovering interesting subsequences in a set of sequences, where the interestingness of a subsequence can be measured in terms of various criteria such as its occurrence frequency, length, and profit. Sequential pattern mining has numerous real-life applications due to the fact that data is naturally encoded as sequences of symbols in many fields such as bioinformatics, e-learning, market basket analysis, texts, and webpage click-stream analysis.

Consider the following sequence database, representing the purchases made by customers in a retail store.

SID	Sequence
1	$\langle \{a,b\},\{c\},\{f,g\},\{g\},\{e\} \rangle$
2	$\langle \{a,d\},\{c\},\{b\},\{a,b,e,f\} \rangle$
3	$\langle \{a,\},\{b\},\{f,g\}\{e\} \rangle$
4	$\langle \{b\},\{f,g\} \rangle$

This database contains four sequences. Each sequence represents the items purchased by a customer at different times. A sequence is an ordered list of itemsets (sets of items bought together). For example, in this database, the first sequence (SID 1) indicates that a customer bought some items a and b together, then purchased an item c, then purchased items f and g together, then purchased an item g, and then finally purchased an item e.

Traditionally, sequential pattern mining is being used to find subsequences that appear often in a sequence database, i.e. that are common to several sequences. Those subsequences are called the frequent sequential patterns. For example, in the context of our example, sequential pattern mining can be used to find the sequences of items frequently bought by customers. This can be useful to understand the behavior of customers to take marketing decisions.

To do sequential pattern mining, a user must provide a sequence database and specify a parameter called the minimum support threshold. This parameter indicates a minimum number of sequences in which a pattern must appear to be considered frequent, and be shown to the user. For example, if a user sets the minimum support threshold to 2 sequences, the task of sequential pattern mining consists of finding all subsequences appearing in at least 2 sequences of the input database. In the example database, 30 subsequences met this requirement. These sequential patterns are shown in the table, where the number of sequences containing each pattern (called the *support*) is indicated in the right column of the table.

Pattern	Sup.
$\langle\{a\}\rangle$	3
$\langle\{a\},\{g\}\rangle$	2
$\langle\{a\},\{g\},\{e\}\rangle$	2
$\langle\{a\},\{f\}\rangle$	3
$\langle\{a\},\{f\},\{e\}\rangle$	2
$\langle\{a\},\{c\}\rangle$	2
$\langle\{a\},\{c\},\{f\}\rangle$	2
$\langle\{a\},\{c\},\{e\}\rangle$	2
$\langle\{a\},\{b\}\rangle$	2
$\langle\{a\},\{b\},\{f\}\rangle$	2
$\langle\{a\},\{b\},\{f\}\rangle$	2
$\langle\{a\},\{e\}\rangle$	3
$\langle\{a,b\}\rangle$	2
$\langle\{b\}\rangle$	4

Pattern	Sup.
$\langle\{b\},\{g\}\rangle$	3
$\langle\{b\},\{g\},\{e\}\rangle$	2
$\langle\{b\},\{f\}\rangle$	4
$\langle\{b\},\{f,g\}\rangle$	3
$\langle\{b\},\{f\},\{e\}\rangle$	2
$\langle\{b\},\{e\}\rangle$	3
$\langle\{c\}\rangle$	2
$\langle\{c\},\{f\}\rangle$	2
$\langle\{c\},\{e\}\rangle$	2
$\langle\{e\}\rangle$	3
$\langle\{f\}\rangle$	4
$\langle\{f,g\}\rangle$	3
$\langle\{f\},\{e\}\rangle$	2
$\langle\{g\}\rangle$	3
$\langle\{g\},\{e\}\rangle$	2

For example, the patterns <{a}> and <{a}, {g}> are frequent and have a support of 3 and 2 sequences, respectively. In other words, these patterns appears in 3 and 2 sequences of the input database, respectively. The pattern <{a}> appears in the sequences 1, 2 and 3, while the pattern <{a}, {g}> appears in sequences 1 and 3. These patterns are interesting as they represent some behavior common to several customers. Of course, this is a toy example. Sequential pattern mining can actually be applied on database containing hundreds of thousands of sequences.

Another example of application of sequential pattern mining is text analysis. In this context, a set of sentences from a text can be viewed as sequence database, and the goal of sequential pattern mining is then to find subsequences of words frequently used in the text. If such sequences are contiguous, they are called "ngrams" in this context.

Can Sequential Pattern Mining be applied to Time Series?

Besides sequences, sequential pattern mining can also be applied to time series (e.g. stock data), when discretization is performed as a pre-processing step. For example, the figure shows a time series (an ordered list of numbers) on the left. On the right, a sequence (a sequence of symbols) is shown representing the same data, after applying a transformation. Various transformations can be done to transform a time series to a sequence such as the popular SAX transformation. After performing the transformation, any sequential pattern mining algorithm can be applied.

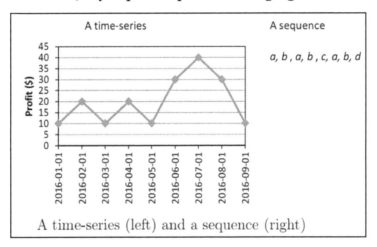

A time-series (left) and a sequence (right)

Sequential Pattern Mining Implementations

To try sequential pattern mining with your datasets, you may try the open-source SPMF data mining software, which provides implementations of numerous sequential pattern mining algorithms. It provides implementations of several algorithms for sequential pattern mining, as well as several variations of the problem such as discovering maximal sequential patterns, closed sequential patterns and sequential rules. Sequential rules are especially useful for the purpose of performing predictions, as they also include the concept of confidence.

Algorithms for Sequential Pattern Mining

There exists several sequential pattern mining algorithms. Some of the classic algorithms for this problem are PrefixSpan, Spade, SPAM, and GSP. However, in the recent decade, several novel and more efficient algorithms have been proposed such as CM-SPADE and CM-SPAM, FCloSM and FGenSM, to name a few. Besides, numerous algorithms have been proposed for extensions of the problem of sequential pattern mining such as finding the sequential patterns that generate the most profit (high utility sequential pattern mining).

Major Issues

Mining Methodology and User-interaction Issues

These reect the kinds of knowledge mined, the ability to mine knowledge at multiple granularities, the use of domain knowledge, ad-hoc mining, and knowledge visualization.

Mining Different kinds of Knowledge in Databases

Since different users can be interested in different kinds of knowledge, data mining should cover a wide spectrum of data analysis and knowledge discovery tasks, including data characterization, discrimination, association, classification, clustering, trend and deviation analysis, and similarity analysis. These tasks may use the same database in different ways and require the development of numerous data mining techniques.

Interactive Mining of Knowledge at Multiple Levels of Abstraction

Since it is difficult to know exactly what can be discovered within a database, the data mining process should be interactive. For databases containing a huge amount of data, appropriate sampling technique can first be applied to facilitate interactive data exploration. Interactive mining allows users to focus the search for patterns, providing and refining data mining requests based on returned results. Specifically, knowledge should be mined by drilling-down, rolling-up, and pivoting through the data space and knowledge space interactively, similar to what OLAP can do on data cubes. In this way, the user can interact with the data mining system to view data and discovered patterns at multiple granularities and from different angles.

Incorporation of Background Knowledge

Background knowledge, or information regarding the domain under study, may be used to guide the discovery process and allow discovered patterns to be expressed in concise terms and at different levels of abstraction. Domain knowledge related to databases, such as integrity constraints and deduction rules, can help focus and speed up a data mining process, or judge the interestingness of discovered patterns.

Data Mining Query Languages and Ad-hoc Data Mining

Relational query languages (such as SQL) allow users to pose ad-hoc queries for data retrieval. In a similar vein, high-level data mining query languages need to be developed to allow users to describe ad-hoc data mining tasks by facilitating the specification of the relevant sets of data for analysis, the domain knowledge, the kinds of knowledge to be mined, and the conditions and interestingness constraints to be enforced on the discovered patterns. Such a language should be integrated with a database or data warehouse query language, and optimized for efficient and exible data mining.

Presentation and Visualization of Data Mining Results

Discovered knowledge should be expressed in high-level languages, visual representations, or other expressive forms so that the knowledge can be easily understood and directly usable by humans. This is especially crucial if the data mining system is to be interactive. This requires the system to adopt expressive knowledge representation techniques, such as trees, tables, rules, graphs, charts, crosstabs, matrices, or curves.

Handling Outlier or Incomplete Data

The data stored in a database may reject outliers noise, exceptional cases, or incomplete data objects. These objects may confuse the analysis process, causing overfitting of the data to the knowledge model constructed. As a result, the accuracy of the discovered patterns can be poor. Data cleaning methods and data analysis methods which can handle outliers are required. While most methods discard outlier data, such data may be of interest in itself such as in fraud detection for Finding unusual usage of tele-communication services or credit cards. This form of data analysis is known as outlier mining.

Pattern Evaluation: The Interestingness Problem

A data mining system can uncover thousands of patterns. Many of the patterns discovered may be uninteresting to the given user, representing common knowledge or lacking novelty. Several challenges remain regarding the development of techniques to assess the interestingness of discovered patterns, particularly with regard to subjective measures which estimate the value of patterns with respect to a given user class, based on user beliefs or expectations. The use of interestingness measures to guide the discovery process and reduce the search space is another active area of research.

Performance Issues

These include efficiency, scalability, and parallelization of data mining algorithms.

Efficiency and Scalability of Data Mining Algorithms

To effectively extract information from a huge amount of data in databases, data mining algorithms must be efficient and scalable. That is, the running time of a data mining algorithm must be predictable and acceptable in large databases. Algorithms with exponential or even medium-order polynomial complexity will not be of practical use. From a database perspective on knowledge discovery, efficiency and scalability are key issues in the implementation of data mining systems. Many of the issues discussed above under mining methodology and user-interaction must also consider efficiency and scalability.

Parallel, Distributed and Incremental Updating Algorithms

The huge size of many databases, the wide distribution of data, and the computational complexity of some data mining methods are factors motivating the development of parallel and distributed data mining algorithms. Such algorithms divide the data into partitions, which are processed in parallel. The results from the partitions are then merged. Moreover, the high cost of some data mining processes promotes the need for incremental data mining algorithms which incorporate database updates without having to mine the entire data again "from scratch". Such algorithms perform knowledge modification incrementally to amend and strengthen what was previously discovered.

Issues Relating to the Diversity of Database Types

Handling of Relational and Complex Types of Data

There are many kinds of data stored in databases and data warehouses. Since relational databases and data warehouses are widely used, the development of efficient and effective data mining systems for such data is important. However, other databases may contain complex data objects, hypertext and multimedia data, spatial data, temporal data, or transaction data. It is unrealistic to expect one system to mine all kinds of data due to the diversity of data types and different goals of data mining. Specific data mining systems should be constructed for mining specific kinds of data. Therefore, one may expect to have different data mining systems for different kinds of data.

Mining Information from Heterogeneous Databases and Global Information Systems

Local and wide-area computer networks (such as the Internet) connect many sources of data, forming huge, distributed, and heterogeneous databases. The discovery of knowledge from different sources of structured, semi-structured, or unstructured data with diverse data semantics poses great challenges to data mining. Data mining may help disclose high-level data regularities in multiple heterogeneous databases that are unlikely to be discovered by simple query systems and may improve information exchange and interoperability in heterogeneous databases.

References

* Data-set-ibm-mainframe, definition: techopedia.Com, retrieved 7 january, 2019

* Data-mining-sources-of-data-that-can-be-mined: geeksforgeeks.Org, retrieved 8 february, 2019

* Data-mining-tutorial: guru99.Com, retrieved 9 march, 2019

* Data-normalization-in-data-mining: geeksforgeeks.Org, retrieved 10 april, 2019

* Data-integration-in-data-mining: geeksforgeeks.Org, retrieved 11 may, 2019

* Introduction-sequential-pattern-mining: data-mining.Philippe-fournier-viger.Com, retrieved 12 june, 2019

2
Concepts of Data Mining

Many concepts and techniques are used for processing gathered data and information. Some of these include association rule learning, regression analysis, anomaly detection and binning. The topics elaborated in this chapter will help in gaining a better perspective about these concepts of data mining.

Concepts and Techniques provides the concepts and techniques in processing gathered data or information, which will be used in various applications. Specifically, it explains data mining and the tools used in discovering knowledge from the collected data. It focuses on the feasibility, usefulness, effectiveness, and scalability of techniques of large data sets. After describing data mining, this edition explains the methods of knowing, preprocessing, processing, and warehousing data.

Anomaly Detection

In data mining, anomaly detection (also outlier detection) is the identification of rare items, events or observations which raise suspicions by differing significantly from the majority of the data. Typically the anomalous items will translate to some kind of problem such as bank fraud, a structural defect, medical problems or errors in a text. Anomalies are also referred to as outliers, novelties, noise, deviations and exceptions.

In particular, in the context of abuse and network intrusion detection, the interesting objects are often not *rare* objects, but unexpected *bursts* in activity. This pattern does not adhere to the common statistical definition of an outlier as a rare object, and many outlier detection methods (in particular unsupervised methods) will fail on such data, unless it has been aggregated appropriately. Instead, a cluster analysis algorithm may be able to detect the micro clusters formed by these patterns.

Three broad categories of anomaly detection techniques exist. Unsupervised anomaly detection techniques detect anomalies in an unlabeled test data set under the assumption that the majority of the instances in the data set are normal by looking for instances that seem to fit least to the remainder of the data set. Supervised anomaly detection techniques require a data set that has been labeled as "normal" and "abnormal" and involves training a classifier (the key difference to many other statistical classification problems is the inherent unbalanced nature of outlier detection).

Semi-supervised anomaly detection techniques construct a model representing normal behavior from a given *normal* training data set, and then test the likelihood of a test instance to be generated by the learnt model.

Applications

Anomaly detection is applicable in a variety of domains, such as intrusion detection, fraud detection, fault detection, system health monitoring, event detection in sensor networks, and detecting ecosystem disturbances. It is often used in preprocessing to remove anomalous data from the dataset. In supervised learning, removing the anomalous data from the dataset often results in a statistically significant increase in accuracy.

Popular Techniques

Several anomaly detection techniques have been proposed in literature. Some of the popular techniques are:

- Density-based techniques (k-nearest neighbor, local outlier factor, isolation forests, and many more variations of this concept).

- Subspace-, correlation-based and tensor-based outlier detection for high-dimensional data.

- One-class support vector machines.

- Replicator neural networks., Autoencoders, Long short-term memory neural networks.

- Bayesian Networks.

- Hidden Markov models (HMMs).

- Cluster analysis-based outlier detection.

- Deviations from association rules and frequent itemsets.

- Fuzzy logic-based outlier detection.

- Ensemble techniques, using feature bagging, score normalization and different sources of diversity.

The performance of different methods depends a lot on the data set and parameters, and methods have little systematic advantages over another when compared across many data sets and parameters.

Application to Data Security

Anomaly detection was proposed for intrusion detection systems (IDS) by Dorothy Denning in 1986. Anomaly detection for IDS is normally accomplished with thresholds and statistics, but can also be done with soft computing, and inductive learning. Types of statistics proposed by 1999 included profiles of users, workstations, networks, remote hosts, groups of users, and programs based on frequencies, means, variances, covariances, and standard deviations. The counterpart of anomaly detection in intrusion detection is misuse detection.

Software

ELKI is an open-source Java data mining toolkit that contains several anomaly detection algorithms, as well as index acceleration for them.

Association Rule Learning

Association rule learning is a rule-based machine learning method for discovering interesting relations between variables in large databases. It is intended to identify strong rules discovered in databases using some measures of interestingness.

Based on the concept of strong rules, Rakesh Agrawal, Tomasz Imieliński and Arun Swami introduced association rules for discovering regularities between products in large-scale transaction data recorded by point-of-sale (POS) systems in supermarkets. For example, the rule {onions,potatoes} $\Rightarrow$ {burger} found in the sales data of a supermarket would indicate that if a customer buys onions and potatoes together, they are likely to also buy hamburger meat. Such information can be used as the basis for decisions about marketing activities such as, e.g., promotional pricing or product placements.

In addition to the above example from market basket analysis association rules are employed today in many application areas including Web usage mining, intrusion detection, continuous production, and bioinformatics. In contrast with sequence mining, association rule learning typically does not consider the order of items either within a transaction or across transactions.

Example database with 5 transactions and 5 items					
Transaction ID	Milk	Bread	Butter	Beer	Diapers
1	1	1	0	0	0
2	0	0	1	0	0
3	0	0	0	1	1
4	1	1	1	0	0
5	0	1	0	0	0

Following the original definition by Agrawal, Imieliński, Swami the problem of association rule mining is defined as:

Let $I = \{i_1, i_2, \ldots, i_n\}$ be a set of n binary attributes called items.

Let $D = \{t_1, t_2, \ldots, t_m\}$ be a set of transactions called the database.

Each *transaction* in D has a unique transaction ID and contains a subset of the items in I.

A *rule* is defined as an implication of the form:

$$X \Rightarrow Y, \text{ where } X, Y \subseteq I.$$

In Agrawal, Imieliński, Swami a *rule* is defined only between a set and a single item,

$$X \Rightarrow i_j \text{ for } i_j \in I.$$

Every rule is composed by two different sets of items, also known as *itemsets*, X and Y, where X is called *antecedent* or left-hand-side (LHS) and Y *consequent* or right-hand-side (RHS).

To illustrate the concepts, we use a small example from the supermarket domain. The set of items is $I = \{$milk, bread, butter, beer, diapers$\}$ and in the table is shown a small database containing the items, where, in each entry, the value 1 means the presence of the item in the corresponding transaction, and the value 0 represents the absence of an item in that transaction.

An example rule for the supermarket could be $\{$butter, bread$\} \Rightarrow \{$milk$\}$ meaning that if butter and bread are bought, customers also buy milk.

This example is extremely small. In practical applications, a rule needs a support of several hundred transactions before it can be considered statistically significant, and datasets often contain thousands or millions of transactions.

Useful Concepts

In order to select interesting rules from the set of all possible rules, constraints on various measures of significance and interest are used. The best-known constraints are minimum thresholds on support and confidence.

Let X, Y be itemsets, $X \Rightarrow Y$ an association rule and T a set of transactions of a given database.

Support

Support is an indication of how frequently the itemset appears in the dataset.

The support of X with respect to T is defined as the proportion of transactions t in the dataset which contains the itemset X.

$$\text{supp}(X) = \frac{|\{t \in T; X \subseteq t\}|}{|T|}$$

In the example dataset, the itemset $X = \{$beer, diapers$\}$ has a support of $1/5 = 0.2$ since it occurs in 20% of all transactions (1 out of 5 transactions). The argument of $\text{supp}()$ is a set of preconditions, and thus becomes more restrictive as it grows (instead of more inclusive).

Confidence

Confidence is an indication of how often the rule has been found to be true.

The *confidence* value of a rule, $X \Rightarrow Y$, with respect to a set of transactions T, is the proportion of the transactions that contains X which also contains Y.

Confidence is defined as:

$$\text{conf}(X \Rightarrow Y) = \text{supp}(X \cup Y) / \text{supp}(X)$$

For example, the rule {butter, bread} $\Rightarrow$ {milk} has a confidence of $0.2/0.2 = 1.0$ in the database, which means that for 100% of the transactions containing butter and bread the rule is correct (100% of the times a customer buys butter and bread, milk is bought as well).

Note that $\text{supp}(X \cup Y)$ means the support of the union of the items in X and Y. This is somewhat confusing since we normally think in terms of probabilities of events and not sets of items. We can rewrite $\text{supp}(X \cup Y)$ as the probability $P(E_X \cap E_Y)$, where E_X and E_Y are the events that a transaction contains itemset X and Y, respectively.

Thus confidence can be interpreted as an estimate of the conditional probability $P(E_Y | E_X)$, the probability of finding the RHS of the rule in transactions under the condition that these transactions also contain the LHS.

Lift

The *lift* of a rule is defined as:

$$\text{lift}(X \Rightarrow Y) = \frac{\text{supp}(X \cup Y)}{\text{supp}(X) \times \text{supp}(Y)}$$

or the ratio of the observed support to that expected if X and Y were independent.

For example, the rule {milk, bread} $\Rightarrow$ {butter} has a lift of $\dfrac{0.2}{0.4 \times 0.4} = 1.25.$

If the rule had a lift of 1, it would imply that the probability of occurrence of the antecedent and that of the consequent are independent of each other. When two events are independent of each other, no rule can be drawn involving those two events.

If the lift is > 1, that lets us know the degree to which those two occurrences are dependent on one another, and makes those rules potentially useful for predicting the consequent in future data sets.

If the lift is < 1, that lets us know the items are substitute to each other. This means that presence of one item has negative effect on presence of other item and vice versa. The value of lift is that it considers both the support of the rule and the overall data set.

Conviction

The *conviction* of a rule is defined as $\text{conv}(X \Rightarrow Y) = \dfrac{1 - \text{supp}(Y)}{1 - \text{conf}(X \Rightarrow Y)}.$

For example, the rule {milk, bread} $\Rightarrow$ {butter} has a conviction of $\dfrac{1 - 0.4}{1 - 0.5} = 1.2,$ and can be interpreted as the ratio of the expected frequency that X occurs without Y (that is to say, the frequency that the rule makes an incorrect prediction) if X and Y were independent divided by the observed frequency of incorrect predictions. In this example, the conviction value of 1.2 shows that the rule {milk, bread} ⇒ {butter} would be incorrect 20% more often (1.2 times as often) if the association between X and Y was purely random chance.

Rule Power Factor

Rule Power Factor is an indication of how intense a rule's items are associated with each other in terms of positive relationship. Rule Power Factor is defined as:

$$\mathrm{rpf}(X \Rightarrow Y) = \mathrm{supp}(X \cup Y) \times \mathrm{supp}(X \cup Y) / \mathrm{supp}(X)$$

(a) If item A appeared in 20 transactions and B in 50 out of total 100 transactions and item A and B both together appear 15 transactions. Then conf(A->B) = 0.15/0.2 = 0.75 = 75%.

(b) If item A appeared in 30 transactions and B in 60 out of total 100 transactions and item A and B both together appear 20 transactions. Then conf = 0.2/0.3 = 0.66 = 66%.

But, in case (b), both antecedent and consequent item's occurrences increased individually and also increased in association (both A and B items together purchased) occurrences. While interest measure confidence says surprisingly that case (a) is more important (75%) than case (b) 66%. If we take the help of Rule Power Factor (RPF) RPF: confidence (A->B) × supp(A B):

(a) 0.75 × 0.15= 0.11,

(b) 0.66 × 0.2= 0.13.

RPF, correctly judge that case (b) is more important.

Process

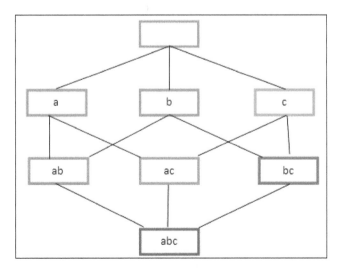

Frequent itemset lattice, where the color of the box indicates how many transactions contain the combination of items. Note that lower levels of the lattice can contain at most the minimum number of their parents' items; e.g. {ac} can have only at most *min(a,c)* items. This is called the downward-closure property.

Association rules are usually required to satisfy a user-specified minimum support and a user-specified minimum confidence at the same time. Association rule generation is usually split up into two separate steps:

1. A minimum support threshold is applied to find all frequent itemsets in a database.

2. A minimum confidence constraint is applied to these frequent itemsets in order to form rules.

While the second step is straightforward, the first step needs more attention.

Finding all frequent itemsets in a database is difficult since it involves searching all possible itemsets (item combinations). The set of possible itemsets is the power set over I and has size $2^n - 1$ (excluding the empty set which is not a valid itemset). Although the size of the power-set grows exponentially in the number of items n in I, efficient search is possible using the *downward-closure property* of support (also called *anti-monotonicity*) which guarantees that for a frequent itemset, all its subsets are also frequent and thus no infrequent itemset can be a subset of a frequent itemset. Exploiting this property, efficient algorithms can find all frequent itemsets.

Alternative Measures of Interestingness

In addition to confidence, other measures of *interestingness* for rules have been proposed. Some popular measures are:

- All-confidence,
- Collective strength,
- Conviction,
- Leverage,
- Lift (originally called interest).

Statistically Sound Associations

One limitation of the standard approach to discovering associations is that by searching massive numbers of possible associations to look for collections of items that appear to be associated, there is a large risk of finding many spurious associations. These are collections of items that co-occur with unexpected frequency in the data, but only do so by chance. For example, suppose we are considering a collection of 10,000 items and looking for rules containing two items in the left-hand-side and 1 item in the right-hand-side. There are approximately 1,000,000,000,000 such rules. If we apply a statistical test for independence with a significance level of 0.05 it means there is only a 5% chance of accepting a rule if there is no association. If we assume there are no associations, we should nonetheless expect to find 50,000,000,000 rules. Statistically sound association discovery controls this risk, in most cases reducing the risk of finding *any* spurious associations to a user-specified significance level.

Algorithms

Many algorithms for generating association rules have been proposed.

Some well-known algorithms are Apriori, Eclat and FP-Growth, but they only do half the job, since they are algorithms for mining frequent itemsets. Another step needs to be done after to generate rules from frequent itemsets found in a database.

Apriori Algorithm

Apriori uses a breadth-first search strategy to count the support of itemsets and uses a candidate generation function which exploits the downward closure property of support.

Eclat Algorithm

Eclat (ECLAT, stands for Equivalence Class Transformation) is a depth-first search algorithm based on set intersection. It is suitable for both sequential as well as parallel execution with locality-enhancing properties.

FP-growth Algorithm

FP stands for frequent pattern. In the first pass, the algorithm counts the occurrences of items (attribute-value pairs) in the dataset of transactions, and stores these counts in a 'header table'. In the second pass, it builds the FP-tree structure by inserting transactions into a trie.

Items in each transaction have to be sorted by descending order of their frequency in the dataset before being inserted so that the tree can be processed quickly. Items in each transaction that do not meet the minimum support requirement are discarded. If many transactions share most frequent items, the FP-tree provides high compression close to tree root.

Recursive processing of this compressed version of the main dataset grows frequent item sets directly, instead of generating candidate items and testing them against the entire database (as in the apriori algorithm).

Growth begins from the bottom of the header table i.e. the item with the smallest support by finding all sorted transactions that end in that item. Call this item I.

A new conditional tree is created which is the original FP-tree projected onto I. The supports of all nodes in the projected tree are re-counted with each node getting the sum of its children counts. Nodes (and hence subtrees) that do not meet the minimum support are pruned. Recursive growth ends when no individual items conditional on I meet the minimum support threshold. The resulting paths from root to I will be frequent itemsets. After this step, processing continues with the next least-supported header item of the original FP-tree. Once the recursive process has completed, all frequent item sets will have been found, and association rule creation begins.

Others Algorithms

AprioriDP

AprioriDP utilizes Dynamic Programming in Frequent itemset mining. The working principle is to eliminate the candidate generation like FP-tree, but it stores support count in specialized data structure instead of tree.

Context based Association Rule Mining Algorithm

CBPNARM is an algorithm, developed in 2013, to mine association rules on the basis of context. It uses context variable on the basis of which the support of an itemset is changed on the basis of which the rules are finally populated to the rule set.

Node-set-based Algorithms

FIN, PrePost and PPV are three algorithms based on node sets. They use nodes in a coding FP-tree to represent itemsets, and employ a depth-first search strategy to discovery frequent itemsets using "intersection" of node sets.

GUHA Procedure ASSOC

GUHA is a general method for exploratory data analysis that has theoretical foundations in observational calculi.

The ASSOC procedure is a GUHA method which mines for generalized association rules using fast bitstrings operations. The association rules mined by this method are more general than those output by apriori, for example "items" can be connected both with conjunction and disjunctions and the relation between antecedent and consequent of the rule is not restricted to setting minimum support and confidence as in apriori: an arbitrary combination of supported interest measures can be used.

OPUS Search

OPUS is an efficient algorithm for rule discovery that, in contrast to most alternatives, does not require either monotone or anti-monotone constraints such as minimum support. Initially used to find rules for a fixed consequent it has subsequently been extended to find rules with any item as a consequent. OPUS search is the core technology in the popular Magnum Opus association discovery system.

Lore

A famous story about association rule mining is the "beer and diaper" story. A purporsed survey of behavior of supermarket shoppers discovered that customers (presumably young men) who buy diapers tend also to buy beer. This anecdote became popular as an example of how unexpected association rules might be found from everyday data. There are varying opinions as to how much of the story is true. Daniel Powers says:

> In 1992, Thomas Blischok, manager of a retail consulting group at Teradata, and his staff prepared an analysis of 1.2 million market baskets from about 25 Osco Drug stores. Database queries were developed to identify affinities. The analysis "did discover that between 5:00 and 7:00 p.m. that consumers bought beer and diapers". Osco managers did not exploit the beer and diapers relationship by moving the products closer together on the shelves.

Other Types of Association Rule Mining

Multi Relation Association Rules: Multi Relation Association Rules (MRAR) are association rules where each item may have several relations. These relations indicate indirect relationship between the entities. Consider the following MRAR where the first item consists of three relations live in, nearby and humid: "Those who live in a place which is nearby a city with humid climate type and also are younger than 20 -> their health condition is good". Such association rules are extractable from RDBMS data or semantic web data.

Context Based Association Rules are a form of association rule. Context Based Association Rules claims more accuracy in association rule mining by considering a hidden variable named context variable which changes the final set of association rules depending upon the value of context variables. For example, the baskets orientation in market basket analysis reflects an odd pattern in the early days of month. This might be because of abnormal context i.e. salary is drawn at the start of the month.

- Contrast set learning is a form of associative learning. Contrast set learners use rules that differ meaningfully in their distribution across subsets.

- Weighted class learning is another form of associative learning in which weight may be assigned to classes to give focus to a particular issue of concern for the consumer of the data mining results.

- High-order pattern discovery facilitate the capture of high-order (polythetic) patterns or event associations that are intrinsic to complex real-world data.

- K-optimal pattern discovery provides an alternative to the standard approach to association rule learning that requires that each pattern appear frequently in the data.

- Approximate Frequent Itemset mining is a relaxed version of Frequent Itemset mining that allows some of the items in some of the rows to be 0.

- Generalized Association Rules hierarchical taxonomy (concept hierarchy).

- Quantitative Association Rules categorical and quantitative data.

- Interval Data Association Rules e.g. partition the age into 5-year-increment ranged

- Sequential pattern mining discovers subsequences that are common to more than minsup sequences in a sequence database, where minsup is set by the user. A sequence is an ordered list of transactions.

- Subspace Clustering, a specific type of Clustering high-dimensional data, is in many variants also based on the downward-closure property for specific clustering models.

- Warmr is shipped as part of the ACE data mining suite. It allows association rule learning for first order relational rules.

Lift

In data mining and association rule learning, lift is a measure of the performance of a targeting model (association rule) at predicting or classifying cases as having an enhanced response (with respect to the population as a whole), measured against a random choice targeting model. A targeting model is doing a good job if the response within the target is much better than the average for the population as a whole. Lift is simply the ratio of these values: target response divided by average response.

For example, suppose a population has an average response rate of 5%, but a certain model (or rule) has identified a segment with a response rate of 20%. Then that segment would have a lift of 4.0 (20%/5%).

Typically, the modeller seeks to divide the population into quantiles, and rank the quantiles by lift. Organizations can then consider each quantile, and by weighing the predicted response rate (and associated financial benefit) against the cost, they can decide whether to market to that quantile or not.

The lift curve can also be considered a variation on the receiver operating characteristic (ROC) curve, and is also known in econometrics as the Lorenz or power curve.

$$lift = \frac{P(A \cap B)}{P(A) \times P(B)}$$

Example:

Assume the data set being mined is,

Antecedent	Consequent
A	0
A	0
A	1
A	0
B	1
B	0
B	1

where the antecedent is the input variable that we can control, and the consequent is the variable we are trying to predict. Real mining problems would typically have more complex antecedents, but usually focus on single-value consequents.

Most mining algorithms would determine the following rules (targeting models):

- Rule 1: A implies 0.

- Rule 2: B implies 1.

Because these are simply the most common patterns found in the data.

The *support* for Rule 1 is 3/7 because that is the number of items in the dataset in which the antecedent is A and the consequent 0. The support for Rule 2 is 2/7 because two of the seven records meet the antecedent of B and the consequent of 1. The supports can be written as:

$$supp(A \Rightarrow 0) = P(A \wedge 0) = P(A)P(0\,|\,A) = P(0)P(A\,|\,0)$$
$$supp(B \Rightarrow 1) = P(B \wedge 1) = P(B)P(1\,|\,B) = P(1)P(B\,|\,1)$$

The *confidence* for Rule 1 is 3/4 because three of the four records that meet the antecedent of A meet the consequent of 0. The confidence for Rule 2 is 2/3 because two of the three records that meet the antecedent of B meet the consequent of 1. The confidences can be written as:

$$\text{conf}(A \Rightarrow 0) = P(0 \mid A)$$
$$\text{conf}(B \Rightarrow 1) = P(1 \mid B)$$

Lift can be found by dividing the confidence by the unconditional probability of the consequent, or by dividing the support by the probability of the antecedent times the probability of the consequent,

- The lift for Rule 1 is $(3/4)/(4/7) = (3 \times 7)/(4 \times 4) = 21/16 \approx 1.31$.

- The lift for Rule 2 is $(2/3)/(3/7) = (2 \times 7)/(3 \times 3) = 14/9 \approx 1.56$.

$$\text{lift}(A \Rightarrow 0) = \frac{P(0 \mid A)}{P(0)} = \frac{P(A \wedge 0)}{P(A)P(0)}$$

$$\text{lift}(B \Rightarrow 1) = \frac{P(1 \mid B)}{P(1)} = \frac{P(B \wedge 1)}{P(B)P(1)}$$

If some rule had a lift of 1, it would imply that the probability of occurrence of the antecedent and that of the consequent are independent of each other. When two events are independent of each other, no rule can be drawn involving those two events.

If the lift is > 1, like it is here for Rules 1 and 2, that lets us know the degree to which those two occurrences are dependent on one another, and makes those rules potentially useful for predicting the consequent in future data sets.

Observe that even though Rule 1 has higher confidence, it has lower lift. Intuitively, it would seem that Rule 1 is more valuable because of its higher confidence—it seems more accurate (better supported). But accuracy of the rule independent of the data set can be misleading. The value of lift is that it considers both the confidence of the rule and the overall data set.

Regression Analysis

Regression analysis is a set of statistical processes for estimating the relationships between a dependent variable (often called the 'outcome variable') and one or more independent variables (often called 'predictors', 'covariates', or 'features'). The most common form of regression analysis is linear regression, in which a researcher finds the line (or a more complex linear function) that most closely fits the data according to a specific mathematical criterion. For example, the method of ordinary least squares computes the unique line (or hyperplane) that minimizes the sum of squared distances between the true data and that line (or hyperplane). For specific mathematical reasons, this allows the researcher to estimate the conditional expectation (or population average value) of the dependent variable when the independent variables take on a given set of values. Less common forms of regression use slightly different procedures to estimate alternative location parameters (e.g., quantile regression or Necessary Condition Analysis) or estimate the conditional expectation across a broader collection of non-linear models (e.g., nonparametric regression).

Regression analysis is primarily used for two conceptually distinct purposes. First, regression analysis is widely used for prediction and forecasting, where its use has substantial overlap with the field of machine learning. Second, in some situations regression analysis can be used to infer causal relationships between the independent and dependent variables. Importantly, regressions by themselves only reveal relationships between a dependent variable and a collection of independent variables in a fixed dataset. To use regressions for prediction or to infer causal relationships, respectively, a researcher must carefully justify why existing relationships have predictive power for a new context or why a relationship between two variables has a causal interpretation. The latter is especially important when a researcher hopes to estimate causal relationships using observational data.

Regression Model

In practice, a researcher first selects a model she would like to estimate and then uses her chosen method (e.g., ordinary least squares) to estimate the parameters of that model. Regression models involve the following components:

- The unknown parameters, often denoted as a scalar or vector β.

- The independent variables, which are observed in data and are often denoted as a vector X_i (where i denotes a row of data).

- The dependent variable, which are observed in data and often denoted using the scalar Y_i.

- The error terms, which are *not* directly observed in data and are often denoted using the scalar e_i.

In various fields of application, different terminologies are used in place of dependent and independent variables.

Most regression models propose that Y_i is a function of X_i and β, with e_i representing and additive error term that may stand in for un-modeled determinants of Y_i or random statistical noise:

$$Y_i = f(X_i, \beta) + e_i$$

The researcher's goal is to estimate the function $f(X_i, \beta)$ that most closely fits the data. To carry out regression analysis, the form of the function f must be specified. Sometimes the form of this function is based on knowledge about the relationship between Y_i and X_i that does not rely on the data. If no such knowledge is available, a flexible or convenient form for f is chosen. For example, a simple univariate regression may propose $f(X_i, \beta) = \beta_0 + \beta_1 X_i$, suggesting that the researcher believes $Y_i = \beta_0 + \beta_1 X_i + e_i$ to be a reasonable approximation for the statistical process generating the data.

Once the researcher determines their preferred statistical model, different forms of regression analysis provide tools to estimate the parameters β. For example, least squares (including its most common variant, ordinary least squares) finds the value of $\hat{\beta}$ that minimizes the sum of squared errors

$$\sum_i (Y_i - f(X_i, \beta))^2.$$

A given regression method will ultimately provide an estimate of β, usually denoted $\hat{\beta}$ to distinguish the estimate from the true (unknown) parameter value that generated the data. Using this estimate, the researcher can then use the *fitted value* $\widehat{Y}_i = f(X_i, \hat{\beta})$ for prediction or to assess the accuracy of the model in explaining the data. Whether the researcher is intrinsically interested in the estimate $\hat{\beta}$ or the predicted value $\widehat{Y}_i$ will depend on context and her goals. As described in ordinary least squares, least squares is widely used because the estimated function $f(X_i, \hat{\beta})$ approximates the conditional expectation $E(Y_i \mid X_i)$. However, alternative variants (e.g., least absolute deviations or quantile regression) are useful when the researcher wants to model other functions $f(X_i, \beta)$.

It it important to note that there must be sufficient data to estimate a regression model. For example, suppose that a researcher has access to N rows of data with three independent variables: (Y_i, X_{1i}, X_{2i}). Suppose further that the researcher wants to estimate a bivariate linear model via least squares: $Y_i = \beta_0 + \beta_1 X_{1i} + \beta_2 X_{2i} + e_i$. If she only has access to $N = 2$ data points, then she could find infinitely many combinations $(\hat{\beta}_0, \hat{\beta}_1, \hat{\beta}_2)$ that explain the data equally well: she can choose any combination that satisfies $\widehat{Y}_i = \hat{\beta}_0 + \hat{\beta}_1 X_{1i} + \hat{\beta}_2 X_{2i}$, all of which lead to $\sum_i \hat{e}_i^2 = \sum_i (\widehat{Y}_i - (\hat{\beta}_0 + \hat{\beta}_1 X_{1i} + \hat{\beta}_2 X_{2i}))^2 = 0$ and are therefore valid solutions that minimize the sum of squared residuals. To understand why she has infinitely many options, note that she is facing a system of $N = 2$ equations and wants to solve for 3 unknowns, which makes the system *underdetermined* in the jargon of linear algebra. Alternatively, one can visualize infinitely many 3-dimensional planes that go through $N = 2$ fixed points.

More generally, to estimate a least squares model with k distinct parameters, one must have $N \geq k$ distinct data points. If $N > k$, then there does not generally exist a set of parameters that will perfectly fit the data. The quantity $(N - k)$ appears often in regression analysis, and is referred to as the degrees of freedom in the model. Moreover, to estimate a least squares model, the independent variables $(X_{1i}, X_{2i}, ..., X_{ki})$ must be linearly independent: one must *not* be able to reconstruct any of the independent variables by adding and multiplying the remaining independent variables. As discussed in ordinary least squares, this condition ensures that $(X^T X)$ is an Invertible matrix and therefore that a solution $\hat{\beta}$ exists.

Underlying Assumptions

By itself, a regression is simply a calculation using the data. In order to interpret the output of a regression as a meaningful statistical quantity that measures real-world relationships, researchers often rely on a number of classical assumptions. These often include:

- The sample is representative of the population at large.

- The independent variables are measured with no error.

- Deviations from the model have an expected value of zero, conditional on covariates:

$$E(e_i \mid X_i) = 0$$

- The variance of the residuals e_i is constant across observations (homoscedasticity).

- The residuals e_i are uncorrelated with one another. Mathematically, the variance–covariance matrix of the errors is diagonal.

A handful of conditions are sufficient for the least-squares estimator to possess desirable properties: in particular, the Gauss–Markov assumptions imply that the parameter estimates will be unbiased, consistent, and efficient in the class of linear unbiased estimators. Practitioners have developed a variety of methods to maintain some or all of these desirable properties in real-world settings, since these classical assumptions are unlikely to hold exactly. For example, modeling errors-in-variables can lead to reasonable estimates independent variables are measured with errors. Heteroscedasticity-consistent standard errors allow the variance of e_i to change across values of X_i. Correlated errors that exist within subsets of the data or follow specific patterns can be handled using *clustered standard errors, geographic weighted regression*, or Newey–West standard errors, among other techniques. When rows of data correspond to locations in space, the choice of how to model e_i within geographic units can have important consequences. The subfield of econometrics is largely focused on developing techniques that allow researchers to make reasonable real-world conclusions in real-world settings, where classical assumptions do not hold exactly.

Linear Regression

In linear regression, the model specification is that the dependent variable, y_i is a linear combination of the *parameters* (but need not be linear in the *independent variables*). For example, in simple linear regression for modeling n data points there is one independent variable: x_i, and two parameters, β_0 and β_1:

straight line: $y_i = \beta_0 + \beta_1 x_i + \varepsilon_i, \quad i = 1,\ldots,n.$

In multiple linear regression, there are several independent variables or functions of independent variables.

Adding a term in x_i^2 to the preceding regression gives:

parabola: $y_i = \beta_0 + \beta_1 x_i + \beta_2 x_i^2 + \varepsilon_i, i = 1,\ldots,n.$

This is still linear regression; although the expression on the right hand side is quadratic in the independent variable x_i, it is linear in the parameters , β_1 and β_2.

In both cases, ε_i is an error term and the subscript i indexes a particular observation.

Returning our attention to the straight line case: Given a random sample from the population, we estimate the population parameters and obtain the sample linear regression model:

$$\hat{y}_i = \hat{\beta}_0 + \hat{\beta}_1 x_i.$$

The residual, $e_i = y_i - \hat{y}_i$, is the difference between the value of the dependent variable predicted by the model, $\hat{y}_i$, and the true value of the dependent variable, $\hat{y}_i$. One method of estimation is ordinary least squares. This method obtains parameter estimates that minimize the sum of squared residuals, SSR:

$$SSR = \sum_{i=1}^{n} e_i^2$$

Minimization of this function results in a set of normal equations, a set of simultaneous linear equations in the parameters, which are solved to yield the parameter estimators, $\hat{\beta}_0$, $\hat{\beta}_1$.

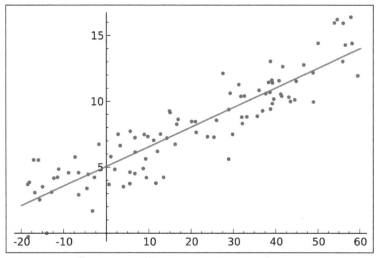

Illustration of linear regression on a data set.

In the case of simple regression, the formulas for the least squares estimates are,

$$\hat{\beta}_1 = \frac{\sum (x_i - \bar{x})(y_i - \bar{y})}{\sum (x_i - \bar{x})^2}$$

$$\hat{\beta}_0 = \bar{y} - \hat{\beta}_1 \bar{x}$$

where $\bar{x}$ is the mean (average) of the x values and $\bar{y}$ is the mean of the y values.

Under the assumption that the population error term has a constant variance, the estimate of that variance is given by:

$$\hat{\sigma}_\varepsilon^2 = \frac{SSR}{n-2}.$$

This is called the mean square error (MSE) of the regression. The denominator is the sample size reduced by the number of model parameters estimated from the same data, $(n-p)$ for p regressors or $(n-p-1)$ if an intercept is used. In this case, $p=1$ so the denominator is $n-2$.

The standard errors of the parameter estimates are given by,

$$\hat{\sigma}_{\beta_1} = \hat{\sigma}_\varepsilon \sqrt{\frac{1}{\sum(x_i - \bar{x})^2}}$$

$$\hat{\sigma}_{\beta_0} = \hat{\sigma}_\varepsilon \sqrt{\frac{1}{n} + \frac{\bar{x}^2}{\sum(x_i - \bar{x})^2}} = \hat{\sigma}_{\beta_1} \sqrt{\frac{\sum x_i^2}{n}}.$$

Under the further assumption that the population error term is normally distributed, the researcher can use these estimated standard errors to create confidence intervals and conduct hypothesis tests about the population parameters.

General Linear Model

In the more general multiple regression model, there are p independent variables:

$$y_i = \beta_1 x_{i1} + \beta_2 x_{i2} + \cdots + \beta_p x_{ip} + \varepsilon_i,$$

where x_{ij} is the i-th observation on the j-th independent variable. If the first independent variable takes the value 1 for all i, $x_{i1} = 1$, then β_1 is called the regression intercept.

The least squares parameter estimates are obtained from p normal equations. The residual can be written as,

$$\varepsilon_i = y_i - \hat{\beta}_1 x_{i1} - \cdots - \hat{\beta}_p x_{ip}.$$

The normal equations are,

$$\sum_{i=1}^{n}\sum_{k=1}^{p} x_{ij} x_{ik} \hat{\beta}_k = \sum_{i=1}^{n} x_{ij} y_i, \ j = 1,\ldots,p.$$

In matrix notation, the normal equations are written as,

$$(\mathbf{X}^\top \mathbf{X})\hat{\beta} = \mathbf{X}^\top \mathbf{Y},$$

where the ij element of $\mathbf{X}$ is x_{ij}, the i element of the column vector Y is y_i, and the j element of $\hat{\beta}$ is $\hat{\beta}_j$. Thus $\mathbf{X}$ is $n \times p$, Y is $n \times 1$, and $\hat{\beta}$ is $p \times 1$. The solution is,

$$\hat{\beta} = (\mathbf{X}^\top \mathbf{X})^{-1} \mathbf{X}^\top \mathbf{Y}.$$

Diagnostics

Once a regression model has been constructed, it may be important to confirm the goodness of fit of the model and the statistical significance of the estimated parameters. Commonly used checks of goodness of fit include the R-squared, analyses of the pattern of residuals and hypothesis testing. Statistical significance can be checked by an F-test of the overall fit, followed by t-tests of individual parameters.

Interpretations of these diagnostic tests rest heavily on the model assumptions. Although examination of the residuals can be used to invalidate a model, the results of a t-test or F-test are sometimes more difficult to interpret if the model's assumptions are violated. For example, if the error term does not have a normal distribution, in small samples the estimated parameters will not follow normal distributions and complicate inference. With relatively large samples, however, a central limit theorem can be invoked such that hypothesis testing may proceed using asymptotic approximations.

Limited Dependent Variables

Limited dependent variables, which are response variables that are categorical variables or are variables constrained to fall only in a certain range, often arise in econometrics.

The response variable may be non-continuous ("limited" to lie on some subset of the real line). For binary (zero or one) variables, if analysis proceeds with least-squares linear regression, the model is called the linear probability model. Nonlinear models for binary dependent variables include the probit and logit model. The multivariate probit model is a standard method of estimating a joint relationship between several binary dependent variables and some independent variables. For categorical variables with more than two values there is the multinomial logit. For ordinal variables with more than two values, there are the ordered logit and ordered probit models. Censored regression models may be used when the dependent variable is only sometimes observed, and Heckman correction type models may be used when the sample is not randomly selected from the population of interest. An alternative to such procedures is linear regression based on polychoric correlation (or polyserial correlations) between the categorical variables. Such procedures differ in the assumptions made about the distribution of the variables in the population. If the variable is positive with low values and represents the repetition of the occurrence of an event, then count models like the Poisson regression or the negative binomial model may be used.

Nonlinear Regression

When the model function is not linear in the parameters, the sum of squares must be minimized by an iterative procedure.

Interpolation and Extrapolation

Regression models predict a value of the *Y* variable given known values of the *X* variables. Prediction *within* the range of values in the dataset used for model-fitting is known informally as interpolation. Prediction *outside* this range of the data is known as extrapolation. Performing extrapolation relies strongly on the regression assumptions. The further the extrapolation goes outside the data, the more room there is for the model to fail due to differences between the assumptions and the sample data or the true values.

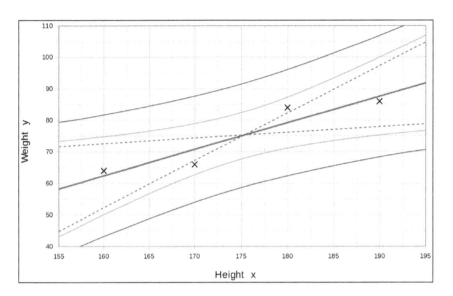

In the middle, the interpolated straight line represents the best balance between the points above and below this line. The dotted lines represent the two extreme lines. The first curves represent the estimated values. The outer curves represent a prediction for a new measurement.

It is generally advised that when performing extrapolation, one should accompany the estimated value of the dependent variable with a prediction interval that represents the uncertainty. Such intervals tend to expand rapidly as the values of the independent variable(s) moved outside the range covered by the observed data. For such reasons and others, some tend to say that it might be unwise to undertake extrapolation.

However, this does not cover the full set of modeling errors that may be made: in particular, the assumption of a particular form for the relation between Y and X. A properly conducted regression analysis will include an assessment of how well the assumed form is matched by the observed data, but it can only do so within the range of values of the independent variables actually available. This means that any extrapolation is particularly reliant on the assumptions being made about the structural form of the regression relationship. Best-practice advice here is that a linear-in-variables and linear-in-parameters relationship should not be chosen simply for computational convenience, but that all available knowledge should be deployed in constructing a regression model. If this knowledge includes the fact that the dependent variable cannot go outside a certain range of values, this can be made use of in selecting the model – even if the observed dataset has no values particularly near such bounds. The implications of this step of choosing an appropriate functional form for the regression can be great when extrapolation is considered. At a minimum, it can ensure that any extrapolation arising from a fitted model is "realistic" (or in accord with what is known).

Power and Sample Size Calculations

There are no generally agreed methods for relating the number of observations versus the number of independent variables in the model. One rule of thumb conjectured by Good and Hardin is $N = m^n$, where   is the sample size, n is the number of independent variables and m is the number of observations needed to reach the desired precision if the model had only one independent variable. For example, a researcher is building a linear regression model using a dataset that contains 1000 patients (N). If the researcher decides that five observations are needed to precisely define a straight line (m), then the maximum number of independent variables the model can support is 4, because:

$$\frac{\log 1000}{\log 5} = 4.29.$$

Other Methods

Although the parameters of a regression model are usually estimated using the method of least squares, other methods which have been used include:

- Bayesian methods, e.g. Bayesian linear regression.
- Percentage regression, for situations where reducing *percentage* errors is deemed more appropriate.
- Least absolute deviations, which is more robust in the presence of outliers, leading to quantile regression.
- Nonparametric regression, requires a large number of observations and is computationally intensive.
- Scenario optimization, leading to interval predictor models.
- Distance metric learning, which is learned by the search of a meaningful distance metric in a given input space.

Software

All major statistical software packages perform least squares regression analysis and inference. Simple linear regression and multiple regression using least squares can be done in some spreadsheet applications and on some calculators. While many statistical software packages can perform various types of nonparametric and robust regression, these methods are less standardized; different software packages implement different methods, and a method with a given name may be implemented differently in different packages. Specialized regression software has been developed for use in fields such as survey analysis and neuroimaging.

Binning in Data Mining

Data binning, bucketing is a data pre-processing method used to minimize the effects of small observation errors. The original data values are divided into small intervals known as bins and then they are replaced by a general value calculated for that bin. This has a smoothing effect on the input data and may also reduce the chances of overfitting in case of small datasets.

There are 2 methods of dividing data into bins:

1. Equal Frequency Binning: Bins have equal frequency.

2. Equal Width Binning: Bins have equal width with a range of each bin are defined as, [min + w], [min + 2w] .... [min + nw] where w = (max − min)/(no of bins).

Equal Frequency

```
Input :[5, 10, 11, 13, 15, 35, 50, 55, 72, 92, 204, 215]
Output :
[5, 10, 11, 13]
[15, 35, 50, 55]
[72, 92, 204, 215]
```

Equal Width

```
Input :[5, 10, 11, 13, 15, 35, 50, 55, 72, 92, 204, 215]
Output :
[10, 11, 13, 15, 35, 50, 55, 72]
[92]
[204]
```

Implementation of Bining Technique

```python
#equal frequency
def equifreq(arr1, m):

    a = len(arr1)
    n = int(a / m)
    for i in range(0, m):
        arr = []
        for j in range(i * n, (i + 1) * n):
            if j >= a:
                break
            arr = arr + [arr1[j]]
        print(arr)


#equal width
def equiwidth(arr1, m):
    a = len(arr1)
    w = int((max(arr1) - min(arr1)) / m)
    min1 = min(arr1)
    arr = []
    for i in range(0, m + 1):
        arr = arr + [min1 + w * i]
```

```
    arri=[]
    for i in range(0, m):
        temp = []
        for j in arr1:
            if j > arr[i] and j < arr[i+1]:
                temp += [j]
        arri += [temp]
    print(arri)

#data to be binned
data = [5, 10, 11, 13, 15, 35, 50, 55, 72, 92, 204, 215]
#no of bins
m = 3

print("equal frequency binning")
equifreq(data, m)

print("\n\nequal width binning")
equiwidth(data, 3)
```

Output

```
equal frequency binning

[5, 10, 11, 13]

[15, 35, 50, 55]

[72, 92, 204, 215]


equal width binning

[[10, 11, 13, 15, 35, 50, 55, 72], [92], [204]]
```

References

- Zimek, Arthur; Schubert, Erich (2017), "Outlier Detection", Encyclopedia of Database Systems, Springer New York, pp. 1–5, doi:10.1007/978-1-4899-7993-3_80719-1, ISBN 9781489979933

- Data-mining-concepts-and-techniques: sciencedirect.com, Retrieved 13 July, 2019

- Lazarevic, A.; Kumar, V. (2005). Feature bagging for outlier detection. Proc. 11th ACM SIGKDD International Conference on Knowledge Discovery in Data Mining. Pp. 157–166. Citeseerx 10.1.1.399.425.Doi:10.1145/1081870.1081891. ISBN 978-1-59593-135-1

- Binning-in-data-mining: geeksforgeeks.org, Retrieved 14 August, 2019

- Ramezani, Reza, Mohamad Sunni ee, and Mohammad Ali Nematbakhsh; MRAR: Mining Multi-Relation Association Rules, Journal of Computing and Security, 1, no. 2 (2014)

- Good, P. I.; Hardin, J. W. (2009). Common Errors in Statistics (And How to Avoid Them) (3rd ed.). Hoboken, New Jersey: Wiley. P. 211. ISBN 978-0-470-45798-6

3
Data Mining Algorithms

Data mining algorithm is a set of heuristics and calculations that creates a model from gathered data. A few of its algorithms are C4.5 algorithm, Apriori algorithm, k-nearest neighbors algorithm, etc. All these types of data mining algorithms have been carefully analyzed in this chapter.

An algorithm in data mining (or machine learning) is a set of heuristics and calculations that creates a model from data. To create a model, the algorithm first analyzes the data you provide, looking for specific types of patterns or trends. The algorithm uses the results of this analysis over many iterations to find the optimal parameters for creating the mining model. These parameters are then applied across the entire data set to extract actionable patterns and detailed statistics.

The mining model that an algorithm creates from your data can take various forms, including:

- A set of clusters that describe how the cases in a dataset are related.

- A decision tree that predicts an outcome, and describes how different criteria affect that outcome.

- A mathematical model that forecasts sales.

- A set of rules that describe how products are grouped together in a transaction, and the probabilities that products are purchased together.

The algorithms provided in SQL Server Data Mining are the most popular, well-researched methods of deriving patterns from data. To take one example, K-means clustering is one of the oldest clustering algorithms and is available widely in many different tools and with many different implementations and options. However, the particular implementation of K-means clustering used in SQL Server Data Mining was developed by Microsoft Research and then optimized for performance with Analysis Services. All of the Microsoft data mining algorithms can be extensively customized and are fully programmable, using the provided APIs. You can also automate the creation, training, and retraining of models by using the data mining components in Integration Services.

You can also use third-party algorithms that comply with the OLE DB for Data Mining specification, or develop custom algorithms that can be registered as services and then used within the SQL Server Data Mining framework.

Choosing the Right Algorithm

Choosing the best algorithm to use for a specific analytical task can be a challenge. While you can use different algorithms to perform the same business task, each algorithm produces a different result, and some algorithms can produce more than one type of result. For example, you can use the Microsoft Decision Trees algorithm not only for prediction, but also as a way to reduce the number of columns in a dataset, because the decision tree can identify columns that do not affect the final mining model.

Choosing an Algorithm by Type

SQL Server Data Mining includes the following algorithm types:

- Classification algorithms predict one or more discrete variables, based on the other attributes in the dataset.

- Regression algorithms predict one or more continuous numeric variables, such as profit or loss, based on other attributes in the dataset.

- Segmentation algorithms divide data into groups, or clusters, of items that have similar properties.

- Association algorithms find correlations between different attributes in a dataset. The most common application of this kind of algorithm is for creating association rules, which can be used in a market basket analysis.

- Sequence analysis algorithms summarize frequent sequences or episodes in data, such as a series of clicks in a web site, or a series of log events preceding machine maintenance.

However, there is no reason that you should be limited to one algorithm in your solutions. Experienced analysts will sometimes use one algorithm to determine the most effective inputs (that is, variables), and then apply a different algorithm to predict a specific outcome based on that data. SQL Server Data Mining lets you build multiple models on a single mining structure, so within a single data mining solution you could use a clustering algorithm, a decision trees model, and a Naive Bayes model to get different views on your data. You might also use multiple algorithms within a single solution to perform separate tasks: for example, you could use regression to obtain financial forecasts, and use a neural network algorithm to perform an analysis of factors that influence forecasts.

C4.5 Algorithm

C4.5 is an algorithm used to generate a decision tree developed by Ross Quinlan. C4.5 is an extension of Quinlan's earlier ID3 algorithm. The decision trees generated by C4.5 can be used for classification, and for this reason, C4.5 is often referred to as a statistical classifier. In 2011, authors of the Weka machine learning software described the C4.5 algorithm as "a landmark decision tree program that is probably the machine learning workhorse most widely used in practice to date".

Algorithm

C4.5 builds decision trees from a set of training data in the same way as ID3, using the concept of information entropy. The training data is a set $S = s_1, s_2, ...$ of already classified samples. Each sample s_i consists of a p-dimensional vector $(x_{1,i}, x_{2,i}, ..., x_{p,i})$, where the represent attribute values or features of the sample, as well as the class in which x_j falls.

At each node of the tree, C4.5 chooses the attribute of the data that most effectively splits its set of samples into subsets enriched in one class or the other. The splitting criterion is the normalized information gain (difference in entropy). The attribute with the highest normalized information gain is chosen to make the decision. The C4.5 algorithm then recurses on the partitioned sublists.

This algorithm has a few base cases:

- All the samples in the list belong to the same class. When this happens, it simply creates a leaf node for the decision tree saying to choose that class.

- None of the features provide any information gain. In this case, C4.5 creates a decision node higher up the tree using the expected value of the class.

- Instance of previously-unseen class encountered. Again, C4.5 creates a decision node higher up the tree using the expected value.

Pseudocode

In pseudocode, the general algorithm for building decision trees is:

- Check for the above base cases.

- For each attribute a, find the normalized information gain ratio from splitting on a.

- Let a_best be the attribute with the highest normalized information gain.

- Create a decision *node* that splits on a_best.

- Recur on the sublists obtained by splitting on a_best, and add those nodes as children of *node*.

Improvements From ID.3 Algorithm

C4.5 made a number of improvements to ID3. Some of these are:

- Handling both continuous and discrete attributes - In order to handle continuous attributes, C4.5 creates a threshold and then splits the list into those whose attribute value is above the threshold and those that are less than or equal to it.

- Handling training data with missing attribute values - C4.5 allows attribute values to be marked as (?) for missing. Missing attribute values are simply not used in gain and entropy calculations.

- Handling attributes with differing costs.

- Pruning trees after creation - C4.5 goes back through the tree once it's been created and attempts to remove branches that do not help by replacing them with leaf nodes.

Improvements in C5.0 and See5 Algorithm

Quinlan went on to create C5.0 and See5 (C5.0 for Unix/Linux, See5 for Windows) which he markets commercially. C5.0 offers a number of improvements on C4.5. Some of these are:

- Speed - C5.0 is significantly faster than C4.5 (several orders of magnitude).

- Memory usage - C5.0 is more memory efficient than C4.5.

- Smaller decision trees - C5.0 gets similar results to C4.5 with considerably smaller decision trees.

- Support for boosting - Boosting improves the trees and gives them more accuracy.

- Weighting - C5.0 allows you to weight different cases and misclassification types.

- Winnowing - a C5.0 option automatically winnows the attributes to remove those that may be unhelpful.

Source for a single-threaded Linux version of C5.0 is available under the GPL.

Support-vector Machine

In machine learning, support-vector machines (SVMs, also support-vector networks) are supervised learning models with associated learning algorithms that analyze data used for classification and regression analysis. Given a set of training examples, each marked as belonging to one or the other of two categories, an SVM training algorithm builds a model that assigns new examples to one category or the other, making it a non-probabilistic binary linear classifier (although methods such as Platt scaling exist to use SVM in a probabilistic classification setting). An SVM model is a representation of the examples as points in space, mapped so that the examples of the separate categories are divided by a clear gap that is as wide as possible. New examples are then mapped into that same space and predicted to belong to a category based on the side of the gap on which they fall.

In addition to performing linear classification, SVMs can efficiently perform a non-linear classification using what is called the kernel trick, implicitly mapping their inputs into high-dimensional feature spaces.

When data are unlabelled, supervised learning is not possible, and an unsupervised learning approach is required, which attempts to find natural clustering of the data to groups, and then map new data to these formed groups. The support-vector clustering algorithm, created by Hava Siegelmann and Vladimir Vapnik, applies the statistics of support vectors, developed in the support vector machines algorithm, to categorize unlabeled data, and is one of the most widely used clustering algorithms in industrial applications.

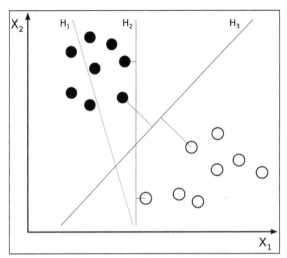

H_1 does not separate the classes. H_2 does, but only with a small margin.
H_3 separates them with the maximal margin.

Classifying data is a common task in machine learning. Suppose some given data points each belong to one of two classes, and the goal is to decide which class a *new* data point will be in. In the case of support-vector machines, a data point is viewed as a p-dimensional vector (a list of p numbers), and we want to know whether we can separate such points with a $(p-1)$-dimensional hyperplane. This is called a linear classifier. There are many hyperplanes that might classify the data. One reasonable choice as the best hyperplane is the one that represents the largest separation, or margin, between the two classes. So we choose the hyperplane so that the distance from it to the nearest data point on each side is maximized. If such a hyperplane exists, it is known as the maximum-margin hyperplane and the linear classifier it defines is known as a maximum-margin classifier; or equivalently, the perceptron of optimal stability.

More formally, a support-vector machine constructs a hyperplane or set of hyperplanes in a high- or infinite-dimensional space, which can be used for classification, regression, or other tasks like outliers detection. Intuitively, a good separation is achieved by the hyperplane that has the largest distance to the nearest training-data point of any class (so-called functional margin), since in general the larger the margin, the lower the generalization error of the classifier.

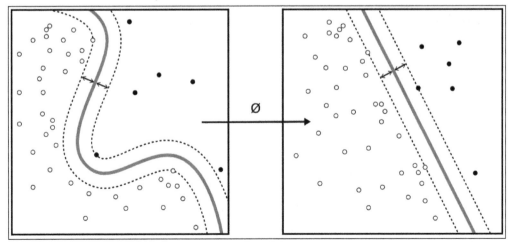

Kernel machine.

Whereas the original problem may be stated in a finite-dimensional space, it often happens that the sets to discriminate are not linearly separable in that space. For this reason, it was proposed that the original finite-dimensional space be mapped into a much higher-dimensional space, presumably making the separation easier in that space. To keep the computational load reasonable, the mappings used by SVM schemes are designed to ensure that dot products of pairs of input data vectors may be computed easily in terms of the variables in the original space, by defining them in terms of a kernel function $k(x,y)$ selected to suit the problem. The hyperplanes in the higher-dimensional space are defined as the set of points whose dot product with a vector in that space is constant, where such a set of vectors is an orthogonal (and thus minimal) set of vectors that defines a hyperplane. The vectors defining the hyperplanes can be chosen to be linear combinations with parameters α_i of images of feature vectors x_i that occur in the data base. With this choice of a hyperplane, the points x in the feature space that are mapped into the hyperplane are defined by the relation $\sum_i \alpha_i k(x_i, x) = \text{constant}$.

Note that if $k(x,y)$ becomes small as y grows further away from x, each term in the sum measures the degree of closeness of the test point x to the corresponding data base point x_i. In this way, the sum of kernels above can be used to measure the relative nearness of each test point to the data points originating in one or the other of the sets to be discriminated. Note the fact that the set of points x mapped into any hyperplane can be quite convoluted as a result, allowing much more complex discrimination between sets that are not convex at all in the original space.

Applications

SVMs can be used to solve various real-world problems:

- SVMs are helpful in text and hypertext categorization, as their application can significantly reduce the need for labeled training instances in both the standard inductive and transductive settings. Some methods for shallow semantic parsing are based on support vector machines.

- Classification of images can also be performed using SVMs. Experimental results show that SVMs achieve significantly higher search accuracy than traditional query refinement schemes after just three to four rounds of relevance feedback. This is also true for image segmentation systems, including those using a modified version SVM that uses the privileged approach as suggested by Vapnik.

- Hand-written characters can be recognized using SVM.

- The SVM algorithm has been widely applied in the biological and other sciences. They have been used to classify proteins with up to 90% of the compounds classified correctly. Permutation tests based on SVM weights have been suggested as a mechanism for interpretation of SVM models. Support-vector machine weights have also been used to interpret SVM models in the past. Posthoc interpretation of support-vector machine models in order to identify features used by the model to make predictions is a relatively new area of research with special significance in the biological sciences.

Linear SVM

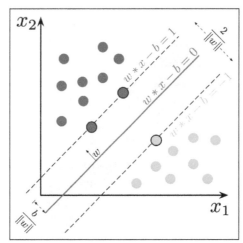

Maximum-margin hyperplane and margins for an SVM trained with samples from two classes. Samples on the margin are called the support vectors.

We are given a training dataset of n points of the form,

$$(\vec{x}_1, y_1), \ldots, (\vec{x}_n, y_n),$$

where the y_i are either 1 or −1, each indicating the class to which the point $\vec{x}_i$ belongs. Each $\vec{x}_i$ is a p-dimensional real vector. We want to find the "maximum-margin hyperplane" that divides the group of points $\vec{x}_i$ for which $y_i = 1$ from the group of points for which $y_i = -1$, which is defined so that the distance between the hyperplane and the nearest point $\vec{x}_i$ from either group is maximized.

Any hyperplane can be written as the set of points $\vec{x}$ satisfying,

$$\vec{w} \cdot \vec{x} - b = 0,$$

where $\vec{w}$ is the (not necessarily normalized) normal vector to the hyperplane. This is much like Hesse normal form, except that $\vec{w}$ is not necessarily a unit vector. The parameter $\dfrac{b}{\|\vec{w}\|}$ determines the offset of the hyperplane from the origin along the normal vector $\vec{w}$.

Hard-margin

If the training data is linearly separable, we can select two parallel hyperplanes that separate the two classes of data, so that the distance between them is as large as possible. The region bounded by these two hyperplanes is called the "margin", and the maximum-margin hyperplane is the hyperplane that lies halfway between them. With a normalized or standardized dataset, these hyperplanes can be described by the equations,

$$\vec{w} \cdot \vec{x} - b = 1 \text{ (anything on or above this boundary is of one class, with label 1),}$$

and

$$\vec{w} \cdot \vec{x} - b = -1 \text{ (anything on or below this boundary is of the other class, with label −1).}$$

Geometrically, the distance between these two hyperplanes is $\dfrac{2}{\|\vec{w}\|}$, so to maximize the distance between the planes we want to minimize $\|\vec{w}\|$. The distance is computed using the distance from a point to a plane equation. We also have to prevent data points from falling into the margin, we add the following constraint: for each i either,

$$\vec{w}\cdot\vec{x}_i - b \geq 1, \text{ if } y_i = 1,,$$

or

$$\vec{w}\cdot\vec{x}_i - b \leq -1, \text{ if } y_i = -1.$$

These constraints state that each data point must lie on the correct side of the margin.

This can be rewritten as,

$$y_i(\vec{w}\cdot\vec{x}_i - b) \geq 1, \quad \text{for all } 1 \leq i \leq n.$$

We can put this together to get the optimization problem:

"Minimize $\|\quad\|$ subject to $y_i(\vec{w}\cdot\vec{x}_i - b) \geq 1$, for $i = 1,\ldots,n$"

The $\vec{w}$ and b that solve this problem determine our classifier, $\vec{x} \mapsto \text{sgn}(\vec{w}\cdot\vec{x} - b)$.

An important consequence of this geometric description is that the max-margin hyperplane is completely determined by those $\vec{x}_i$ that lie nearest to it. These $\vec{x}_i$ are called support vectors.

Soft-margin

To extend SVM to cases in which the data are not linearly separable, we introduce the *hinge loss* function,

$$\max\left(0, 1 - y_i(\vec{w}\cdot\vec{x}_i - b)\right).$$

Note that y_i is the i-th target (i.e., in this case, 1 or −1), and $\vec{w}\cdot\vec{x}_i - b$ is the current output.

This function is zero if the constraint in $y_i\ \vec{w}\ \vec{x}_i - b\ \geq 1$ is satisfied, in other words, if $\vec{x}_i$ lies on the correct side of the margin. For data on the wrong side of the margin, the function's value is proportional to the distance from the margin.

We then wish to minimize,

$$\left[\frac{1}{n}\sum_{i=1}^{n}\max\left(0, 1 - y_i(\vec{w}\cdot\vec{x}_i - b)\right)\right] + \lambda\|\vec{w}\|^2,$$

where the parameter λ determines the trade-off between increasing the margin size and ensuring that the $\vec{x}_i$ lie on the correct side of the margin. Thus, for sufficiently small values of λ, the second term in the loss function will become negligible, hence, it will behave similar to the hard-margin SVM, if the input data are linearly classifiable, but will still learn if a classification rule is viable or not.

Nonlinear Classification

The original maximum-margin hyperplane algorithm proposed by Vapnik in 1963 constructed a linear classifier. However, in 1992, Bernhard E. Boser, Isabelle M. Guyon and Vladimir N. Vapnik suggested a way to create nonlinear classifiers by applying the kernel trick to maximum-margin hyperplanes. The resulting algorithm is formally similar, except that every dot product is replaced by a nonlinear kernel function. This allows the algorithm to fit the maximum-margin hyperplane in a transformed feature space. The transformation may be nonlinear and the transformed space high-dimensional; although the classifier is a hyperplane in the transformed feature space, it may be nonlinear in the original input space.

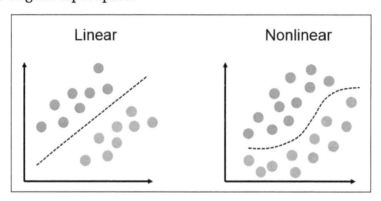

It is noteworthy that working in a higher-dimensional feature space increases the generalization error of support-vector machines, although given enough samples the algorithm still performs well.

Some common kernels include:

- Polynomial (homogeneous): $k(\vec{x_i}, \vec{x_j}) = (\vec{x_i} \cdot \vec{x_j})^d$.

- Polynomial (inhomogeneous): $k(\vec{x_i}, \vec{x_j}) = (\vec{x_i} \cdot \vec{x_j} + 1)^d$.

- Gaussian radial basis function: $k(\vec{x_i}, \vec{x_j}) = \exp(-\gamma \| \vec{x_i} - \vec{x_j} \|^2)$ for $\gamma > 0$. Sometimes parametrized using $\gamma = 1 / (2\sigma^2)$.

- Hyperbolic tangent: $k(\vec{x_i}, \vec{x_j}) = \tanh(\kappa \vec{x_i} \cdot \vec{x_j} + c)$ for some (not every) $\kappa > 0$ and $c < 0$.

The kernel is related to the transform $\varphi(\vec{x_i})$ by the equation $k(\vec{x_i}, \vec{x_j}) = \varphi(\vec{x_i}) \cdot \varphi(\vec{x_j})$. The value w is also in the transformed space, with $\vec{w} = \sum_i \alpha_i y_i \varphi(\vec{x_i})$. Dot products with w for classification can again be computed by the kernel trick, i.e. $\vec{w} \cdot \varphi(\vec{x}) = \sum_i \alpha_i y_i k(\vec{x_i}, \vec{x})$.

Computing the SVM Classifier

Computing the (soft-margin) SVM classifier amounts to minimizing an expression of the form

$$\left[\frac{1}{n}\sum_{i=1}^{n} \max(0, 1 - y_i(w \cdot x_i - b))\right] + \lambda \| w \|^2 .$$

We focus on the soft-margin classifier since, choosing a sufficiently small value for λ yields the hard-margin classifier for linearly classifiable input data.

Primal

Minimizing $\left[\dfrac{1}{n}\sum_{i=1}^{n}\max\left(0,1-y_i(w{\cdot}x_i-b)\right)\right]+\lambda\,\|w\|^2$ can be rewritten as a constrained optimization problem with a differentiable objective function in the following way.

For each $i\in\{1,\ldots,n\}$ we introduce a variable $\zeta_i=\max\left(0,1-y_i(w{\cdot}x_i-b)\right)$. Note that ζ_i is the smallest nonnegative number satisfying $y_i(w{\cdot}x_i-b)\geq1-\zeta_i$.

Thus we can rewrite the optimization problem as follows,

$$\text{minimize}\;\frac{1}{n}\sum_{i=1}^{n}\zeta_i+\lambda\,\|w\|^2$$

$$\text{subject to } y_i(w{\cdot}x_i-b)\geq1-\zeta_i \text{ and } \zeta_i\geq0, \text{for all } i.$$

This is called the *primal* problem.

Dual

By solving for the Lagrangian dual of the above problem, one obtains the simplified problem

$$\text{maximize } f(c_1\ldots c_n)=\sum_{i=1}^{n}c_i-\frac{1}{2}\sum_{i=1}^{n}\sum_{j=1}^{n}y_ic_i(x_i{\cdot}x_j)y_jc_j,$$

$$\text{subject to }\sum_{i=1}^{n}c_iy_i=0, \text{and } 0\leq c_i\leq\frac{1}{2n\lambda} \text{ for all } i.$$

This is called the *dual* problem. Since the dual maximization problem is a quadratic function of the c_i subject to linear constraints, it is efficiently solvable by quadratic programming algorithms.

Here, the variables c_i are defined such that,

$$\vec{w}=\sum_{i=1}^{n}c_iy_i\vec{x}_i.$$

Moreover, $c_i=0$ exactly when $\vec{x}_i$ lies on the correct side of the margin, and $0<c_i<(2n\lambda)^{-1}$ when $\vec{x}_i$ lies on the margin's boundary. It follows that $\vec{w}$ can be written as a linear combination of the support vectors.

The offset, b, can be recovered by finding an $\vec{x}_i$ on the margin's boundary and solving,

$$y_i(\vec{w}{\cdot}\vec{x}_i-b)=1\Leftrightarrow b=\vec{w}{\cdot}\vec{x}_i-y_i.$$

Note that $y_i^{-1}=y_i$ since $y_i=\pm1$.

Kernel Trick

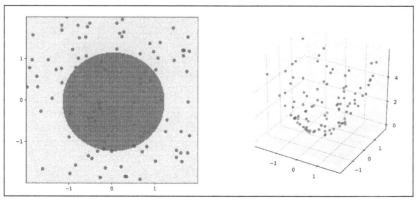

A training example of SVM with kernel given by $\varphi((a, b)) = (a, b, a^2 + b^2)$.

Suppose now that we would like to learn a nonlinear classification rule which corresponds to a linear classification rule for the transformed data points $\varphi(\vec{x}_i)$. Moreover, we are given a kernel function k which satisfies $k(\vec{x}_i, \vec{x}_j) = \varphi(\vec{x}_i) \cdot \varphi(\vec{x}_j)$.

We know the classification vector $\vec{w}$ in the transformed space satisfies,

$$\vec{w} = \sum_{i=1}^{n} c_i y_i \varphi(\vec{x}_i),$$

where, the c_i are obtained by solving the optimization problem,

$$\text{maximize } f(c_1 \ldots c_n) = \sum_{i=1}^{n} c_i - \frac{1}{2} \sum_{i=1}^{n} \sum_{j=1}^{n} y_i c_i (\varphi(\vec{x}_i) \cdot \varphi(\vec{x}_j)) y_j c_j$$

$$= \sum_{i=1}^{n} c_i - \frac{1}{2} \sum_{i=1}^{n} \sum_{j=1}^{n} y_i c_i k(\vec{x}_i, \vec{x}_j) y_j c_j$$

$$\text{subject to } \sum_{i=1}^{n} c_i y_i = 0, \text{ and } 0 \le c_i \le \frac{1}{2n\lambda}, \text{ for all } i.$$

The coefficients c_i can be solved for using quadratic programming, as before. Again, we can find some index i such that $0 < c_i < (2n\lambda)^{-1}$, so that $\varphi(\vec{x}_i)$ lies on the boundary of the margin in the transformed space, and then solve

$$b = \vec{w} \cdot \varphi(\vec{x}_i) - y_i = \left[\sum_{j=1}^{n} c_j y_j \varphi(\vec{x}_j) \cdot \varphi(\vec{x}_i) \right] - y_i$$

$$= \left[\sum_{j=1}^{n} c_j y_j k(\vec{x}_j, \vec{x}_i) \right] - y_i.$$

Finally,

$$\vec{z} \mapsto \text{sgn}(\vec{w} \cdot \varphi(\vec{z}) - b) = \text{sgn}\left(\left[\sum_{i=1}^{n} c_i y_i k(\vec{x}_i, \vec{z}) \right] - b \right).$$

Modern Methods

Recent algorithms for finding the SVM classifier include sub-gradient descent and coordinate descent. Both techniques have proven to offer significant advantages over the traditional approach when dealing with large, sparse datasets—sub-gradient methods are especially efficient when there are many training examples, and coordinate descent when the dimension of the feature space is high.

Sub-gradient Descent

Sub-gradient descent algorithms for the SVM work directly with the expression,

$$f(\vec{w},b) = \left[\frac{1}{n} \sum_{i=1}^{n} \max\left(0, 1 - y_i(\vec{w} \cdot \vec{x}_i - b)\right) \right] + \lambda \| \vec{w} \|^2 .$$

Note that f is a convex function of $\vec{w}$ and b. As such, traditional gradient descent (or SGD) methods can be adapted, where instead of taking a step in the direction of the functions gradient, a step is taken in the direction of a vector selected from the function's sub-gradient. This approach has the advantage that, for certain implementations, the number of iterations does not scale with n, the number of data points.

Coordinate Descent

Coordinate descent algorithms for the SVM work from the dual problem,

$$\text{maximize } f(c_1 \ldots c_n) = \sum_{i=1}^{n} c_i - \frac{1}{2} \sum_{i=1}^{n} \sum_{j=1}^{n} y_i c_i (x_i \cdot x_j) y_j c_j,$$

$$\text{subject to } \sum_{i=1}^{n} c_i y_i = 0, \text{ and } 0 \le c_i \le \frac{1}{2n\lambda}, \text{for all } i.$$

For each $i \in \{1, \ldots, n\}$, iteratively, the coefficient c_i is adjusted in the direction of $\partial f / \partial c_i$. Then, the resulting vector of coefficients $(c_1', \ldots, c_n')$ is projected onto the nearest vector of coefficients that satisfies the given constraints. (Typically Euclidean distances are used.) The process is then repeated until a near-optimal vector of coefficients is obtained. The resulting algorithm is extremely fast in practice, although few performance guarantees have been proven.

Empirical Risk Minimization

The soft-margin support vector machine described above is an example of an empirical risk minimization (ERM) algorithm for the *hinge loss*. Seen this way, support vector machines belong to a natural class of algorithms for statistical inference, and many of its unique features are due to the behavior of the hinge loss. This perspective can provide further insight into how and why SVMs work, and allow us to better analyze their statistical properties.

Risk Minimization

In supervised learning, one is given a set of training examples $X_1 \ldots X_n$ with labels $y_1 \ldots y_n$, and wishes to predict y_{n+1} given X_{n+1}. To do so one forms a hypothesis, f, such that $f(X_{n+1})$ is a "good" approximation of y_{n+1}. A "good" approximation is usually defined with the help of a *loss function, $\ell(y,z)$*, which characterizes how bad z is as a prediction of y. We would then like to choose a hypothesis that minimizes the *expected risk:*

$$\varepsilon(f) = \mathbb{E}\left[\ell(y_{n+1}, f(X_{n+1}))\right].$$

In most cases, we don't know the joint distribution of X_{n+1}, y_{n+1} outright. In these cases, a common strategy is to choose the hypothesis that minimizes the empirical risk:

$$\hat{\varepsilon}(f) = \frac{1}{n}\sum_{k=1}^{n}\ell(y_k, f(X_k)).$$

Under certain assumptions about the sequence of random variables X_k, y_k (for example, that they are generated by a finite Markov process), if the set of hypotheses being considered is small enough, the minimizer of the empirical risk will closely approximate the minimizer of the expected risk as n grows large. This approach is called *empirical risk minimization*, or ERM.

Regularization and Stability

In order for the minimization problem to have a well-defined solution, we have to place constraints on the set $\mathcal{H}$ of hypotheses being considered. If $\mathcal{H}$ is a normed space (as is the case for SVM), a particularly effective technique is to consider only those hypotheses f for which $\| f \|_{\mathcal{H}} < k$. This is equivalent to imposing a *regularization penalty* $\mathcal{R}(f) = \lambda_k \| f \|_{\mathcal{H}}$, and solving the new optimization problem,

$$\hat{f} = \arg \min_{f \in \mathcal{H}} \hat{\varepsilon}(f) + \mathcal{R}(f).$$

This approach is called Tikhonov regularization.

More generally, $\mathcal{R}(f)$ can be some measure of the complexity of the hypothesis f, so that simpler hypotheses are preferred.

SVM and the Hinge Loss

Recall that the (soft-margin) SVM classifier $\hat{w}, b : x \mapsto \mathrm{sgn}(\hat{w} \cdot x - b)$ is chosen to minimize the following expression,

$$\left[\frac{1}{n}\sum_{i=1}^{n}\max\left(0, 1 - y_i(w \cdot x_i - b)\right)\right] + \lambda \| w \|^2 .$$

We see that the SVM technique is equivalent to empirical risk minimization with Tikhonov regularization, where in this case the loss function is the hinge loss,

$$\ell(y,z) = \max\left(0, 1 - yz\right).$$

From this perspective, SVM is closely related to other fundamental classification algorithms such as regularized least-squares and logistic regression. The difference between the three lies in the choice of loss function: regularized least-squares amounts to empirical risk minimization with the square-loss,

$$_{sq}(y,z) = (y-z) \ ;$$

logistic regression employs the log-loss,

$$\ell_{\log}(y,z) = \ln(1 + e^{-yz}).$$

Target Functions

The difference between the hinge loss and these other loss functions is best stated in terms of *target functions* - the function that minimizes expected risk for a given pair of random variables X, y.

In particular, let y_x denote y conditional on the event that $X = x$. In the classification setting, we have:

$$y_x = \begin{cases} 1 & \text{with probability } p_x \\ -1 & \text{with probability } 1 - p_x \end{cases}$$

The optimal classifier is therefore:

$$f^*(x) = \begin{cases} 1 & \text{if } p_x \geq 1/2 \\ -1 & \text{otherwise} \end{cases}$$

For the square-loss, the target function is the conditional expectation function, $f_{sq}(x) = \mathbb{E}[y_x]$. For the logistic loss, it's the logit function, $f_{\log}(x) = \ln(p_x / (1 - p_x))$. While both of these target functions yield the correct classifier, as $\operatorname{sgn}(f_{sq}) = \operatorname{sgn}(f_{\log}) = f^*$, they give us more information than we need. In fact, they give us enough information to completely describe the distribution of y_x.

On the other hand one can check that the target function for the hinge loss is *exactly* f^*. Thus, in a sufficiently rich hypothesis space—or equivalently, for an appropriately chosen kernel—the SVM classifier will converge to the simplest function (in terms of $\mathcal{R}$) that correctly classifies the data. This extends the geometric interpretation of SVM—for linear classification, the empirical risk is minimized by any function whose margins lie between the support vectors, and the simplest of these is the max-margin classifier.

Properties

SVMs belong to a family of generalized linear classifiers and can be interpreted as an extension of the perceptron. They can also be considered a special case of Tikhonov regularization. A special property is that they simultaneously minimize the empirical *classification error* and maximize the *geometric margin*; hence they are also known as maximum margin classifiers. A comparison of the SVM to other classifiers has been made by Meyer, Leisch and Hornik.

Parameter Selection

The effectiveness of SVM depends on the selection of kernel, the kernel's parameters, and soft margin parameter C. A common choice is a Gaussian kernel, which has a single parameter γ. The best combination of C and γ is often selected by a grid search with exponentially growing sequences of C and γ, for example, $C \in \{2^{-5}, 2^{-3}, ..., 2^{13}, 2^{15}\}$; $\gamma \in \{2^{-15}, 2^{-13}, ..., 2^{1}, 2^{3}\}$. Typically, each combination of parameter choices is checked using cross validation, and the parameters with best cross-validation accuracy are picked. Alternatively, recent work in Bayesian optimization can be used to select C and γ, often requiring the evaluation of far fewer parameter combinations than grid search. The final model, which is used for testing and for classifying new data, is then trained on the whole training set using the selected parameters.

Issues

Potential drawbacks of the SVM include the following aspects:

- Requires full labeling of input data.

- Uncalibrated class membership probabilities—SVM stems from Vapnik's theory which avoids estimating probabilities on finite data.

- The SVM is only directly applicable for two-class tasks. Therefore, algorithms that reduce the multi-class task to several binary problems have to be applied.

- Parameters of a solved model are difficult to interpret.

Extensions

Support-vector Clustering

SVC is a similar method that also builds on kernel functions but is appropriate for unsupervised learning. It is considered a fundamental method in data science.

Multiclass SVM

Multiclass SVM aims to assign labels to instances by using support-vector machines, where the labels are drawn from a finite set of several elements.

The dominant approach for doing so is to reduce the single multiclass problem into multiple binary classification problems. Common methods for such reduction include:

- Building binary classifiers that distinguish between one of the labels and the rest (*one-versus-all*) or between every pair of classes (*one-versus-one*). Classification of new instances for the one-versus-all case is done by a winner-takes-all strategy, in which the classifier with the highest-output function assigns the class (it is important that the output functions be calibrated to produce comparable scores). For the one-versus-one approach, classification is done by a max-wins voting strategy, in which every classifier assigns the instance to one of the two classes, then the vote for the assigned class is increased by one vote, and finally the class with the most votes determines the instance classification.

- Directed acyclic graph SVM (DAGSVM).

- Error-correcting output codes.

Crammer and Singer proposed a multiclass SVM method which casts the multiclass classification problem into a single optimization problem, rather than decomposing it into multiple binary classification problems.

Transductive Support-vector Machines

Transductive support-vector machines extend SVMs in that they could also treat partially labeled data in semi-supervised learning by following the principles of transduction. Here, in addition to the training set $\mathcal{D}$, the learner is also given a set.

$$\mathcal{D}^\star = \{\vec{x}_i^\star \mid \vec{x}_i^\star \in \mathbb{R}^p\}_{i=1}^k$$

of test examples to be classified. Formally, a transductive support-vector machine is defined by the following primal optimization problem:

Minimize (in $\vec{w}, b, \overrightarrow{y^\star}$),

$$\frac{1}{2}\|\vec{w}\|^2$$

subject to (for any $i = 1, \dots, n$ and any $j = 1, \dots, k$),

$$y_i(\vec{w} \cdot \overrightarrow{x_i} - b) \geq 1,$$

$$y_j^\star(\vec{w} \cdot \overrightarrow{x_j^\star} - b) \geq 1,$$

and

$$y_j^\star \in \{-1, 1\}.$$

Structured SVM

SVMs have been generalized to structured SVMs, where the label space is structured and of possibly infinite size.

Regression

A version of SVM for regression was proposed in 1996 by Vladimir N. Vapnik, Harris Drucker, Christopher J. C. Burges, Linda Kaufman and Alexander J. Smola. This method is called support-vector regression (SVR). The model produced by support-vector classification depends only on a subset of the training data, because the cost function for building the model does not care about training points that lie beyond the margin. Analogously, the model produced by SVR depends only on a subset of the training data, because the cost function for building the model ignores any training data close to the model prediction. Another SVM version known as least-squares support-vector machine (LS-SVM) has been proposed by Suykens and Vandewalle.

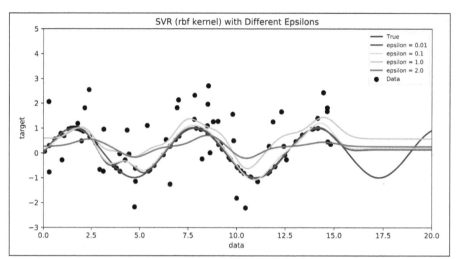

Support-vector regression (prediction) with different thresholds ε.
As ε increases, the prediction becomes less sensitive to errors.

Training the original SVR means solving,

$$\text{minimize } \frac{1}{2}\| w \|^2$$

$$\text{subject to } | y_i - \langle w, x_i \rangle - b | \leq \varepsilon$$

where x_i is a training sample with target value y_i. The inner product plus intercept $\langle w, x_i \rangle + b$ is the prediction for that sample, and ε is a free parameter that serves as a threshold: all predictions have to be within an ε range of the true predictions. Slack variables are usually added into the above to allow for errors and to allow approximation in the case the above problem is infeasible.

Bayesian SVM

In 2011, it was shown by Polson and Scott that the SVM admits a Bayesian interpretation through the technique of data augmentation. In this approach the SVM is viewed as a graphical model (where the parameters are connected via probability distributions). This extended view allows the application of Bayesian techniques to SVMs, such as flexible feature modeling, automatic hyperparameter tuning, and predictive uncertainty quantification. Recently, a scalable version of the Bayesian SVM was developed by Wenzel et al. enabling the application of Bayesian SVMs to big data.

Implementation

The parameters of the maximum-margin hyperplane are derived by solving the optimization. There exist several specialized algorithms for quickly solving the quadratic programming (QP) problem that arises from SVMs, mostly relying on heuristics for breaking the problem down into smaller, more manageable chunks.

Another approach is to use an interior-point method that uses Newton-like iterations to find a solution of the Karush–Kuhn–Tucker conditions of the primal and dual problems. Instead of solving a sequence of broken-down problems, this approach directly solves the problem altogether. To avoid solving a linear system involving the large kernel matrix, a low-rank approximation to the matrix is often used in the kernel trick.

Another common method is Platt's sequential minimal optimization (SMO) algorithm, which breaks the problem down into 2-dimensional sub-problems that are solved analytically, eliminating the need for a numerical optimization algorithm and matrix storage. This algorithm is conceptually simple, easy to implement, generally faster, and has better scaling properties for difficult SVM problems.

The special case of linear support-vector machines can be solved more efficiently by the same kind of algorithms used to optimize its close cousin, logistic regression; this class of algorithms includes sub-gradient descent (e.g., PEGASOS) and coordinate descent (e.g., LIBLINEAR). LIBLINEAR has some attractive training-time properties. Each convergence iteration takes time linear in the time taken to read the train data, and the iterations also have a Q-linear convergence property, making the algorithm extremely fast.

The general kernel SVMs can also be solved more efficiently using sub-gradient descent (e.g. P-packSVM), especially when parallelization is allowed.

Kernel SVMs are available in many machine-learning toolkits, including LIBSVM, MATLAB, SAS, SVMlight, kernlab, scikit-learn, Shogun, Weka, Shark, JKernelMachines, OpenCV and others.

Apriori Algorithm

Apriori is an algorithm for frequent item set mining and association rule learning over relational databases. It proceeds by identifying the frequent individual items in the database and extending them to larger and larger item sets as long as those item sets appear sufficiently often in the database. The frequent item sets determined by Apriori can be used to determine association rules which highlight general trends in the database: this has applications in domains such as market basket analysis.

The Apriori algorithm was proposed by Agrawal and Srikant in 1994. Apriori is designed to operate on databases containing transactions (for example, collections of items bought by customers, or details of a website frequentation or IP addresses). Other algorithms are designed for finding association rules in data having no transactions, or having no timestamps (DNA sequencing). Each transaction is seen as a set of items (an *itemset*). Given a threshold C, the Apriori algorithm identifies the item sets which are subsets of at least C transactions in the database.

Apriori uses a "bottom up" approach, where frequent subsets are extended one item at a time (a step known as *candidate generation*), and groups of candidates are tested against the data. The algorithm terminates when no further successful extensions are found.

Apriori uses breadth-first search and a Hash tree structure to count candidate item sets efficiently. It generates candidate item sets of length k from item sets of length $k-1$. Then it prunes the candidates which have an infrequent sub pattern. According to the downward closure lemma, the candidate set contains all frequent k-length item sets. After that, it scans the transaction database to determine frequent item sets among the candidates.

The pseudo code for the algorithm is given below for a transaction database T, and a support threshold of ϵ. Usual set theoretic notation is employed, though note that T is a multiset. C_k is the candidate set for level k. At each step, the algorithm is assumed to generate the candidate sets from the large item sets of the preceding level, heeding the downward closure lemma. $count[c]$ accesses a field of the data structure that represents candidate set c, which is initially assumed to be zero.

$$\text{Apriori}(T,\epsilon)$$
$$L_1 \leftarrow \{\text{large 1-itemsets}\}$$
$$k \leftarrow 2$$
$$\text{while } L_{k-1} \neq \phi$$
$$C_k \leftarrow \{c = a \cup \{b\} \mid a \in L_{k-1} \wedge b \notin a, \{s \subseteq c \mid\mid s \mid = k-1\} \subseteq L_{k-1}\}$$
$$\text{for transactions } t \in T$$
$$D_t \leftarrow \{c \in C_k \mid c \subseteq t\}$$
$$\text{for candidates } c \in D_t$$
$$count[c] \leftarrow count[c] + 1$$
$$L_k \leftarrow \{c \in C_k \mid count[c] \geq \epsilon\}$$
$$k \leftarrow k+1$$
$$\text{return} \bigcup_k L_k$$

Examples:

Consider the following database, where each row is a transaction and each cell is an individual item of the transaction:

alpha	beta	epsilon
alpha	beta	theta
alpha	beta	epsilon
alpha	beta	theta

The association rules that can be determined from this database are the following:

1. 100% of sets with alpha also contain beta.

2. 50% of sets with alpha, beta also have epsilon.

3. 50% of sets with alpha, beta also have theta.

We can also illustrate this through a variety of examples.

Example:

Assume that a large supermarket tracks sales data by stock-keeping unit (SKU) for each item: each item, such as "butter" or "bread", is identified by a numerical SKU. The supermarket has a database of transactions where each transaction is a set of SKUs that were bought together.

Let the database of transactions consist of following itemsets:

Itemsets
{1, 2, 3, 4}
{1, 2, 4}
{1, 2}
{2, 3, 4}
{2, 3}
{3, 4}
{2, 4}

We will use Apriori to determine the frequent item sets of this database. To do this, we will say that an item set is frequent if it appears in at least 3 transactions of the database: the value 3 is the support threshold.

The first step of Apriori is to count up the number of occurrences, called the support, of each member item separately. By scanning the database for the first time, we obtain the following result:

Item	Support
{1}	3
{2}	6
{3}	4
{4}	5

All the itemsets of size 1 have a support of at least 3, so they are all frequent.

The next step is to generate a list of all pairs of the frequent items.

For example, regarding the pair {1, 2}: the first table shows items 1 and 2 appearing together in three of the itemsets; therefore, we say item {1, 2} has support of three.

Item	Support
{1, 2}	3
{1, 3}	1
{1, 4}	2
{2, 3}	3
{2, 4}	4
{3, 4}	3

The pairs {1, 2}, {2, 3}, {2, 4}, and {3, 4} all meet or exceed the minimum support of 3, so they are frequent. The pairs {1, 3} and {1, 4} are not. Now, because {1, 3} and {1, 4} are not frequent, any larger set which contains {1, 3} or {1, 4} cannot be frequent. In this way, we can *prune* sets: we will now look for frequent triples in the database, but we can already exclude all the triples that contain one of these two pairs:

Item	Support
{2, 3, 4}	2

In the example, there are no frequent triplets. {2, 3, 4} is below the minimal threshold, and the other triplets were excluded because they were super sets of pairs that were already below the threshold.

We have thus determined the frequent sets of items in the database, and illustrated how some items were not counted because one of their subsets was already known to be below the threshold.

Limitations

Apriori, while historically significant, suffers from a number of inefficiencies or trade-offs, which have spawned other algorithms. Candidate generation generates large numbers of subsets (the algorithm attempts to load up the candidate set with as many as possible before each scan). Bottom-up subset exploration (essentially a breadth-first traversal of the subset lattice) finds any maximal subset S only after all $2^{|S|} - 1$ of its proper subsets.

The algorithm scans the database too many times, which reduces the overall performance. Due to this, the algorithm assumes that the database is Permanent in the memory.

Also, both the time and space complexity of this algorithm are very high: $O(2^{|D|})$, thus exponential, where $|D|$ is the horizontal width (the total number of items) present in the database.

Later algorithms such as Max-Miner try to identify the maximal frequent item sets without enumerating their subsets, and perform "jumps" in the search space rather than a purely bottom-up approach.

Expectation–maximization Algorithm

In statistics, an expectation–maximization (EM) algorithm is an iterative method to find maximum likelihood or maximum a posteriori (MAP) estimates of parameters in statistical models, where the model depends on unobserved latent variables. The EM iteration alternates between performing an expectation (E) step, which creates a function for the expectation of the log-likelihood evaluated using the current estimate for the parameters, and a maximization (M) step, which computes parameters maximizing the expected log-likelihood found on the E step. These parameter-estimates are then used to determine the distribution of the latent variables in the next E step.

The EM algorithm is used to find (local) maximum likelihood parameters of a statistical model in cases where the equations cannot be solved directly. Typically these models involve latent variables in addition to unknown parameters and known data observations. That is, either missing values exist among the data, or the model can be formulated more simply by assuming the existence of further unobserved data points. For example, a mixture model can be described more simply by assuming that each observed data point has a corresponding unobserved data point, or latent variable, specifying the mixture component to which each data point belongs.

Finding a maximum likelihood solution typically requires taking the derivatives of the likelihood function with respect to all the unknown values, the parameters and the latent variables, and simultaneously solving the resulting equations. In statistical models with latent variables, this is usually impossible. Instead, the result is typically a set of interlocking equations in which the solution to the parameters requires the values of the latent variables and vice versa, but substituting one set of equations into the other produces an unsolvable equation.

The EM algorithm proceeds from the observation that there is a way to solve these two sets of equations numerically. One can simply pick arbitrary values for one of the two sets of unknowns, use them to estimate the second set, then use these new values to find a better estimate of the first set, and then keep alternating between the two until the resulting values both converge to fixed points. It's not obvious that this will work, but it can be proven that in this context it does, and that the derivative of the likelihood is (arbitrarily close to) zero at that point, which in turn means that the point is either a maximum or a saddle point. In general, multiple maxima may occur, with no guarantee that the global maximum will be found. Some likelihoods also have singularities in them, i.e., nonsensical maxima. For example, one of the *solutions* that may be found by EM in a mixture model involves setting one of the components to have zero variance and the mean parameter for the same component to be equal to one of the data points.

Given the statistical model which generates a set $\mathbf{X}$ of observed data, a set of unobserved latent data or missing values $\mathbf{Z}$, and a vector of unknown parameters θ, along with a likelihood function, $L(\theta;\mathbf{X},\mathbf{Z}) = p(\mathbf{X},\mathbf{Z},\theta)$, the maximum likelihood estimate (MLE) of the unknown parameters is determined by maximizing the marginal likelihood of the observed data,

$$L(\theta;\mathbf{X}) = p(\mathbf{X}\,|\,\theta) = \int p(\mathbf{X},\mathbf{Z}\,|\,\theta)d\mathbf{Z}$$

However, this quantity is often intractable, e.g. if $\mathbf{Z}$ is a sequence of events, so that the number of values grows exponentially with the sequence length, the exact calculation of the sum will be extremely difficult.

The EM algorithm seeks to find the MLE of the marginal likelihood by iteratively applying these two steps:

1. Expectation step (E step): Define $Q\left(\theta\,|\,\theta^{(t)}\right)$ as the expected value of the log likelihood function of θ, with respect to the current conditional distribution of $\mathbf{Z}$ given $\mathbf{X}$ and the current estimates of the parameters $\theta^{(t)}$:

$$Q(\theta\,|\,\theta^{(t)}) = \mathrm{E}_{\mathbf{Z}|\mathbf{X},\theta^{(t)}}\left[\log L(\theta;\mathbf{X},\mathbf{Z})\right]$$

2. Maximization step (M step): Find the parameters that maximize this quantity:

$$\theta^{(t+1)} = \arg\max_{\theta} Q(\theta\,|\,\theta^{(t)})$$

The typical models to which EM is applied use $\mathbf{Z}$ as a latent variable indicating membership in one of a set of groups:

1. The observed data points $\mathbf{X}$ may be discrete (taking values in a finite or countably infinite

set) or continuous (taking values in an uncountably infinite set). Associated with each data point may be a vector of observations.

2. The missing values (aka latent variables) **Z** are discrete, drawn from a fixed number of values, and with one latent variable per observed unit.

3. The parameters are continuous, and are of two kinds: Parameters that are associated with all data points, and those associated with a specific value of a latent variable (i.e., associated with all data points which corresponding latent variable has that value).

However, it is possible to apply EM to other sorts of models. The motive is as follows. If the value of the parameters θ is known, usually the value of the latent variables **Z** can be found by maximizing the log-likelihood over all possible values of **Z**, either simply by iterating over **Z** or through an algorithm such as the Baum–Welch algorithm for hidden Markov models. Conversely, if we know the value of the latent variables **Z**, we can find an estimate of the parameters θ fairly easily, typically by simply grouping the observed data points according to the value of the associated latent variable and averaging the values, or some function of the values, of the points in each group. This suggests an iterative algorithm, in the case where both θ and **Z** are unknown:

1. First, initialize the parameters θ to some random values.

2. Compute the probability of each possible value of **Z**, given θ.

3. Then, use the just-computed values of **Z** to compute a better estimate for the parameters θ.

4. Iterate steps 2 and 3 until convergence.

The algorithm as just described monotonically approaches a local minimum of the cost function.

Properties

Speaking of an expectation (E) step is a bit of a misnomer. What are calculated in the first step are the fixed, data-dependent parameters of the function Q. Once the parameters of Q are known, it is fully determined and is maximized in the second (M) step of an EM algorithm.

Although an EM iteration does increase the observed data (i.e., marginal) likelihood function, no guarantee exists that the sequence converges to a maximum likelihood estimator. For multimodal distributions, this means that an EM algorithm may converge to a local maximum of the observed data likelihood function, depending on starting values. A variety of heuristic or metaheuristic approaches exist to escape a local maximum, such as random-restart hill climbing (starting with several different random initial estimates $\theta^{(t)}$), or applying simulated annealing methods.

EM is especially useful when the likelihood is an exponential family: the E step becomes the sum of expectations of sufficient statistics, and the M step involves maximizing a linear function. In such a case, it is usually possible to derive closed-form expression updates for each step, using the Sundberg formula.

The EM method was modified to compute maximum a posteriori (MAP) estimates for Bayesian inference.

Other methods exist to find maximum likelihood estimates, such as gradient descent, conjugate gradient, or variants of the Gauss–Newton algorithm. Unlike EM, such methods typically require the evaluation of first and second derivatives of the likelihood function.

Proof of Correctness

Expectation-maximization works to improve $Q(\theta \mid \theta^{(t)})$ rather than directly improving $\log p(\mathbf{X} \mid \theta)$. Here is shown that improvements to the former imply improvements to the latter.

For any $\mathbf{Z}$ with non-zero probability $p(\mathbf{Z} \mid \mathbf{X}, \theta)$, we can write:

$$\log p(\mathbf{X} \mid \theta) = \log p(\mathbf{X}, \mathbf{Z} \mid \theta) - \log p(\mathbf{Z} \mid \mathbf{X}, \theta).$$

We take the expectation over possible values of the unknown data $\mathbf{Z}$ under the current parameter estimate $\theta^{(t)}$ by multiplying both sides by $p(\mathbf{Z} \mid \mathbf{X}, \theta^{(t)})$ and summing (or integrating) over $\mathbf{Z}$. The left-hand side is the expectation of a constant, so we get,

$$\log p(\mathbf{X} \mid \theta) = \sum_{\mathbf{Z}} p(\mathbf{Z} \mid \mathbf{X}, \theta^{(t)}) \log p(\mathbf{X}, \mathbf{Z} \mid \theta) - \sum_{\mathbf{Z}} p(\mathbf{Z} \mid \mathbf{X}, \theta^{(t)}) \log p(\mathbf{Z} \mid \mathbf{X}, \theta)$$

$$= Q(\theta \mid \theta^{(t)}) + H(\theta \mid \theta^{(t)}),$$

where $H(\theta \mid \theta^{(t)})$ is defined by the negated sum it is replacing. This last equation holds for every value of θ including $Q(\theta \mid \theta^{(t)})$,

$$\log p(\mathbf{X} \mid \theta^{(t)}) = Q(\theta^{(t)} \mid \theta^{(t)}) + H(\theta^{(t)} \mid \theta^{(t)}),$$

and subtracting this last equation from the previous equation gives,

$$\log p(\mathbf{X} \mid \theta) - \log p(\mathbf{X} \mid \theta^{(t)}) = Q(\theta \mid \theta^{(t)}) - Q(\theta^{(t)} \mid \theta^{(t)}) + H(\theta \mid \theta^{(t)}) - H(\theta^{(t)} \mid \theta^{(t)}),$$

However, Jensen's inequality tells us that $H(\theta \mid \theta^{(t)}) \geq H(\theta^{(t)} \mid \theta^{(t)})$, so we can conclude that:

$$\log p(\mathbf{X} \mid \theta) - \log p(\mathbf{X} \mid \theta^{(t)}) \geq Q(\theta \mid \theta^{(t)}) - Q(\theta^{(t)} \mid \theta^{(t)}).$$

In words, choosing θ to improve $Q(\theta \mid \theta^{(t)})$ causes $\log p(\mathbf{X} \mid \theta)$ to improve at least as much.

As a Maximization–maximization Procedure

The EM algorithm can be viewed as two alternating maximization steps, that is, as an example of coordinate ascent. Consider the function,

$$F(q, \theta) := \mathrm{E}_q[\log L(\theta; x, Z)] + H(q),$$

where q is an arbitrary probability distribution over the unobserved data z and $H(q)$ is the entropy of the distribution q. This function can be written as,

$$F(q, \theta) = -D_{KL}\big(q \parallel p_{Z \mid X}(\cdot \mid x; \theta)\big) + \log L(\theta; x),$$

where $p_{Z|X}(\cdot | x; \theta)$ is the conditional distribution of the unobserved data given the observed data x and D_{KL} is the Kullback–Leibler divergence.

Then the steps in the EM algorithm may be viewed as:

- Expectation step – Choose q to maximize F:

$$q^{(t)} = \arg\max_q F(q, \theta^{(t)})$$

- Maximization step – Choose θ to maximize F:

$$\theta^{(t+1)} = \arg\max_\theta F(q^{(t)}, \theta)$$

Applications

EM is frequently used for data clustering in machine learning and computer vision. In natural language processing, two prominent instances of the algorithm are the Baum–Welch algorithm for hidden Markov models, and the inside-outside algorithm for unsupervised induction of probabilistic context-free grammars.

EM is frequently used for parameter estimation of mixed models, notably in quantitative genetics. In psychometrics, EM is almost indispensable for estimating item parameters and latent abilities of item response theory models.

With the ability to deal with missing data and observe unidentified variables, EM is becoming a useful tool to price and manage risk of a portfolio.

The EM algorithm (and its faster variant ordered subset expectation maximization) is also widely used in medical image reconstruction, especially in positron emission tomography and single photon emission computed tomography.

In structural engineering, the Structural Identification using Expectation Maximization (STRIDE) algorithm is an output-only method for identifying natural vibration properties of a structural system using sensor data.

Filtering and Smoothing EM Algorithms

A Kalman filter is typically used for on-line state estimation and a minimum-variance smoother may be employed for off-line or batch state estimation. However, these minimum-variance solutions require estimates of the state-space model parameters. EM algorithms can be used for solving joint state and parameter estimation problems.

Filtering and smoothing EM algorithms arise by repeating this two-step procedure:

E-step

Operate a Kalman filter or a minimum-variance smoother designed with current parameter estimates to obtain updated state estimates.

M-step

Use the filtered or smoothed state estimates within maximum-likelihood calculations to obtain updated parameter estimates.

Suppose that a Kalman filter or minimum-variance smoother operates on measurements of a single-input-single-output system that possess additive white noise. An updated measurement noise variance estimate can be obtained from the maximum likelihood calculation,

$$\hat{\sigma}_v^2 = \frac{1}{N}\sum_{k=1}^{N}(z_k - \hat{x}_k)^2$$

where $\hat{x}_k$ are scalar output estimates calculated by a filter or a smoother from N scalar measurements z_k. The above update can also be applied to updating a Poisson measurement noise intensity. Similarly, for a first-order auto-regressive process, an updated process noise variance estimate can be calculated by,

$$\hat{\sigma}_w^2 = \frac{1}{N}\sum_{k=1}^{N}(\hat{x}_{k+1} - \hat{F}\hat{x}_k)^2$$

where $\hat{x}_k$ and $\hat{x}_{k+1}$ are scalar state estimates calculated by a filter or a smoother. The updated model coefficient estimate is obtained via,

$$\hat{F} = \frac{\sum_{k=1}^{N}(\hat{x}_{k+1} - \hat{F}\hat{x}_k)}{\sum_{k=1}^{N}\hat{x}_k^2}.$$

Variants

A number of methods have been proposed to accelerate the sometimes slow convergence of the EM algorithm, such as those using conjugate gradient and modified Newton's methods (Newton–Raphson). Also, EM can be used with constrained estimation methods.

Parameter-expanded expectation maximization (PX-EM) algorithm often provides speed up by "using a 'covariance adjustment' to correct the analysis of the M step, capitalising on extra information captured in the imputed complete data".

Expectation conditional maximization (ECM) replaces each M step with a sequence of conditional maximization (CM) steps in which each parameter θ_i is maximized individually, conditionally on the other parameters remaining fixed. Itself can be extended into the Expectation conditional maximization either (ECME) algorithm.

This idea is further extended in *generalized expectation maximization (GEM)* algorithm, in which is sought only an increase in the objective function *F* for both the E step and M step GEM is further developed in a distributed environment and shows promising results.

It is also possible to consider the EM algorithm as a subclass of the MM (Majorize/Minimize or Minorize/Maximize, depending on context) algorithm, and therefore use any machinery developed in the more general case.

α-EM Algorithm

The Q-function used in the EM algorithm is based on the log likelihood. Therefore, it is regarded as the log-EM algorithm. The use of the log likelihood can be generalized to that of the α-log likelihood ratio. Then, the α-log likelihood ratio of the observed data can be exactly expressed as equality by using the Q-function of the α-log likelihood ratio and the α-divergence. Obtaining this Q-function is a generalized E step. Its maximization is a generalized M step. This pair is called the α-EM algorithm which contains the log-EM algorithm as its subclass. Thus, the α-EM algorithm by Yasuo Matsuyama is an exact generalization of the log-EM algorithm. No computation of gradient or Hessian matrix is needed. The α-EM shows faster convergence than the log-EM algorithm by choosing an appropriate α. The α-EM algorithm leads to a faster version of the Hidden Markov model estimation algorithm α-HMM.

Relation to Variational Bayes Methods

EM is a partially non-Bayesian, maximum likelihood method. Its final result gives a probability distribution over the latent variables (in the Bayesian style) together with a point estimate for θ (either a maximum likelihood estimate or a posterior mode). A fully Bayesian version of this may be wanted, giving a probability distribution over θ and the latent variables. The Bayesian approach to inference is simply to treat θ as another latent variable. In this paradigm, the distinction between the E and M steps disappears. If using the factorized Q approximation (variational Bayes), solving can iterate over each latent variable (now including θ) and optimize them one at a time. Now, k steps per iteration are needed, where k is the number of latent variables. For graphical models this is easy to do as each variable's new Q depends only on its Markov blanket, so local message passing can be used for efficient inference.

Geometric Interpretation

In information geometry, the E step and the M step are interpreted as projections under dual affine connections, called the e-connection and the m-connection; the Kullback–Leibler divergence can also be understood in these terms.

Examples:

Gaussian Mixture

Let $x = (x_1, x_2, \ldots, x_n)$ be a sample of n independent observations from a mixture of two multivariate normal distributions of dimension d, and let $z = (z_1, z_2, \ldots, z_n)$ be the latent variables that determine the component from which the observation originates.

$$X_i \mid (Z_i = 1) \sim \mathcal{N}_d(\mu_1, \Sigma_1) \text{ and } X_i \mid (Z_i = 2) \sim \mathcal{N}_d(\mu_2, \Sigma_2)$$

where,

$$P(Z_i = 1) = \tau_1 \text{ and } P(Z_i = 2) = \tau_2 = 1 - \tau_1$$

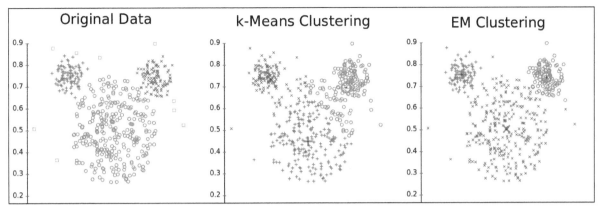

Comparison of k-means and EM on artificial data visualized with ELKI. Using the variances, the EM algorithm can describe the normal distributions exactly, while k-means splits the data in Voronoi-cells. The cluster center is indicated by the lighter, bigger symbol.

The aim is to estimate the unknown parameters representing the *mixing* value between the Gaussians and the means and covariances of each,

$$\theta = \left(\tau, \mu_1, \mu_2, \Sigma_1, \Sigma_2\right)$$

where the incomplete-data likelihood function is,

$$L(\theta; \mathbf{x}) = \prod_{i=1}^{n} \sum_{j=1}^{2} \tau_j\, f(\mathbf{x}_i; \mu_j, \Sigma_j),$$

and the complete-data likelihood function is,

$$L(\theta; \mathbf{x}, \mathbf{z}) = p(\mathbf{x}, \mathbf{z} \mid \theta) = \prod_{i=1}^{n} \prod_{j=1}^{2} \left[f(\mathbf{x}_i; \mu_j, \Sigma_j) \tau_j \right]^{\mathbb{I}(z_i = j)}$$

or

$$L(\theta; \mathbf{x}, \mathbf{z}) = \exp\left\{ \sum_{i=1}^{n} \sum_{j=1}^{2} \mathbb{I}(z_i = j) \left[\log \tau_j - \tfrac{1}{2} \log |\Sigma_j| - \tfrac{1}{2}(\mathbf{x}_i - \mu_j)^{\top} \Sigma_j^{-1}(\mathbf{x}_i - \mu_j) - \tfrac{d}{2}\log(2\pi) \right] \right\}.$$

where $\mathbb{I}$ is an indicator function and f is the probability density function of a multivariate normal.

In the last equality, for each i, one indicator $\mathbb{I}(z_i = j)$ is equal to zero, and one indicator is equal to one. The inner sum thus reduces to one term.

E Step

Given our current estimate of the parameters $\theta^{(t)}$, the conditional distribution of the Z_i is determined by Bayes theorem to be the proportional height of the normal density weighted by τ:

$$T_{j,i}^{(t)} := \mathrm{P}(Z_i = j \mid X_i = \mathbf{x}_i; \theta^{(t)}) = \frac{\tau_j^{(t)} f(\mathbf{x}_i; \mu_j^{(t)}, \Sigma_j^{(t)})}{\tau_1^{(t)} f(\mathbf{x}_i; \mu_1^{(t)}, \Sigma_1^{(t)}) + \tau_2^{(t)} f(\mathbf{x}_i; \mu_2^{(t)}, \Sigma_2^{(t)})}$$

These are called the "membership probabilities" which are normally considered the output of the E step (although this is not the Q function of below).

This E step corresponds with setting up this function for Q:

$$Q(\theta \mid \theta^{(t)}) = E_{Z \mid X, \theta^{(t)}}[\log L(\theta; \mathbf{x}, \mathbf{Z})]$$

$$= E_{Z \mid X, \theta^{(t)}}[\log \prod_{i=1}^{n} L(\theta; \mathbf{x}_i, Z_i)]$$

$$= E_{Z \mid X, \theta^{(t)}}[\sum_{i=1}^{n} \log L(\theta; \mathbf{x}_i, Z_i)]$$

$$= \sum_{i=1}^{n} E_{Z_i \mid X; \theta^{(t)}}[\log L(\theta; \mathbf{x}_i, Z_i)]$$

$$= \sum_{i=1}^{n} \sum_{j=1}^{2} P(Z_i = j \mid X_i = \mathbf{x}_i; \theta^{(t)}) \log L(\theta_j; \mathbf{x}_i, j)$$

$$= \sum_{i=1}^{n} \sum_{j=1}^{2} T_{j,i}^{(t)} \left[\log \tau_j - \tfrac{1}{2} \log |\Sigma_j| - \tfrac{1}{2}(\mathbf{x}_i - \mu_j)^{\top} \Sigma_j^{-1}(\mathbf{x}_i - \mu_j) - \tfrac{d}{2} \log (2\pi) \right]$$

The expectation of $\log L(\theta; \mathbf{x}_i, Z_i)$ inside the sum is taken with respect to the probability density function $P(Z_i \mid X_i = \mathbf{x}_i; \theta^{(t)})$, which might be different for each $\mathbf{x}_i$ of the training set. Everything in the E step is known before the step is taken except $T_{j,i}$, which is computed according to the equation at the beginning of the E step section.

This full conditional expectation does not need to be calculated in one step, because τ and μ/Σ appear in separate linear terms and can thus be maximized independently.

M Step

$Q(\theta \mid \theta^{(t)})$ being quadratic in form means that determining the maximizing values of θ is relatively straightforward. Also, τ, (μ_1, Σ_1) and (μ_2, Σ_2) may all be maximized independently since they all appear in separate linear terms.

To begin, consider τ, which has the constraint $\tau_1 + \tau_2 = 1$:

$$\tau^{(t+1)} = \arg \max_{\tau} Q(\theta \mid \theta^{(t)})$$

$$= \arg \max_{\tau} \left\{ \left[\sum_{i=1}^{n} T_{1,i}^{(t)} \right] \log \tau_1 + \left[\sum_{i=1}^{n} T_{2,i}^{(t)} \right] \log \tau_2 \right\}$$

This has the same form as the MLE for the binomial distribution. So,

$$\tau_j^{(t+1)} = \frac{\sum_{i=1}^{n} T_{j,i}^{(t)}}{\sum_{i=1}^{n} (T_{1,i}^{(t)} + T_{2,i}^{(t)})} = \frac{1}{n} \sum_{i=1}^{n} T_{j,i}^{(t)}.$$

For the next estimates of (μ_1, Σ_1):

$$\left(\mu_1^{(t+1)}, \sum{}_1^{(t+1)}\right) = \arg\max_{\mu_1, \Sigma_1} Q\left(\theta \mid \theta^{(t)}\right)$$

$$= \arg\max_{\mu_1, \Sigma_1} \sum_{i=1}^{n} T_{1,i}^{(t)} \left\{ -\frac{1}{2}\log\left|\sum{}_1\right| - \frac{1}{2}(x_i - \mu_1)^{\top}\sum{}_1^{-1}(x_i - \mu_1) \right\}$$

This has the same form as a weighted MLE for a normal distribution. So,

$$\mu_1^{(t+1)} = \frac{\sum_{i=1}^{n} T_{1,i}^{(t)} x_i}{\sum_{i=1}^{n} T_{1,i}^{(t)}} \quad \text{and} \quad \Sigma_1^{(t+1)} = \frac{\sum_{i=1}^{n} T_{1,i}^{(t)}(x_i - \mu_1^{(t+1)})(x_i - \mu_1^{(t+1)})^{\top}}{\sum_{i=1}^{n} T_{1,i}^{(t)}}$$

and by symmetry:

$$\mu_2^{(t+1)} = \frac{\sum_{i=1}^{n} T_{2,i}^{(t)} x_i}{\sum_{i=1}^{n} T_{2,i}^{(t)}} \quad \text{and} \quad \Sigma_2^{(t+1)} = \frac{\sum_{i=1}^{n} T_{2,i}^{(t)}(x_i - \mu_2^{(t+1)})(x_i - \mu_2^{(t+1)})^{\top}}{\sum_{i=1}^{n} T_{2,i}^{(t)}}.$$

Termination

Conclude the iterative process if $E_{Z\mid\theta^{(t)}, \mathbf{x}}[\log L(\theta^{(t)}; \mathbf{x}, \mathbf{Z})] \leq E_{Z\mid\theta^{(t-1)}, \mathbf{x}}[\log L(\theta^{(t-1)}; \mathbf{x}, \mathbf{Z})] + \varepsilon$ for ε below some preset threshold.

Generalization

The algorithm illustrated above can be generalized for mixtures of more than two multivariate normal distributions.

Truncated and Censored Regression

The EM algorithm has been implemented in the case where an underlying linear regression model exists explaining the variation of some quantity, but where the values actually observed are censored or truncated versions of those represented in the model. Special cases of this model include censored or truncated observations from one normal distribution.

Alternatives

EM typically converges to a local optimum, not necessarily the global optimum, with no bound on the convergence rate in general. It is possible that it can be arbitrarily poor in high dimensions and there can be an exponential number of local optima. Hence, a need exists for alternative methods for guaranteed learning, especially in the high-dimensional setting. Alternatives to EM exist with better guarantees for consistency, which are termed *moment-based approaches* or the so-called *spectral techniques*. Moment-based approaches to learning the parameters of a probabilistic model are of increasing interest recently since they enjoy guarantees such as global convergence under certain conditions unlike EM which is often plagued by the issue of getting stuck in local optima. Algorithms with guarantees for learning can be derived for a number of important models such as mixture models, HMMs etc. For these spectral methods, no spurious local optima occur, and the true parameters can be consistently estimated under some regularity conditions.

PageRank

PageRank (PR) is an algorithm used by Google Search to rank web pages in their search engine results. PageRank was named after Larry Page, one of the founders of Google. PageRank is a way of measuring the importance of website pages.

PageRank works by counting the number and quality of links to a page to determine a rough estimate of how important the website is. The underlying assumption is that more important websites are likely to receive more links from other websites.

Currently, PageRank is not the only algorithm used by Google to order search results, but it is the first algorithm that was used by the company, and it is the best known.

PageRank is a link analysis algorithm and it assigns a numerical weighting to each element of a hyperlinked set of documents, such as the World Wide Web, with the purpose of "measuring" its relative importance within the set. The algorithm may be applied to any collection of entities with reciprocal quotations and references. The numerical weight that it assigns to any given element E is referred to as the *PageRank of E* and denoted by $PR(E)$.

The basic principle of PageRank. The size of each face is
proportional to the total size of the other faces which are pointing to it.

A PageRank results from a mathematical algorithm based on the webgraph, created by all World Wide Web pages as nodes and hyperlinks as edges, taking into consideration authority hubs. The rank value indicates an importance of a particular page. A hyperlink to a page counts as a vote of support. The PageRank of a page is defined recursively and depends on the number and PageRank metric of all pages that link to it ("incoming links"). A page that is linked to by many pages with high PageRank receives a high rank itself.

In practice, the PageRank concept may be vulnerable to manipulation. Research has been conducted into identifying falsely influenced PageRank rankings. The goal is to find an effective means of ignoring links from documents with falsely influenced PageRank.

Other link-based ranking algorithms for Web pages include the HITS algorithm invented by Jon Kleinberg, the IBM CLEVER project, the TrustRank algorithm and the Hummingbird algorithm.

Algorithm

The PageRank algorithm outputs a probability distribution used to represent the likelihood that a person randomly clicking on links will arrive at any particular page. PageRank can be calculated for collections of documents of any size. It is assumed that the distribution is evenly divided among all documents in the collection at the beginning of the computational process. The PageRank computations require several passes, called "iterations", through the collection to adjust approximate PageRank values to more closely reflect the theoretical true value.

A probability is expressed as a numeric value between 0 and 1. A 0.5 probability is commonly expressed as a "50% chance" of something happening. Hence, a PageRank of 0.5 means there is a 50% chance that a person clicking on a random link will be directed to the document with the 0.5 PageRank.

Simplified Algorithm

Assume a small universe of four web pages: **A, B, C** and **D.** Links from a page to itself are ignored. Multiple outbound links from one page to another page are treated as a single link. PageRank is initialized to the same value for all pages. In the original form of PageRank, the sum of PageRank over all pages was the total number of pages on the web at that time, so each page in this example would have an initial value of 1. However, later versions of PageRank, assume a probability distribution between 0 and 1. Hence the initial value for each page in this example is 0.25.

The PageRank transferred from a given page to the targets of its outbound links upon the next iteration is divided equally among all outbound links.

If the only links in the system were from pages **B, C,** and **D** to **A**, each link would transfer 0.25 PageRank to A upon the next iteration, for a total of 0.75.

$$PR(A) = PR(B) + PR(C) + PR(D).$$

Suppose instead that page **B** had a link to pages **C** and **A**, page **C** had a link to page A, and page D had links to all three pages. Thus, upon the first iteration, page B would transfer half of its existing value, or 0.125, to page A and the other half, or 0.125, to page C. Page C would transfer all of its existing value, 0.25, to the only page it links to, A. Since **D** had three outbound links, it would transfer one third of its existing value, or approximately 0.083, to A. At the completion of this iteration, page A will have a PageRank of approximately 0.458.

$$PR(A) = \frac{PR(B)}{2} + \frac{PR(C)}{1} + \frac{PR(D)}{3}.$$

In other words, the PageRank conferred by an outbound link is equal to the document's own Page-eRank score divided by the number of outbound links L( ).

$$PR(A) = \frac{PR(B)}{L(B)} + \frac{PR(C)}{L(C)} + \frac{PR(D)}{L(D)}.$$

In the general case, the PageRank value for any page u can be expressed as:

$$PR(u) = \sum_{v \in B_u} \frac{PR(v)}{L(v)}$$

i.e. the PageRank value for a page u is dependent on the PageRank values for each page v contained in the set B_u (the set containing all pages linking to page u), divided by the number $L(v)$ of links from page v.

Damping Factor

The PageRank theory holds that an imaginary surfer who is randomly clicking on links will eventually stop clicking. The probability, at any step, that the person will continue is a damping factor d. Various studies have tested different damping factors, but it is generally assumed that the damping factor will be set around 0.85. In applications of PageRank to biological data, a Bayesian analysis finds the optimal value of d to be 0.31.

The damping factor is subtracted from 1 (and in some variations of the algorithm, the result is divided by the number of documents (N) in the collection) and this term is then added to the product of the damping factor and the sum of the incoming PageRank scores.

That is,

$$PR(A) = \frac{1-d}{N} + d\left(\frac{PR(B)}{L(B)} + \frac{PR(C)}{L(C)} + \frac{PR(D)}{L(D)} + \cdots \right).$$

So any page's PageRank is derived in large part from the PageRanks of other pages. The damping factor adjusts the derived value downward. The original paper, however, gave the following formula, which has led to some confusion:

$$PR(A) = 1 - d + d\left(\frac{PR(B)}{L(B)} + \frac{PR(C)}{L(C)} + \frac{PR(D)}{L(D)} + \cdots \right).$$

The difference between them is that the PageRank values in the first formula sum to one, while in the second formula each PageRank is multiplied by N and the sum becomes N. A statement in Page and Brin's paper that "the sum of all PageRanks is one" and claims by other Google employees support the first variant of the formula above.

Google recalculates PageRank scores each time it crawls the Web and rebuilds its index. As Google increases the number of documents in its collection, the initial approximation of PageRank decreases for all documents.

The formula uses a model of a *random surfer* who gets bored after several clicks and switches to a random page. The PageRank value of a page reflects the chance that the random surfer will land on that page by clicking on a link. It can be understood as a Markov chain in which the states are pages, and the transitions, which are all equally probable, are the links between pages.

If a page has no links to other pages, it becomes a sink and therefore terminates the random surfing process. If the random surfer arrives at a sink page, it picks another URL at random and continues surfing again.

When calculating PageRank, pages with no outbound links are assumed to link out to all other pages in the collection. Their PageRank scores are therefore divided evenly among all other pages. In other words, to be fair with pages that are not sinks, these random transitions are added to all nodes in the Web. This residual probability, d, is usually set to 0.85, estimated from the frequency that an average surfer uses his or her browser's bookmark feature. So, the equation is as follows:

$$PR(p_i) = \frac{1-d}{N} + d \sum_{p_j \in M(p_i)} \frac{PR(p_j)}{L(p_j)}$$

where $p_1, p_2,..., p_N$ are the pages under consideration, $M(p_i)$ is the set of pages that link to p_i, $L(p_j)$ is the number of outbound links on page p_j, and $L(p_j)$ is the total number of pages.

The PageRank values are the entries of the dominant right eigenvector of the modified adjacency matrix rescaled so that each column adds up to one. This makes PageRank a particularly elegant metric: the eigenvector is,

$$\mathbf{R} = \begin{bmatrix} PR(p_1) \\ PR(p_2) \\ \vdots \\ PR(p_N) \end{bmatrix}$$

where R is the solution of the equation.

$$\mathbf{R} = \begin{bmatrix} (1-d)/N \\ (1-d)/N \\ \vdots \\ (1-d)/N \end{bmatrix} + d \begin{bmatrix} \ell(p_1,p_1) & \ell(p_1,p_2) & \cdots & \ell(p_1,p_N) \\ \ell(p_2,p_1) & \ddots & & \vdots \\ \vdots & & \ell(p_i,p_j) & \\ \ell(p_N,p_1) & \cdots & & \ell(p_N,p_N) \end{bmatrix} \mathbf{R}$$

where the adjacency function $\ell(p_i,p_j)$ is the ratio between number of links outbound from page j to page i to the total number of outbound links of page j. The adjacency function is 0 if page p_j does not link to p_i, and normalized such that, for each j,

$$\sum_{i=1}^{N} \ell(p_i,p_j) = 1,$$

i.e. the elements of each column sum up to 1, so the matrix is a stochastic matrix. Thus this is a variant of the eigenvector centrality measure used commonly in network analysis. Because of the large eigengap of the modified adjacency matrix above, the values of the PageRank eigenvector can be approximated to within a high degree of accuracy within only a few iterations.

Google's founders, reported that the PageRank algorithm for a network consisting of 322 million links (in-edges and out-edges) converges to within a tolerable limit in 52 iterations. The convergence in a network of half the above size took approximately 45 iterations. Through this data, they concluded the algorithm can be scaled very well and that the scaling factor for extremely large networks would be roughly linear in $\log n$, where n is the size of the network.

As a result of Markov theory, it can be shown that the PageRank of a page is the probability of arriving at that page after a large number of clicks. This happens to equal t^{-1} where t is the expectation of the number of clicks (or random jumps) required to get from the page back to itself.

One main disadvantage of PageRank is that it favors older pages. A new page, even a very good one, will not have many links unless it is part of an existing site. Several strategies have been proposed to accelerate the computation of PageRank.

Various strategies to manipulate PageRank have been employed in concerted efforts to improve search results rankings and monetize advertising links. These strategies have severely impacted the reliability of the PageRank concept, which purports to determine which documents are actually highly valued by the Web community.

Since December 2007, when it started *actively* penalizing sites selling paid text links, Google has combatted link farms and other schemes designed to artificially inflate PageRank. How Google identifies link farms and other PageRank manipulation tools is among Google's trade secrets.

Computation

PageRank can be computed either iteratively or algebraically. The iterative method can be viewed as the power iteration method or the power method. The basic mathematical operations performed are identical.

Iterative

At $t = 0$, an initial probability distribution is assumed, usually,

$$PR(p_i;0) = \frac{1}{N}$$

where N is the total number of pages, and $p_i;0$ is page i at time 0.

At each time step, the computation, yields,

$$PR(p_i;t+1) = \frac{1-d}{N} + d \sum_{p_j \in M(p_i)} \frac{PR(p_j;t)}{L(p_j)}$$

where d is the damping factor,

or in matrix notation,

$$\mathbf{R}(t+1) = d\mathcal{M}\mathbf{R}(t) + \frac{1-d}{N}\mathbf{1}$$

where $\mathbf{R}_i(t) = PR(p_i;t)$ and $\mathbf{1}$ is the column vector of length N containing only ones.

The matrix $\mathcal{M}$ is defined as,

$$\mathcal{M}_{ij} = \begin{cases} 1/L(p_j), & \text{if } j \text{ links to } i \\ 0, & \text{otherwise} \end{cases}$$

i.e.,

$$\mathcal{M} := (K^{-1}A)^T,$$

where A denotes the adjacency matrix of the graph and K is the diagonal matrix with the outdegrees in the diagonal.

The probability calculation is made for each page at a time point, then repeated for the next time point. The computation ends when for some small ϵ,

$$|\mathbf{R}(t+1) - \mathbf{R}(t)| < \epsilon,$$

i.e., when convergence is assumed.

Algebraic

For $t \to \infty$ (i.e., in the steady state), the equation,

$$\mathbf{R}(t+1) = d\mathcal{M}\mathbf{R}(t) + \frac{1-d}{N}\mathbf{1}$$

reads,

$$\mathbf{R} = d\mathcal{M}\mathbf{R} + \frac{1-d}{N}\mathbf{1}.$$

The solution is given by,

$$\mathbf{R} = (\mathbf{I} - d\mathcal{M})^{-1}\frac{1-d}{N}\mathbf{1},$$

with the identity matrix $\mathbf{I}$.

The solution exists and is unique for $0 < d < 1$. This can be seen by noting that $\mathcal{M}$ is by construction a stochastic matrix and hence has an eigenvalue equal to one as a consequence of the Perron–Frobenius theorem.

Power Method

If the matrix $\mathcal{M}$ is a transition probability, i.e., column-stochastic and $\mathbf{R}$ is a probability distribution (i.e., $|\mathbf{R}|=1$, $\mathbf{ER}=1$ where $\mathbf{E}$ is matrix of all ones), then equation, $\mathbf{R} = d\mathcal{M}\mathbf{R} + \dfrac{1-d}{N}\mathbf{1}$ is equivalent to,

$$\mathbf{R} = \left(d\mathcal{M} + \frac{1-d}{N}\mathbf{E}\right)\mathbf{R} =: \widehat{\mathcal{M}}\mathbf{R}.$$

Hence, PageRank $\mathbf{R}$ is the principal eigenvector of $\widehat{\mathcal{M}}$. A fast and easy way to compute this is using the power method: starting with an arbitrary vector $x(0)$, the operator $\widehat{\mathcal{M}}$. is applied in succession, i.e.,

$$x(t+1) = \widehat{\mathcal{M}}x(t),$$

until,

$$|x(t+1) - x(t)| < \epsilon.$$

Note that in equation, $\mathbf{R} = \left(d\mathcal{M} + \dfrac{1-d}{N}\mathbf{E}\right)\mathbf{R} =: \widehat{\mathcal{M}}\mathbf{R}$ the matrix on the right-hand side in the parenthesis can be interpreted as,

$$\frac{1-d}{N}\mathbf{E} = (1-d)\mathbf{P1}^t,$$

where $\mathbf{P}$ is an initial probability distribution. In the current case,

$$\mathbf{P} := \frac{1}{N}\mathbf{1}.$$

Finally, if $\mathcal{M}$ has columns with only zero values, they should be replaced with the initial probability vector $\mathbf{P}$. In other words,

$$\mathcal{M}' := \mathcal{M} + \mathcal{D},$$

where the matrix $\mathcal{D}$ is defined as,

$$\mathcal{D} := \mathbf{PD}^t,$$

with,

$$\mathbf{D}_i = \begin{cases} 1, & \text{if } L(p_i) = 0 \\ 0, & \text{otherwise} \end{cases}$$

In this case, the two computations using $\mathcal{M}$ only give the same PageRank if their results are normalized:

$$\mathbf{R}_{power} = \frac{\mathbf{R}_{iterative}}{|\mathbf{R}_{iterative}|} = \frac{\mathbf{R}_{algebraic}}{|\mathbf{R}_{algebraic}|}.$$

Implementation

MATLAB/Octave

```
% Parameter M adjacency matrix where M_i,j represents the link from 'j'
to 'i', such that for all 'j'
%       sum(i, M_i,j) = 1
% Parameter d damping factor
% Parameter v_quadratic_error quadratic error for v
% Return v, a vector of ranks such that v_i is the i-th rank from [0, 1]
function [v] = rank2(M, d, v_quadratic_error)
N = size(M, 2); % N is equal to either dimension of M and the number of
documents
v = rand(N, 1);
v = v ./ norm(v, 1);    % This is now L1, not L2
last_v = ones(N, 1) * inf;
M_hat = (d .* M) + (((1 - d) / N) .* ones(N, N));
while(norm(v - last_v, 2) > v_quadratic_error)
        last_v = v;
        v = M_hat * v;
          % removed the L2 norm of the iterated PR
end
end %function
```

Example of code calling the rank function:

```
M = [0 0 0 0 1 ; 0.5 0 0 0 0 ; 0.5 0 0 0 0 ; 0 1 0.5 0 0 ; 0 0 0.5 1 0];
rank2(M, 0.80, 0.001)
```

Python

```
"""Pagerank algorithm with explicit number of iterations.

Returns

-------

ranking of nodes (pages) in the adjacency matrix

"""
```

```python
import numpy as np

def pagerank(M, num_iterations=100, d=0.85):
    """pagerank: The trillion dollar algorithm.

    Parameters
    ----------

    M : numpy array

        adjacency matrix where M_i,j represents the link from 'j' to 'i',
such that for all 'j'

        sum(i, M_i,j) = 1]
    num_iterations : int, optional

        number of iterations, by default 100

    d : float, optional

        damping factor, by default 0.85

    Returns
    -------

    numpy array

        a vector of ranks such that v_i is the i-th rank from [0, 1],

        v sums to 1
    """

    N = M.shape[1]

    v = np.random.rand(N, 1)

    v = v / np.linalg.norm(v, 1)

    iteration = 0

    while iteration < num_iterations:

        iteration += 1

        v = d * np.matmul(M, v) + (1 - d) / N

    return v
```

```
M = np.array([[0, 0, 0, 0, 1],

              [0.5, 0, 0, 0, 0],

              [0.5, 0, 0, 0, 0],

              [0, 1, 0.5, 0, 0],

              [0, 0, 0.5, 1, 0]])
v = pagerank(M, 0.001, 0.85)
```

This example takes 13 iterations to converge.

Variations

PageRank of an Undirected Graph

The PageRank of an undirected graph G is statistically close to the degree distribution of the graph G, but they are generally not identical: If R is the PageRank vector defined above, and D is the degree distribution vector,

$$D = \frac{1}{2|E|} \begin{bmatrix} \deg(p_1) \\ \deg(p_2) \\ \vdots \\ \deg(p_N) \end{bmatrix}$$

where $\deg(p_i)$ denotes the degree of vertex p_i, and E is the edge-set of the graph, then, with

$Y = \frac{1}{N}\mathbf{1}$, shows that:

$$\frac{1-d}{1+d} \|Y-D\|_1 \le \|R-D\|_1 \le \|Y-D\|_1,$$

that is, the PageRank of an undirected graph equals to the degree distribution vector if and only if the graph is regular, i.e., every vertex has the same degree.

Generalization of PageRank and Eigenvector Centrality for Ranking Objects of Two Kinds

In applications it may be necessary to model systems having objects of two kinds where a weighted relation is defined on object pairs. This leads to considering bipartite graphs. For such graphs two related positive or nonnegative irreducible matrices corresponding to vertex partition sets can be defined. One can compute rankings of objects in both groups as eigenvectors corresponding to the maximal positive eigenvalues of these matrices. Normed eigenvectors exist and are unique by the Perron or Perron–Frobenius theorem. Example: consumers and products. The relation weight is the product consumption rate.

Distributed Algorithm for PageRank Computation

Sarma et al. describe two random walk-based distributed algorithms for computing PageRank of nodes in a network. One algorithm takes $O(\log n / \epsilon)$ rounds with high probability on any graph (directed or undirected), where n is the network size and ϵ is the reset probability $(1-\epsilon)$, which is called the damping factor) used in the PageRank computation. They also present a faster algorithm that takes $O(\sqrt{\log n} / \epsilon)$ rounds in undirected graphs. In both algorithms, each node processes and sends a number of bits per round that are polylogarithmic in n, the network size.

Google Toolbar

The Google Toolbar long had a PageRank feature which displayed a visited page's PageRank as a whole number between 0 and 10. The most popular websites displayed a PageRank of 10. The least showed a PageRank of 0. Google has not disclosed the specific method for determining a Toolbar PageRank value, which is to be considered only a rough indication of the value of a website. In March 2016 Google announced it would no longer support this feature, and the underlying API would soon cease to operate.

SERP Rank

The search engine results page (SERP) is the actual result returned by a search engine in response to a keyword query. The SERP consists of a list of links to web pages with associated text snippets. The SERP rank of a web page refers to the placement of the corresponding link on the SERP, where higher placement means higher SERP rank. The SERP rank of a web page is a function not only of its PageRank, but of a relatively large and continuously adjusted set of factors (over 200). Search engine optimization (SEO) is aimed at influencing the SERP rank for a website or a set of web pages.

Positioning of a webpage on Google SERPs for a keyword depends on relevance and reputation, also known as authority and popularity. PageRank is Google's indication of its assessment of the reputation of a webpage: it is non-keyword specific. Google uses a combination of webpage and website authority to determine the overall authority of a webpage competing for a keyword. The PageRank of the HomePage of a website is the best indication Google offers for website authority.

After the introduction of Google Places into the mainstream organic SERP, numerous other factors in addition to PageRank affect ranking a business in Local Business Results.

Google Directory PageRank

The Google Directory PageRank was an 8-unit measurement. Unlike the Google Toolbar, which shows a numeric PageRank value upon mouseover of the green bar, the Google Directory only displayed the bar, never the numeric values. Google Directory was closed on July 20, 2011.

Spoofed PageRank

In the past, the PageRank shown in the Toolbar was easily manipulated. Redirection from one page to another, either via a HTTP 302 response or a "Refresh" meta tag, caused the source page to acquire the PageRank of the destination page. Hence, a new page with PR 0 and no incoming links could have acquired PR 10 by redirecting to the Google home page. This spoofing technique was a known vulnerability. Spoofing can generally be detected by performing a Google search for a source URL; if the URL of an entirely different site is displayed in the results, the latter URL may represent the destination of a redirection.

Manipulating PageRank

For search engine optimization purposes, some companies offer to sell high PageRank links to webmasters. As links from higher-PR pages are believed to be more valuable, they tend to be more expensive. It can be an effective and viable marketing strategy to buy link advertisements on content pages of quality and relevant sites to drive traffic and increase a webmaster's link popularity. However, Google has publicly warned webmasters that if they are or were discovered to be selling links for the purpose of conferring PageRank and reputation, their links will be devalued (ignored in the calculation of other pages' PageRanks). The practice of buying and selling links is intensely debated across the Webmaster community. Google advises webmasters to use the nofollow HTML attribute value on sponsored links. According to Matt Cutts, Google is concerned about webmasters who try to game the system, and thereby reduce the quality and relevance of Google search results.

Directed Surfer Model

A more intelligent surfer that probabilistically hops from page to page depending on the content of the pages and query terms the surfer that it is looking for. This model is based on a query-dependent PageRank score of a page which as the name suggests is also a function of query. When given a multiple-term query, Q = {q1, q2,...}, the surfer selects a q according to some probability distribution, P(q) and uses that term to guide its behavior for a large number of steps. It then selects another term according to the distribution to determine its behavior, and so on. The resulting distribution over visited web pages is QD-PageRank.

Social Components

The PageRank algorithm has major effects on society as it contains a social influence. As opposed to the scientific viewpoint of PageRank as an algorithm the humanities instead view it through a lens examining its social components. In these instances, it is dissected and reviewed not for its technological advancement in the field of search engines, but for its societal influences. Laura Granka discusses PageRank by describing how the pages are not simply ranked via popularity as they contain a reliability that gives them a trustworthy quality. This has led to a development of behavior that is directly linked to PageRank. PageRank is viewed as the definitive rank of products and businesses and thus, can manipulate thinking. The information that is available to individuals is what shapes thinking and ideology and PageRank is the device that displays this information. The results shown are the forum to which information is delivered to the public and these results have a societal impact as they will affect how a person thinks and acts.

Katja Mayer views PageRank as a social network as it connects differing viewpoints and thoughts in a single place. People go to PageRank for information and are flooded with citations of other authors who also have an opinion on the topic. This creates a social aspect where everything can be discussed and collected to provoke thinking. There is a social relationship that exists between PageRank and the people who use it as it is constantly adapting and changing to the shifts in modern society. Viewing the relationship between PageRank and the individual through sociometry allows for an in-depth look at the connection that results.

Matteo Pasquinelli reckons the basis for the belief that PageRank has a social component lies in the idea of attention economy. With attention economy, value is placed on products that receive a greater amount of human attention and the results at the top of the PageRank garner a larger amount of focus then those on subsequent pages. The outcomes with the higher PageRank will therefore enter the human consciousness to a larger extent. These ideas can influence decision-making and the actions of the viewer have a direct relation to the PageRank. They possess a higher potential to attract a user's attention as their location increases the attention economy attached to the site. With this location they can receive more traffic and their online marketplace will have more purchases. The PageRank of these sites allow them to be trusted and they are able to parlay this trust into increased business.

Other Uses

The mathematics of PageRank are entirely general and apply to any graph or network in any domain. Thus, PageRank is now regularly used in bibliometrics, social and information network analysis, and for link prediction and recommendation. It's even used for systems analysis of road networks, as well as biology, chemistry, neuroscience, and physics.

Scientific Impact

Pagerank has recently been used to quantify the scientific impact of researchers. The underlying citation and collaboration networks are used in conjunction with pagerank algorithm in order to come up with a ranking system for individual publications which propagates to individual authors. The new index known as pagerank-index (Pi) is demonstrated to be fairer compared to h-index in the context of many drawbacks exhibited by h-index.

For the analysis of protein networks in biology PageRank is also a useful tool. In any ecosystem, a modified version of PageRank may be used to determine species that are essential to the continuing health of the environment.

A similar new use of PageRank is to rank academic doctoral programs based on their records of placing their graduates in faculty positions. In PageRank terms, academic departments link to each other by hiring their faculty from each other (and from themselves).

A version of PageRank has recently been proposed as a replacement for the traditional Institute for Scientific Information (ISI) impact factor, and implemented at Eigenfactor as well as at SCImago. Instead of merely counting total citation to a journal, the "importance" of each citation is determined in a PageRank fashion.

In neuroscience, the PageRank of a neuron in a neural network has been found to correlate with its relative firing rate.

Internet Use

Personalized PageRank is used by Twitter to present users with other accounts they may wish to follow.

Swiftype's site search product builds a "PageRank that's specific to individual websites" by looking at each website's signals of importance and prioritizing content based on factors such as number of links from the home page.

A Web crawler may use PageRank as one of a number of importance metrics it uses to determine which URL to visit during a crawl of the web. One of the early working papers that were used in the creation of Google is *Efficient crawling through URL ordering*, which discusses the use of a number of different importance metrics to determine how deeply, and how much of a site Google will crawl. PageRank is presented as one of a number of these importance metrics, though there are others listed such as the number of inbound and outbound links for a URL, and the distance from the root directory on a site to the URL.

The PageRank may also be used as a methodology to measure the apparent impact of a community like the Blogosphere on the overall Web itself. This approach uses therefore the PageRank to measure the distribution of attention in reflection of the Scale-free network paradigm.

Other Applications

In 2005, in a pilot study in Pakistan, *Structural Deep Democracy, SD2* was used for leadership selection in a sustainable agriculture group called Contact Youth. SD2 uses *PageRank* for the processing of the transitive proxy votes, with the additional constraints of mandating at least two initial proxies per voter, and all voters are proxy candidates. More complex variants can be built on top of SD2, such as adding specialist proxies and direct votes for specific issues, but SD2 as the underlying umbrella system, mandates that generalist proxies should always be used.

In sport the PageRank algorithm has been used to rank the performance of: teams in the National Football League (NFL) in the USA; individual soccer players; and athletes in the Diamond League.

PageRank has been used to rank spaces or streets to predict how many people (pedestrians or vehicles) come to the individual spaces or streets. In lexical semantics it has been used to perform Word Sense Disambiguation, Semantic similarity, and also to automatically rank WordNet synsets according to how strongly they possess a given semantic property, such as positivity or negativity.

Nofollow

In early 2005, Google implemented a new value, nofollow, for the rel attribute of HTML link and anchor elements, so that website developers and bloggers can make links that Google will not consider for the purposes of PageRank—they are links that no longer constitute a "vote" in the PageRank system. The nofollow relationship was added in an attempt to help combat spamdexing.

As an example, people could previously create many message-board posts with links to their website to artificially inflate their PageRank. With the nofollow value, message-board administrators can modify their code to automatically insert rel = nofollow to all hyperlinks in posts, thus preventing PageRank from being affected by those particular posts. This method of avoidance, however, also has various drawbacks, such as reducing the link value of legitimate comments.

In an effort to manually control the flow of PageRank among pages within a website, many webmasters practice what is known as PageRank Sculpting—which is the act of strategically placing the nofollow attribute on certain internal links of a website in order to funnel PageRank towards those pages the webmaster deemed most important. This tactic has been used since the inception of the nofollow attribute, but may no longer be effective since Google announced that blocking PageRank transfer with nofollow does not redirect that PageRank to other links.

AdaBoost

AdaBoost, is a machine learning meta-algorithm formulated by Yoav Freund and Robert Schapire, who won the 2003 Gödel Prize for their work. It can be used in conjunction with many other types of learning algorithms to improve performance. The output of the other learning algorithms ('weak learners') is combined into a weighted sum that represents the final output of the boosted classifier. AdaBoost is adaptive in the sense that subsequent weak learners are tweaked in favor of those instances misclassified by previous classifiers. AdaBoost is sensitive to noisy data and outliers. In some problems it can be less susceptible to the overfitting problem than other learning algorithms. The individual learners can be weak, but as long as the performance of each one is slightly better than random guessing, the final model can be proven to converge to a strong learner.

Every learning algorithm tends to suit some problem types better than others, and typically has many different parameters and configurations to adjust before it achieves optimal performance on a dataset, AdaBoost (with decision trees as the weak learners) is often referred to as the best out-of-the-box classifier. When used with decision tree learning, information gathered at each stage of the AdaBoost algorithm about the relative 'hardness' of each training sample is fed into the tree growing algorithm such that later trees tend to focus on harder-to-classify examples.

Problems in machine learning often suffer from the curse of dimensionality — each sample may consist of a huge number of potential features (for instance, there can be 162,336 Haar features, as used by the Viola–Jones object detection framework, in a 24×24 pixel image window), and evaluating every feature can reduce not only the speed of classifier training and execution, but in fact reduce predictive power. Unlike neural networks and SVMs, the AdaBoost training process selects only those features known to improve the predictive power of the model, reducing dimensionality and potentially improving execution time as irrelevant features need not be computed.

Training

AdaBoost refers to a particular method of training a boosted classifier. A boost classifier is a classifier in the form,

$$F_T(x) = \sum_{t=1}^{T} f_t(x)$$

where each f_t is a weak learner that takes an object x as input and returns a value indicating the class of the object. For example, in the two-class problem, the sign of the weak learner output identifies the predicted object class and the absolute value gives the confidence in that classification. Similarly, the Tth classifier is positive if the sample is in a positive class and negative otherwise.

Each weak learner produces an output hypothesis, $h(x_i)$, for each sample in the training set. At each iteration t, a weak learner is selected and assigned a coefficient α_t such that the sum training error E_t of the resulting t-stage boost classifier is minimized.

$$E_t = \sum_i E[F_{t-1}(x_i) + \alpha_t h(x_i)]$$

Here $F_{t-1}(x)$ is the boosted classifier that has been built up to the previous stage of training, $E(F)$ is some error function and $f_t(x) = \alpha_t h(x)$ is the weak learner that is being considered for addition to the final classifier.

Weighting

At each iteration of the training process, a weight $w_{i,t}$ is assigned to each sample in the training set equal to the current error $E(F_{t-1}(x_i))$ on that sample. These weights can be used to inform the training of the weak learner, for instance, decision trees can be grown that favor splitting sets of samples with high weights.

Derivation

Suppose we have a data set $\{(x_1, y_1), \ldots, (x_N, y_N)\}$ where each item x_i has an associated class $y_i \in \{-1, 1\}$, and a set of weak classifiers $\{k_1, \ldots, k_L\}$ each of which outputs a classification $k_j(x_i) \in \{-1, 1\}$ for each item. After the $(m-1)$-th iteration our boosted classifier is a linear combination of the weak classifiers of the form:

$$C_{(m-1)}(x_i) = \alpha_1 k_1(x_i) + \cdots + \alpha_{m-1} k_{m-1}(x_i)$$

At the m-th iteration we want to extend this to a better boosted classifier by adding another weak classifier k_m, with another weight α_m:

$$C_m(x_i) = C_{(m-1)}(x_i) + \alpha_m k_m(x_i)$$

So it remains to determine which weak classifier is the best choice for k_m, and what its weight α_m should be. We define the total error E of C_m as the sum of its exponential loss on each data point, given as follows:

$$E = \sum_{i=1}^{N} e^{-y_i C_m(x_i)} = \sum_{i=1}^{N} e^{-y_i C_{(m-1)}(x_i)} e^{-y_i \alpha_m k_m(x_i)}$$

Letting $w_i^{(1)} = 1$ and $w^{(\ )}\ e^{\ y_i C_m\ (x_i)}$ for $m > 1$, we have:

$$E = \sum_{i=1}^{N} w_i^{(m)} e^{-y_i \alpha_m k_m (x_i)}$$

We can split this summation between those data points that are correctly classified by k_m (so $y_i k_m(x_i) = 1$) and those that are misclassified (so $y_i k_m(x_i) = -1$):

$$E = \sum_{y_i = k_m(x_i)} w_i^{(m)} e^{-\alpha_m} + \sum_{y_i \neq k_m(x_i)} w_i^{(m)} e^{\alpha_m}$$

$$= \sum_{i=1}^{N} w_i^{(m)} e^{-\alpha_m} + \sum_{y_i \neq k_m(x_i)} w_i^{(m)} (e^{\alpha_m} - e^{-\alpha_m})$$

Since the only part of the right-hand side of this equation that depends on k_m is $\sum_{y_i \neq k_m(x_i)} w_i^{(m)}$, we see that the k_m that minimizes E is the one that minimizes $\sum_{y_i \neq k_m(x_i)} w_i^{(m)}$ [assuming that $\alpha_m > 0$],

i.e. the weak classifier with the lowest weighted error (with weights $w_i^{(m)} = e^{-y_i C_{m-1}(x_i)}$).

To determine the desired weight α_m that minimizes E with the k_m that we just determined, we differentiate:

$$\frac{dE}{d\alpha_m} = \frac{d\left(\sum_{y_i = k_m(x_i)} w_i^{(m)} e^{-\alpha_m} + \sum_{y_i \neq k_m(x_i)} w_i^{(m)} e^{\alpha_m} \right)}{d\alpha_m}$$

Setting this to zero and solving for α_m yields:

$$\alpha_m = \frac{1}{2} \ln \left(\frac{\sum\limits_{y_i = k_m(x_i)} w_i^{(m)}}{\sum\limits_{y_i \neq k_m(x_i)} w_i^{(m)}} \right)$$

Proof:

$$\frac{dE}{d\alpha_m} = - \sum_{y_i = k_m(x_i)} w_i^{(m)} e^{-\alpha_m} + \sum_{y_i \neq k_m(x_i)} w_i^{(m)} e^{\alpha_m} = 0$$

because $e^{-\alpha_m}$ does not depend on i,

$$e^{-\alpha_m} \sum_{y_i = k_m(x_i)} w_i^{(m)} = e^{\alpha_m} \sum_{y_i \neq k_m(x_i)} w_i^{(m)}$$

$$-\alpha_m + \log\left(\sum_{y_i=k_m(x_i)} w_i^{(m)}\right) = \alpha_m + \log\left(\sum_{y_i \neq k_m(x_i)} w_i^{(m)}\right)$$

$$-2\alpha_m = \log\left(\frac{\sum_{y_i \neq k_m(x_i)} w_i^{(m)}}{\sum_{y_i=k_m(x_i)} w_i^{(m)}}\right)$$

$$\alpha_m = -\frac{1}{2}\log\left(\frac{\sum_{y_i \neq k_m(x_i)} w_i^{(m)}}{\sum_{y_i=k_m(x_i)} w_i^{(m)}}\right)$$

$$\alpha_m = \frac{1}{2}\log\left(\frac{\sum_{y_i=k_m(x_i)} w_i^{(m)}}{\sum_{y_i \neq k_m(x_i)} w_i^{(m)}}\right)$$

We calculate the weighted error rate of the weak classifier to be $\epsilon_m = \sum_{y_i \neq k_m(x_i)} w_i^{(m)} / \sum_{i=1}^{N} w_i^{(m)}$, so it follows that,

$$\alpha_m = \frac{1}{2}\ln\left(\frac{1-\epsilon_m}{\epsilon_m}\right)$$

which is the negative logit function multiplied by 0.5.

Thus we have derived the AdaBoost algorithm: At each iteration, choose the classifier k_m, which minimizes the total weighted error $\sum_{y_i \neq k_m(x_i)} w_i^{(m)}$, use this to calculate the error rate $\epsilon_m = \sum_{y_i \neq k_m(x_i)} w_i^{(m)} / \sum_{i=1}^{N} w_i^{(m)}$, use this to calculate the weight $\alpha_m = \frac{1}{2}\ln\left(\frac{1-\epsilon_m}{\epsilon_m}\right)$, and finally use this to improve the boosted classifier C_{m-1} to $C_m = C_{(m-1)} + \alpha_m k_m$.

Statistical Understanding of Boosting

Boosting is a form of linear regression in which the features of each sample x_i are the outputs of some weak learner h applied to x_i.

While regression tries to fit $F(x)$ to $y(x)$ as precisely as possible without loss of generalization, typically using least square error $E(f) = (y(x) - f(x))^2$, the AdaBoost error function $E(f) = e^{-y(x)f(x)}$ takes into account the fact that only the sign of the final result is used, thus $|F(x)|$ can be far larger than 1 without increasing error. However, the exponential increase in the error for sample x_i as $-y(x_i)f(x_i)$ increases results in excessive weight being assigned to outliers.

One feature of the choice of exponential error function is that the error of the final additive model is the product of the error of each stage, that is, $e^{\sum_i -y_i f(x_i)} = \prod_i e^{-y_i f(x_i)}$. Thus it can be seen that the weight update in the AdaBoost algorithm is equivalent to recalculating the error on $F_t(x)$ after each stage.

There is a lot of flexibility allowed in the choice of loss function. As long as the loss function is monotonic and continuously differentiable, the classifier is always driven toward purer solutions. Zhang provides a loss function based on least squares, a modified Huber loss function:

$$\phi(y, f(x)) = \begin{cases} -4yf(x) & \text{if } yf(x) < -1, \\ (yf(x)-1)^2 & \text{if } -1 \le yf(x) \le 1, \\ 0 & \text{if } yf(x) > 1. \end{cases}$$

This function is more well-behaved than LogitBoost for $f(x)$ close to 1 or -1, does not penalise 'overconfident' predictions ($yf(x) > 1$), unlike unmodified least squares, and only penalises samples misclassified with confidence greater than 1 linearly, as opposed to quadratically or exponentially, and is thus less susceptible to the effects of outliers.

Boosting as Gradient Descent

Boosting can be seen as minimization of a convex loss function over a convex set of functions. Specifically, the loss being minimized by AdaBoost is the exponential loss $\sum_i \phi(i, y, f) = \sum_i e^{-y_i f(x_i)}$, whereas LogitBoost performs logistic regression, minimizing $\sum_i \phi(i, y, f) = \sum_i \ln\left(1 + e^{-y_i f(x_i)}\right)$.

In the gradient descent analogy, the output of the classifier for each training point is considered a point $\left(F_t(x_1), \ldots, F_t(x_n)\right)$ in n-dimensional space, where each axis corresponds to a training sample, each weak learner $h(x)$ corresponds to a vector of fixed orientation and length, and the goal is to reach the target point $(y, \ldots, y)$ (or any region where the value of loss function $E_T(x_1, \ldots, x_n)$ is less than the value at that point), in the least number of steps. Thus, AdaBoost algorithms perform either Cauchy (find $h(x)$ with the steepest gradient, choose α to minimize test error) or Newton (choose some target point, find $\alpha h(x)$ that brings F_t closest to that point) optimization of training error.

Examples of Algorithm: Discrete AdaBoost

With:

- Samples $x_1 \ldots x_n$,
- Desired outputs $y_1 \ldots y_n$, $y \in \{-1, 1\}$,
- Initial weights $w_{1,1} \ldots w_{n,1}$ set to $\dfrac{1}{n}$,

- Error function $E(f(x), y, i) = e^{-y_i f(x_i)}$,
- Weak learners $h : x \rightarrow \{-1, 1\}$.

For t in $1 \ldots T$:

- Choose $h_t(x)$:
  - Find weak learner $h_t(x)$ that minimizes ϵ_t, the weighted sum error for misclassified

    points $\epsilon_t = \sum_{\substack{i=1 \\ h_t(x_i) \neq y_i}}^{n} w_{i,t}$,

  - Choose $\alpha_t = \dfrac{1}{2} \ln \left(\dfrac{1 - \epsilon_t}{\epsilon_t} \right)$,

- Add to ensemble:
  - $F_t(x) = F_{t-1}(x) + \alpha_t h_t(x)$.

- Update weights:
  - $w_{i,t+1} = w_{i,t} e^{-y_i \alpha_t h_t(x_i)}$, for all i,
  - Renormalize $w_{i,t+1}$ such that $\sum_i w_{i,t+1} = 1$,

  - It can be shown that $\dfrac{\sum_{h_{t+1}(x_i)=y_i} w_{i,t+1}}{\sum_{h_{t+1}(x_i) \neq y_i} w_{i,t+1}} = \dfrac{\sum_{h_t(x_i)=y_i} w_{i,t}}{\sum_{h_t(x_i) \neq y_i} w_{i,t}}$ at every step, which can simplify the

    calculation of the new weights.

Choosing α_t

The αt is chosen as it can be analytically shown to be the minimizer of the exponential error function for Discrete AdaBoost.

Minimize:

$$\sum_i w_i e^{-y_i h_i \alpha_t}$$

Using the convexity of the exponential function, and assuming that $\forall i, h_i \in [-1, 1]$ we have:

$$\sum_i w_i e^{-y_i h_i \alpha_t} \leq \sum_i \left(\frac{1 - y_i h_i}{2} \right) w_i e^{\alpha_t} + \sum_i \left(\frac{1 + y_i h_i}{2} \right) w_i e^{-\alpha_t}$$

$$= \left(\frac{\epsilon_t}{2} \right) e^{\alpha_t} + \left(\frac{1 - \epsilon_t}{2} \right) e^{-\alpha_t}$$

We then differentiate that expression with respect to α_t and set it to zero to find the minimum of the upper bound:

$$\left(\frac{\epsilon_t}{2}\right)e^{\alpha_t} - \left(\frac{1-\epsilon_t}{2}\right)e^{-\alpha_t} = 0$$

$$\alpha_t = \frac{1}{2}\ln\left(\frac{1-\epsilon_t}{\epsilon_t}\right)$$

Note that this only applies when $h_i \in \{-1,1\}$, though it can be a good starting guess in other cases, such as when the weak learner is biased ($h(x) \in \{a,b\}, a \neq -b$, has multiple leaves ($h(x) \in \{a,b,\ldots,n\}$ or is some other function $h(x) \in \mathbb{R}$. In such cases the choice of weak learner and coefficient can be condensed to a single step in which $f_t = \alpha_t h_t(x)$ is chosen from all possible α,h as the minimizer of $\sum_i w_{i,t} e^{-y_i f_t(x_i)}$ by some numerical searching routine.

Variants

Real AdaBoost

The output of decision trees is a class probability estimate $p(x) = P(y=1|x)$, the probability that x is in the positive class. Friedman, Hastie and Tibshirani derive an analytical minimizer for $e^{-y(F_{t-1}(x)+f_t(p(x)))}$ for some fixed $p(x)$ (typically chosen using weighted least squares error):

$$f_t(x) = \frac{1}{2}\ln\left(\frac{x}{1-x}\right)$$

Thus, rather than multiplying the output of the entire tree by some fixed value, each leaf node is changed to output half the logit transform of its previous value.

LogitBoost

LogitBoost represents an application of established logistic regression techniques to the AdaBoost method. Rather than minimizing error with respect to y, weak learners are chosen to minimize the (weighted least-squares) error of $f_t(x)$ with respect to,

$$z_t = \frac{y^* - p_t(x)}{2p_t(x)(1-p_t(x))},$$

where,

$$p_t(x) = \frac{e^{F_{t-1}(x)}}{e^{F_{t-1}(x)} + e^{-F_{t-1}(x)}},$$

$$w_t = p_t(x)(1-p_t(x))$$

$$y^* = \frac{y+1}{2}.$$

That is z_t is the Newton–Raphson approximation of the minimizer of the log-likelihood error at stage t, and the weak learner f_t is chosen as the learner that best approximates z_t by weighted least squares.

As p approaches either 1 or 0, the value of $p_t(x_i)(1 - p_t(x_i))$ becomes very small and the z term, which is large for misclassified samples, can become numerically unstable, due to machine precision rounding errors. This can be overcome by enforcing some limit on the absolute value of z and the minimum value of w.

Gentle AdaBoost

While previous boosting algorithms choose f_t greedily, minimizing the overall test error as much as possible at each step, GentleBoost features a bounded step size. f_t is chosen to minimize $\sum_i w_{t,i}(y_i - f_t(x_i))^2$, and no further coefficient is applied. Thus, in the case where a weak learner exhibits perfect classification performance, GentleBoost chooses $f_t(x) = \alpha_t h_t(x)$ exactly equal to y, while steepest descent algorithms try to set $\alpha_t = \infty$. Empirical observations about the good performance of GentleBoost appear to back up Schapire and Singer's remark that allowing excessively large values of α can lead to poor generalization performance.

Early Termination

A technique for speeding up processing of boosted classifiers, early termination refers to only testing each potential object with as many layers of the final classifier necessary to meet some confidence threshold, speeding up computation for cases where the class of the object can easily be determined. One such scheme is the object detection framework introduced by Viola and Jones: in an application with significantly more negative samples than positive, a cascade of separate boost classifiers is trained, the output of each stage biased such that some acceptably small fraction of positive samples is mislabeled as negative, and all samples marked as negative after each stage are discarded. If 50% of negative samples are filtered out by each stage, only a very small number of objects would pass through the entire classifier, reducing computation effort. This method has since been generalized, with a formula provided for choosing optimal thresholds at each stage to achieve some desired false positive and false negative rate.

In the field of statistics, where AdaBoost is more commonly applied to problems of moderate dimensionality, early stopping is used as a strategy to reduce overfitting. A validation set of samples is separated from the training set, performance of the classifier on the samples used for training is compared to performance on the validation samples, and training is terminated if performance on the validation sample is seen to decrease even as performance on the training set continues to improve.

Totally Corrective Algorithms

For steepest descent versions of AdaBoost, where is chosen at each layer t to minimize test error, the next layer added is said to be *maximally independent* of layer t: it is unlikely to choose a weak learner $t+1$ that is similar to learner t. However, there remains the possibility that $t+1$ produces similar information to some other earlier layer. Totally corrective algorithms, such as LPBoost, optimize the value of every coefficient after each step, such that new layers added are always maximally independent of every previous layer. This can be accomplished by backfitting, linear programming or some other method.

Pruning

Pruning is the process of removing poorly performing weak classifiers to improve memory and execution-time cost of the boosted classifier. The simplest methods, which can be particularly effective in conjunction with totally corrective training, are weight- or margin-trimming: when the coefficient, or the contribution to the total test error, of some weak classifier falls below a certain threshold, that classifier is dropped. Margineantu & Dietterich suggest an alternative criterion for trimming: weak classifiers should be selected such that the diversity of the ensemble is maximized. If two weak learners produce very similar outputs, efficiency can be improved by removing one of them and increasing the coefficient of the remaining weak learner.

Naive Bayes Classifier

In machine learning, naive Bayes classifiers are a family of simple "probabilistic classifiers" based on applying Bayes' theorem with strong (naive) independence assumptions between the features.

Naive Bayes has been studied extensively since the 1960s. It was introduced (though not under that name) into the text retrieval community in the early 1960s, and remains a popular (baseline) method for text categorization, the problem of judging documents as belonging to one category or the other (such as spam or legitimate, sports or politics, etc.) with word frequencies as the features. With appropriate pre-processing, it is competitive in this domain with more advanced methods including support vector machines. It also finds application in automatic medical diagnosis.

Naive Bayes classifiers are highly scalable, requiring a number of parameters linear in the number of variables (features/predictors) in a learning problem. Maximum-likelihood training can be done by evaluating a closed-form expression, which takes linear time, rather than by expensive iterative approximation as used for many other types of classifiers.

In the statistics and computer science literature, naive Bayes models are known under a variety of names, including simple Bayes and independence Bayes. All these names reference the use of Bayes' theorem in the classifier's decision rule, but naive Bayes is not (necessarily) a Bayesian method.

Naive Bayes is a simple technique for constructing classifiers: models that assign class labels to problem instances, represented as vectors of feature values, where the class labels are drawn from some finite set. There is not a single algorithm for training such classifiers, but a family of algorithms based on a common principle: all naive Bayes classifiers assume that the value of a particular feature is independent of the value of any other feature, given the class variable. For example, a fruit may be considered to be an apple if it is red, round, and about 10 cm in diameter. A naive

Bayes classifier considers each of these features to contribute independently to the probability that this fruit is an apple, regardless of any possible correlations between the color, roundness, and diameter features.

For some types of probability models, naive Bayes classifiers can be trained very efficiently in a supervised learning setting. In many practical applications, parameter estimation for naive Bayes models uses the method of maximum likelihood; in other words, one can work with the naive Bayes model without accepting Bayesian probability or using any Bayesian methods.

Despite their naive design and apparently oversimplified assumptions, naive Bayes classifiers have worked quite well in many complex real-world situations. In 2004, an analysis of the Bayesian classification problem showed that there are sound theoretical reasons for the apparently implausible efficacy of naive Bayes classifiers. Still, a comprehensive comparison with other classification algorithms in 2006 showed that Bayes classification is outperformed by other approaches, such as boosted trees or random forests.

An advantage of naive Bayes is that it only requires a small number of training data to estimate the parameters necessary for classification.

Probabilistic Model

Abstractly, naive Bayes is a conditional probability model: given a problem instance to be classified, represented by a vector $\mathbf{x} = (x_1, \ldots, x_n)$ representing some n features (independent variables), it assigns to this instance probabilities,

$$p(C_k \mid x_1, \ldots, x_n)$$

for each of K possible outcomes or *classes* C_k.

The problem with the above formulation is that if the number of features n is large or if a feature can take on a large number of values, then basing such a model on probability tables is infeasible. We therefore reformulate the model to make it more tractable. Using Bayes' theorem, the conditional probability can be decomposed as,

$$p(C_k \mid \mathbf{x}) = \frac{p(C_k)\, p(\mathbf{x} \mid C_k)}{p(\mathbf{x})}$$

In plain English, using Bayesian probability terminology, the above equation can be written as,

$$\text{posterior} = \frac{\text{prior} \times \text{likelihood}}{\text{evidence}}$$

In practice, there is interest only in the numerator of that fraction, because the denominator does not depend on C and the values of the features x_i are given, so that the denominator is effectively constant. The numerator is equivalent to the joint probability model,

$$p(C_k, x_1, \ldots, x_n)$$

which can be rewritten as follows, using the chain rule for repeated applications of the definition of conditional probability:

$$
\begin{aligned}
p(C_k, x_1, \ldots, x_n) &= p(x_1, \ldots, x_n, C_k) \\
&= p(x_1 \mid x_2, \ldots, x_n, C_k)\, p(x_2, \ldots, x_n, C_k) \\
&= p(x_1 \mid x_2, \ldots, x_n, C_k)\, p(x_2 \mid x_3, \ldots, x_n, C_k)\, p(x_3, \ldots, x_n, C_k) \\
&= \ldots \\
&= p(x_1 \mid x_2, \ldots, x_n, C_k)\, p(x_2 \mid x_3, \ldots, x_n, C_k) \ldots p(x_{n-1} \mid x_n, C_k)\, p(x_n \mid C_k)\, p(C_k)
\end{aligned}
$$

Now the "naive" conditional independence assumptions come into play: assume that all features in $\mathbf{x}$ are mutually independent, conditional on the category C_k. Under this assumption,

$$
p(x_i \mid x_{i+1}, \ldots, x_n, C_k) = p(x_i \mid C_k).
$$

Thus, the joint model can be expressed as,

$$
\begin{aligned}
p(C_k \mid x_1, \ldots, x_n) &\propto p(C_k, x_1, \ldots, x_n) \\
&= p(C_k)\, p(x_1 \mid C_k)\, p(x_2 \mid C_k)\, p(x_3 \mid C_k) \cdots \\
&= p(C_k) \prod_{i=1}^{n} p(x_i \mid C_k),
\end{aligned}
$$

where $\propto$ denotes proportionality.

This means that under the above independence assumptions, the conditional distribution over the class variable C is:

$$
p(C_k \mid x_1, \ldots, x_n) = \frac{1}{Z} p(C_k) \prod_{i=1}^{n} p(x_i \mid C_k)
$$

where the evidence $Z = p(\mathbf{x}) = \sum_k p(C_k)\, p(\mathbf{x} \mid C_k)$ is a scaling factor dependent only on $x_1, \ldots, x_n$, that is, a constant if the values of the feature variables are known.

Constructing a Classifier from the Probability Model

The discussion so far has derived the independent feature model, that is, the naive Bayes probability model. The naive Bayes classifier combines this model with a decision rule. One common rule is to pick the hypothesis that is most probable; this is known as the *maximum a posteriori* or *MAP* decision rule. The corresponding classifier, a Bayes classifier, is the function that assigns a class label $\hat{y} = C_k$ for some k as follows:

$$
\hat{y} = \operatorname*{argmax}_{k \in \{1, \ldots, K\}} p(C_k) \prod_{i=1}^{n} p(x_i \mid C_k).
$$

Parameter Estimation and Event Models

A class's prior may be calculated by assuming equiprobable classes (i.e., priors = 1/(number of classes)), or by calculating an estimate for the class probability from the training set (i.e., (prior for a given class) = (number of samples in the class)/(total number of samples)). To estimate the parameters for a feature's distribution, one must assume a distribution or generate nonparametric models for the features from the training set.

The assumptions on distributions of features are called the *event model* of the Naive Bayes classifier. For discrete features like the ones encountered in document classification (include spam filtering), multinomial and Bernoulli distributions are popular. These assumptions lead to two distinct models, which are often confused.

Gaussian Naive Bayes

When dealing with continuous data, a typical assumption is that the continuous values associated with each class are distributed according to a normal (or Gaussian) distribution. For example, suppose the training data contains a continuous attribute, x. We first segment the data by the class, and then compute the mean and variance of x in each class. Let μ_k be the mean of the values in x associated with class C_k, and let σ_k^2 be the Bessel corrected variance of the values in x associated with class C_k. Suppose we have collected some observation value v. Then, the probability *distribution* of v given a class C_k, $p(x = v \mid C_k)$, can be computed by plugging v into the equation for a normal distribution parameterized by μ_k and σ_k^2. That is,

$$p(x = v \mid C_k) = \frac{1}{\sqrt{2\pi\sigma_k^2}} e^{-\frac{(v-\mu_k)^2}{2\sigma_k^2}}$$

Another common technique for handling continuous values is to use binning to discretize the feature values, to obtain a new set of Bernoulli-distributed features; some literature in fact suggests that this is necessary to apply naive Bayes, but it is not, and the discretization may throw away discriminative information.

Multinomial Naive Bayes

With a multinomial event model, samples (feature vectors) represent the frequencies with which certain events have been generated by a multinomial $(p, ..., p)$ where p_i is the probability that event i occurs (or K such multinomials in the multiclass case). A feature vector $\mathbf{x} = (x_1,...,x_n)$ is then a histogram, with x_i counting the number of times event i was observed in a particular instance. This is the event model typically used for document classification, with events representing the occurrence of a word in a single document. The likelihood of observing a histogram $\mathbf{x}$ is given by,

$$p(\mathbf{x} \mid C_k) = \frac{(\sum_i x_i)!}{\prod_i x_i!} \prod_i p_{ki}^{x_i}$$

The multinomial naive Bayes classifier becomes a linear classifier when expressed in log-space:

$$\log p(C_k \mid \mathbf{x}) \propto \log \left(p(C_k) \prod_{i=1}^{n} p_{ki}^{x_i} \right)$$

$$= \log p(C_k) + \sum_{i=1}^{n} x_i \cdot \log p_{ki}$$

$$= b + \mathbf{w}_k^{\top} \mathbf{x}$$

where $b = \log p(C_k)$ and $w_{ki} = \log p_{ki}$.

If a given class and feature value never occur together in the training data, then the frequency-based probability estimate will be zero. This is problematic because it will wipe out all information in the other probabilities when they are multiplied. Therefore, it is often desirable to incorporate a small-sample correction, called pseudocount, in all probability estimates such that no probability is ever set to be exactly zero. This way of regularizing naive Bayes is called Laplace smoothing when the pseudocount is one, and Lidstone smoothing in the general case.

Rennie *et al.* discuss problems with the multinomial assumption in the context of document classification and possible ways to alleviate those problems, including the use of tf–idf weights instead of raw term frequencies and document length normalization, to produce a naive Bayes classifier that is competitive with support vector machines.

Bernoulli Naive Bayes

In the multivariate Bernoulli event model, features are independent booleans (binary variables) describing inputs. Like the multinomial model, this model is popular for document classification tasks, where binary term occurrence features are used rather than term frequencies. If x_i is a boolean expressing the occurrence or absence of the i-th term from the vocabulary, then the likelihood of a document given a class C_k is given by,

$$p(\mathbf{x} \mid C_k) = \prod_{i=1}^{n} p_{ki}^{x_i} (1 - p_{ki})^{(1-x_i)}$$

where p_{ki} is the probability of class C_k generating the term x_i. This event model is especially popular for classifying short texts. It has the benefit of explicitly modeling the absence of terms. Note that a naive Bayes classifier with a Bernoulli event model is not the same as a multinomial NB classifier with frequency counts truncated to one.

Semi-supervised Parameter Estimation

Given a way to train a naive Bayes classifier from labeled data, it's possible to construct a semi-supervised training algorithm that can learn from a combination of labeled and unlabeled data by running the supervised learning algorithm in a loop:

> Given a collection $D = L \uplus U$ of labeled samples L and unlabeled samples U, start by training a naive Bayes classifier on L.

Until convergence, do:

- Predict class probabilities $P(C \mid x)$ for all examples x in D.

- Re-train the model based on the *probabilities* (not the labels) predicted in the previous step.

Convergence is determined based on improvement to the model likelihood $P(D \mid \theta)$, where θ denotes the parameters of the naive Bayes model.

This training algorithm is an instance of the more general expectation–maximization algorithm (EM): the prediction step inside the loop is the E-step of EM, while the re-training of naive Bayes is the M-step. The algorithm is formally justified by the assumption that the data are generated by a mixture model, and the components of this mixture model are exactly the classes of the classificatio problem.

Sex Classification

Problem: classify whether a given person is a male or a female based on the measured features. The features include height, weight, and foot size.

Training

Table: Example training set below.

Person	Height (feet)	Weight (lbs)	Foot size (inches)
Male	6	180	12
Male	5.92 (5'11")	190	11
Male	5.58 (5'7")	170	12
Male	5.92 (5'11")	165	10
Female	5	100	6
Female	5.5 (5'6")	150	8
Female	5.42 (5'5")	130	7
Female	5.75 (5'9")	150	9

Table: The classifier created from the training set using a Gaussian distribution assumption would be (given variances are *unbiased* sample variances):

Person	Mean (height)	Variance (height)	Mean (weight)	Variance (weight)	Mean (foot size)	Variance (foot size)
Male	5.855	3.5033×10^{-2}	176.25	1.2292×10^{2}	11.25	9.1667×10^{-1}
Female	5.4175	9.7225×10^{-2}	132.5	5.5833×10^{2}	7.5	1.6667

Let's say we have equiprobable classes so P(male)= P(female) = 0.5. This prior probability distribution might be based on our knowledge of frequencies in the larger population, or on frequency in the training set.

Testing

Table: A sample to be classified as male or female.

Person	Height (feet)	Weight (lbs)	Foot size (inches)
Sample	6	130	8

We wish to determine which posterior is greater, male or female. For the classification as male the posterior is given by:

$$\text{posterior (male)} = \frac{P(\text{male})\,p(\text{height}\mid\text{male})\,p(\text{weight}\mid\text{male})\,p(\text{foot size}\mid\text{male})}{\text{evidence}}$$

For the classification as female the posterior is given by:

$$\text{posterior (female)} = \frac{P(\text{female})\,p(\text{height}\mid\text{female})\,p(\text{weight}\mid\text{female})\,p(\text{foot size}\mid\text{female})}{\text{evidence}}$$

The evidence (also termed normalizing constant) may be calculated:

$$\text{evidence} = P(\text{male})\,p(\text{height}\mid\text{male})\,p(\text{weight}\mid\text{male})\,p(\text{foot size}\mid\text{male})$$

$$+P(\text{female})\,p(\text{height}\mid\text{female})\,p(\text{weight}\mid\text{female})\,p(\text{foot size}\mid\text{female})$$

However, given the sample, the evidence is a constant and thus scales both posteriors equally. It therefore does not affect classification and can be ignored. We now determine the probability distribution for the sex of the sample.

$$P(\text{male}) = 0.5$$

$$p(\text{height}\mid\text{male}) = \frac{1}{\sqrt{2\pi\sigma^2}}\exp\left(\frac{-(6-\mu)^2}{2\sigma^2}\right) \approx 1.5789$$

where $\mu = 5.855$ and $\sigma^2 = 3.5033\cdot10^{-2}$ are the parameters of normal distribution which have been previously determined from the training set. Note that a value greater than 1 is OK here − it is a probability density rather than a probability, because *height* is a continuous variable.

$$p(\text{weight}\mid\text{male}) = \frac{1}{\sqrt{2\pi\sigma^2}}\exp\left(\frac{-(130-\mu)^2}{2\sigma^2}\right) = 5.9881\cdot10^{-6}$$

$$p(\text{foot size}\mid\text{male}) = \frac{1}{\sqrt{2\pi\sigma^2}}\exp\left(\frac{-(8-\mu)^2}{2\sigma^2}\right) = 1.3112\cdot10^{-3}$$

posterior numerator (male) = their product = $6.1984\cdot10^{-9}$

$$P(\text{female}) = 0.5$$

$$p(\text{height} \mid FC \text{ female}) = 2.2346{\cdot}10^{-1}$$

$$p(\text{weight} \mid \text{female}) = 1.6789{\cdot}10^{-2}$$

$$p(\text{foot size} \mid \text{female}) = 2.8669{\cdot}10^{-1}$$

posterior numerator (female) = their product = $5.3778{\cdot}10^{-4}$

Since posterior numerator is greater in the female case, we predict the sample is female.

Document Classification

Here is a worked example of naive Bayesian classification to the document classification problem. Consider the problem of classifying documents by their content, for example into spam and non-spam e-mails. Imagine that documents are drawn from a number of classes of documents which can be modeled as sets of words where the (independent) probability that the i-th word of a given document occurs in a document from class C can be written as,

$$p(w_i \mid C)$$

For this treatment, we simplify things further by assuming that words are randomly distributed in the document - that is, words are not dependent on the length of the document, position within the document with relation to other words, or other document-context.

Then the probability that a given document D contains all of the words w_i, given a class C, is,

$$p(D \mid C) = \prod_i p(w_i \mid C)$$

The question that we desire to answer is: "what is the probability that a given document D belongs to a given class C?" In other words, what is $p(C \mid D)$?

Now,

$$p(D \mid C) = \frac{p(D \cap C)}{p(C)}$$

and

$$p(C \mid D) = \frac{p(D \cap C)}{p(D)}$$

Bayes' theorem manipulates these into a statement of probability in terms of likelihood.

$$p(C \mid D) = \frac{p(C)\,p(D \mid C)}{p(D)}$$

Assume for the moment that there are only two mutually exclusive classes, S and $\neg S$ (e.g. spam and not spam), such that every element (email) is in either one or the other;

$$p(D \mid S) = \prod_i p(w_i \mid S)$$

and

$$p(D \mid \neg S) = \prod_i p(w_i \mid \neg S)$$

Using the Bayesian result above, we can write:

$$p(S \mid D) = \frac{p(S)}{p(D)} \prod_i p(w_i \mid S)$$

$$p(\neg S \mid D) = \frac{p(\neg S)}{p(D)} \prod_i p(w_i \mid \neg S)$$

Dividing one by the other gives:

$$\frac{p(S \mid D)}{p(\neg S \mid D)} = \frac{p(S) \prod_i p(w_i \mid S)}{p(\neg S) \prod_i p(w_i \mid \neg S)}$$

Which can be re-factored as:

$$\frac{p(S \mid D)}{p(\neg S \mid D)} = \frac{p(S)}{p(\neg S)} \prod_i \frac{p(w_i \mid S)}{p(w_i \mid \neg S)}$$

Thus, the probability ratio $p(S \mid D)/p(\neg S \mid D)$ can be expressed in terms of a series of likelihood ratios. The actual probability $p(S \mid D)$ can be easily computed from log $(p(S \mid D)/p(\neg S \mid D))$ based on the observation that $p(S \mid D) + p(\neg S \mid D) = 1$.

Taking the logarithm of all these ratios, we have:

$$\ln \frac{p(S \mid D)}{p(\neg S \mid D)} = \ln \frac{p(S)}{p(\neg S)} + \sum_i \ln \frac{p(w_i \mid S)}{p(w_i \mid \neg S)}$$

This technique of "log-likelihood ratios" is a common technique in statistics. In the case of two mutually exclusive alternatives (such as this example), the conversion of a log-likelihood ratio to a probability takes the form of a sigmoid curve.

Finally, the document can be classified as follows. It is spam if $p(S \mid D) > p(\neg S \mid D)$ (i. e., $\ln \frac{p(S \mid D)}{p(\neg S \mid D)} > 0$), otherwise it is not spam.

k-nearest Neighbors Algorithm

In pattern recognition, the k-nearest neighbors algorithm (k-NN) is a non-parametric method used for classification and regression. In both cases, the input consists of the k closest training examples in the feature space. The output depends on whether k-NN is used for classification or regression:

- In k-NN *classification*, the output is a class membership. An object is classified by a plurality vote of its neighbors, with the object being assigned to the class most common among its k nearest neighbors (k is a positive integer, typically small). If k = 1, then the object is simply assigned to the class of that single nearest neighbor.

- In k-NN *regression*, the output is the property value for the object. This value is the average of the values of k nearest neighbors.

k-NN is a type of instance-based learning, or lazy learning, where the function is only approximated locally and all computation is deferred until classification.

Both for classification and regression, a useful technique can be to assign weights to the contributions of the neighbors, so that the nearer neighbors contribute more to the average than the more distant ones. For example, a common weighting scheme consists in giving each neighbor a weight of $1/d$, where d is the distance to the neighbor.

The neighbors are taken from a set of objects for which the class (for k-NN classification) or the object property value (for k-NN regression) is known. This can be thought of as the training set for the algorithm, though no explicit training step is required.

A peculiarity of the k-NN algorithm is that it is sensitive to the local structure of the data.

Statistical Setting

Suppose we have pairs $(X_1,Y_1),(X_2,Y_2),...,(X_n,Y_n)$ taking values in $\mathbb{R}^d \times \{1,2\}$, where Y is the class label of X, so that $X \mid Y = r \sim P_r$ for $r = 1,2$ (and probability distributions P_r). Given some norm $\|\cdot\|$ on $\mathbb{R}^d$ and a point $x \in \mathbb{R}^d$, let $(X_{(1)},Y_{(1)}),...,(X_{(n)},Y_{(n)})$ be a reordering of the training data such that $\| X_{(1)} - x \| \le ... \le \| X_{(n)} - x \|$.

Algorithm

The training examples are vectors in a multidimensional feature space, each with a class label. The training phase of the algorithm consists only of storing the feature vectors and class labels of the training samples.

In the classification phase, k is a user-defined constant, and an unlabeled vector (a query or test point) is classified by assigning the label which is most frequent among the k training samples nearest to that query point.

A commonly used distance metric for continuous variables is Euclidean distance. For discrete variables, such as for text classification, another metric can be used, such as the overlap metric (or

Hamming distance). In the context of gene expression microarray data, for example, k-NN has been employed with correlation coefficients, such as Pearson and Spearman, as a metric. Often, the classification accuracy of k-NN can be improved significantly if the distance metric is learned with specialized algorithms such as Large Margin Nearest Neighbor or Neighborhood components analysis.

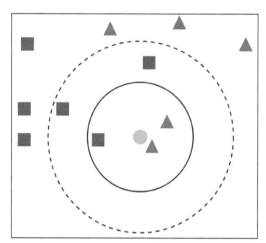

The test sample (green dot) should be classified either to blue squares or to red triangles. If $k = 3$ (solid line circle) it is assigned to the red triangles because there are 2 triangles and only 1 square inside the inner circle. If $k = 5$ (dashed line circle) it is assigned to the blue squares (3 squares vs. 2 triangles inside the outer circle).

A drawback of the basic "majority voting" classification occurs when the class distribution is skewed. That is, examples of a more frequent class tend to dominate the prediction of the new example, because they tend to be common among the k nearest neighbors due to their large number. One way to overcome this problem is to weight the classification, taking into account the distance from the test point to each of its k nearest neighbors. The class (or value, in regression problems) of each of the k nearest points is multiplied by a weight proportional to the inverse of the distance from that point to the test point. Another way to overcome skew is by abstraction in data representation. For example, in a self-organizing map (SOM), each node is a representative (a center) of a cluster of similar points, regardless of their density in the original training data. K-NN can then be applied to the SOM.

Parameter Selection

The best choice of k depends upon the data; generally, larger values of k reduces effect of the noise on the classification, but make boundaries between classes less distinct. A good k can be selected by various heuristic techniques. The special case where the class is predicted to be the class of the closest training sample (i.e. when $k = 1$) is called the nearest neighbor algorithm.

The accuracy of the k-NN algorithm can be severely degraded by the presence of noisy or irrelevant features, or if the feature scales are not consistent with their importance. Much research effort has been put into selecting or scaling features to improve classification. A particularly popular approach is the use of evolutionary algorithms to optimize feature scaling. Another popular approach is to scale features by the mutual information of the training data with the training classes.

In binary (two class) classification problems, it is helpful to choose k to be an odd number as this avoids tied votes. One popular way of choosing the empirically optimal k in this setting is via bootstrap method.

1-nearest Neighbor Classifier

The most intuitive nearest neighbor type classifier is the one nearest neighbor classifier that assigns a point x to the class of its closest neighbor in the feature space, that is $C_n^{1nn}(x) = Y_{(1)}$.

As the size of training data set approaches infinity, the one nearest neighbor classifier guarantees an error rate of no worse than twice the Bayes error rate (the minimum achievable error rate given the distribution of the data).

Weighted Nearest Neighbor Classifier

The k-nearest neighbor classifier can be viewed as assigning the k nearest neighbors a weight $1/k$ and all others 0 weight. This can be generalised to weighted nearest neighbor classifiers. That is, where the ith nearest neighbor is assigned a weight w_{ni}, with $\sum_{i=1}^{n} w_{ni} = 1$. An analogous result on the strong consistency of weighted nearest neighbor classifiers also holds.

Let C_n^{wnn} denote the weighted nearest classifier with weights $\{w_{ni}\}_{i=1}^{n}$. Subject to regularity conditions on the class distributions the excess risk has the following asymptotic expansion,

$$\mathcal{R}_\mathcal{R}(C_n^{wnn}) - \mathcal{R}_\mathcal{R}(C^{Bayes}) = \left(B_1 s_n^2 + B_2 t_n^2\right)\{1 + o(1)\},$$

for constants B_1 and B_2 where $s_n^2 = \sum_{i=1}^{n} w_{ni}^2$ and $t_n = n^{-2/d}\sum_{i=1}^{n} w_{ni}\{i^{1+2/d} - (i-1)^{1+2/d}\}$.

The optimal weighting scheme $\{w_{ni}^*\}_{i=1}^{n}$, that balances the two terms in the display above, is given as follows: set $k^* = \left\lfloor Bn^{\frac{4}{d+4}} \right\rfloor$,

$$w_{ni}^* = \frac{1}{k^*}\left[1 + \frac{d}{2} - \frac{d}{2k^{*2/d}}\{i^{1+2/d} - (i-1)^{1+2/d}\}\right] \text{ for } i = 1,2,\ldots,k^* \text{ and}$$

$$w_{ni}^* = 0 \text{ for } i = k^* + 1,\ldots,n.$$

With optimal weights the dominant term in the asymptotic expansion of the excess risk is $\mathcal{O}(n^{-\frac{4}{d+4}})$. Similar results are true when using a bagged nearest neighbor classifier.

Properties

k-NN is a special case of a variable-bandwidth, kernel density "balloon" estimator with a uniform kernel.

The naive version of the algorithm is easy to implement by computing the distances from the test example to all stored examples, but it is computationally intensive for large training sets. Using an approximate nearest neighbor search algorithm makes k-NN computationally tractable even for large data sets. Many nearest neighbor search algorithms have been proposed over the years; these generally seek to reduce the number of distance evaluations actually performed.

k-NN has some strong consistency results. As the amount of data approaches infinity, the two-class k-NN algorithm is guaranteed to yield an error rate no worse than twice the Bayes error rate (the minimum achievable error rate given the distribution of the data). Various improvements to the k-NN speed are possible by using proximity graphs.

For multi-class k-NN classification, Cover and Hart prove an upper bound error rate of,

$$R^* \leq R_{kNN} \leq R^* \left(2 - \frac{MR^*}{M-1} \right)$$

where R^* is the Bayes error rate (which is the minimal error rate possible), R_{kNN} is the k-NN error rate, and M is the number of classes in the problem. For $M = 2$ and as the Bayesian error rate R^* approaches zero, this limit reduces to "not more than twice the Bayesian error rate".

Error Rates

There are many results on the error rate of the k nearest neighbor classifiers. The k-nearest neighbor classifier is strongly (that is for any joint distribution on (X, Y)) consistent provided $k := k_n$ diverges and k_n / n converges to zero as $n \to \infty$.

Let C_n^{knn} denote the k nearest neighbor classifier based on a training set of size n. Under certain regularity conditions, the excess risk yields the following asymptotic expansion,

$$\mathcal{R}_{\mathcal{R}}(C_n^{knn}) - \mathcal{R}_{\mathcal{R}}(C^{Bayes}) = \left\{ B_1 \frac{1}{k} + B_2 \left(\frac{k}{n} \right)^{4/d} \right\} \{1 + o(1)\},$$

for some constants B_1 and   .

The choice $k^* = \left\lfloor Bn^{\frac{4}{d+4}} \right\rfloor$ offers a trade off between the two terms in the above display, for which

the k^*-nearest neighbor error converges to the Bayes error at the optimal (minimax) rate $\mathcal{O}(n^{-\frac{4}{d+4}})$.

Metric Learning

The K-nearest neighbor classification performance can often be significantly improved through (supervised) metric learning. Popular algorithms are neighborhood components analysis and large margin nearest neighbor. Supervised metric learning algorithms use the label information to learn a new metric or pseudo-metric.

Feature Extraction

When the input data to an algorithm is too large to be processed and it is suspected to be redundant (e.g. the same measurement in both feet and meters) then the input data will be transformed into a reduced representation set of features (also named features vector). Transforming the input data into the set of features is called feature extraction. If the features extracted are carefully chosen it is expected that the features set will extract the relevant information from the input data in order to perform the desired task using this reduced representation instead of the full size input. Feature extraction is performed on raw data prior to applying k-NN algorithm on the transformed data in feature space.

An example of a typical computer vision computation pipeline for face recognition using k-NN including feature extraction and dimension reduction pre-processing steps (usually implemented with OpenCV):

- Haar face detection.

- Mean-shift tracking analysis.

- PCA or Fisher LDA projection into feature space, followed by k-NN classification.

Dimension Reduction

For high-dimensional data (e.g., with number of dimensions more than 10) dimension reduction is usually performed prior to applying the k-NN algorithm in order to avoid the effects of the curse of dimensionality.

The curse of dimensionality in the k-NN context basically means that Euclidean distance is unhelpful in high dimensions because all vectors are almost equidistant to the search query vector (imagine multiple points lying more or less on a circle with the query point at the center; the distance from the query to all data points in the search space is almost the same).

Feature extraction and dimension reduction can be combined in one step using principal component analysis (PCA), linear discriminant analysis (LDA), or canonical correlation analysis (CCA) techniques as a pre-processing step, followed by clustering by k-NN on feature vectors in reduced-dimension space. In machine learning this process is also called low-dimensional embedding.

For very-high-dimensional datasets (e.g. when performing a similarity search on live video streams, DNA data or high-dimensional time series) running a fast approximate k-NN search using locality sensitive hashing, "random projections", "sketches" or other high-dimensional similarity search techniques from the VLDB toolbox might be the only feasible option.

Decision Boundary

Nearest neighbor rules in effect implicitly compute the decision boundary. It is also possible to compute the decision boundary explicitly, and to do so efficiently, so that the computational complexity is a function of the boundary complexity.

Data Reduction

Data reduction is one of the most important problems for work with huge data sets. Usually, only some of the data points are needed for accurate classification. Those data are called the *prototypes* and can be found as follows:

- Select the *class-outliers*, that is, training data that are classified incorrectly by k-NN (for a given k).

- Separate the rest of the data into two sets: (i) the prototypes that are used for the classification decisions and (ii) the *absorbed points* that can be correctly classified by k-NN using prototypes. The absorbed points can then be removed from the training set.

Selection of Class-outliers

A training example surrounded by examples of other classes is called a class outlier. Causes of class outliers include:

- Random error.

- Insufficient training examples of this class (an isolated example appears instead of a cluster)

- Missing important features (the classes are separated in other dimensions which we do not know)

- Too many training examples of other classes (unbalanced classes) that create a "hostile" background for the given small class

Class outliers with k-NN produce noise. They can be detected and separated for future analysis. Given two natural numbers, $k>r>0$, a training example is called a (k,r)NN class-outlier if its k nearest neighbors include more than r examples of other classes.

CNN for Data Reduction

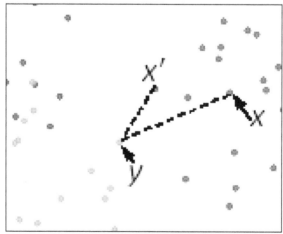

Calculation of the border ratio.

Condensed nearest neighbor (CNN, the Hart algorithm) is an algorithm designed to reduce the data set for k-NN classification. It selects the set of prototypes U from the training data, such that 1NN with U can classify the examples almost as accurately as 1NN does with the whole data set.

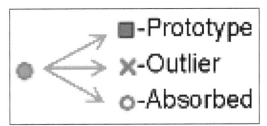

Three types of points: prototypes, class-outliers, and absorbed points.

Given a training set X, CNN works iteratively:

1. Scan all elements of X, looking for an element x whose nearest prototype from U has a different label than x.

2. Remove x from X and add it to U.

3. Repeat the scan until no more prototypes are added to U.

Use U instead of X for classification. The examples that are not prototypes are called "absorbed" points.

It is efficient to scan the training examples in order of decreasing border ratio. The border ratio of a training example x is defined as,

$$a(x) = \frac{\|x'-y\|}{\|x-y\|}$$

where $\|x\text{-}y\|$ is the distance to the closest example y having a different color than x, and $\|x'\text{-}y\|$ is the distance from y to its closest example x' with the same label as x.

The border ratio is in the interval $[0, 1]$ because $\|x'\text{-}y\|$ never exceeds $\|x\text{-}y\|$. This ordering gives preference to the borders of the classes for inclusion in the set of prototypes U. A point of a different label than x is called external to x. The calculation of the border ratio is illustrated by the figure on the right. The data points are labeled by colors: the initial point is x and its label is red. External points are blue and green. The closest to x external point is y. The closest to y red point is x'. The border ratio $a(x) = \|x'\text{-}y\|/\|x\text{-}y\|$ is the attribute of the initial point x.

Below is an illustration of CNN in a series of figures. There are three classes (red, green and blue). Figure initially there are 60 points in each class. Figure shows the 1NN classification map: each pixel is classified by 1NN using all the data. Figure shows the 5NN classification map. White areas correspond to the unclassified regions, where 5NN voting is tied (for example, if there are two green, two red and one blue points among 5 nearest neighbors). Fig. shows the reduced data set. The crosses are the class-outliers selected by the $(3, 2)$NN rule (all the three nearest neighbors of these instances belong to other classes); the squares are the prototypes, and the empty circles are the absorbed points. The left bottom corner shows the numbers of the class-outliers, prototypes and absorbed points for all three classes. The number of prototypes varies from 15% to 20% for different classes in this example. Figure below shows that the 1NN classification map with the prototypes is very similar to that with the initial data set. The figures were produced using the Mirkes applet.

CNN Model Reduction for k-NN Classifiers

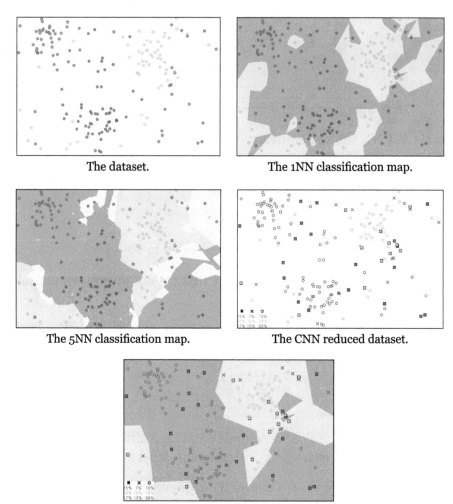

The dataset.

The 1NN classification map.

The 5NN classification map.

The CNN reduced dataset.

The 1NN classification map based on the CNN extracted prototypes.

FCNN (for Fast Condensed Nearest Neighbor) is a variant of CNN, which turns out to be one of the fastest data set reduction algorithms for k-NN classification.

k-NN Regression

In *k*-NN regression, the *k*-NN algorithm is used for estimating continuous variables. One such algorithm uses a weighted average of the *k* nearest neighbors, weighted by the inverse of their distance. This algorithm works as follows:

1. Compute the Euclidean or Mahalanobis distance from the query example to the labeled examples.

2. Order the labeled examples by increasing distance.

3. Find a heuristically optimal number *k* of nearest neighbors, based on RMSE. This is done using cross validation.

4. Calculate an inverse distance weighted average with the *k*-nearest multivariate neighbors.

k-NN Outlier

The distance to the kth nearest neighbor can also be seen as a local density estimate and thus is also a popular outlier score in anomaly detection. The larger the distance to the k-NN, the lower the local density, the more likely the query point is an outlier. To take into account the whole neighborhood of the query point, the average distance to the k-NN can be used. Although quite simple, this outlier model, along with another classic data mining method, local outlier factor, works quite well also in comparison to more recent and more complex approaches, according to a large scale experimental analysis.

Validation of Results

A confusion matrix or "matching matrix" is often used as a tool to validate the accuracy of k-NN classification. More robust statistical methods such as likelihood-ratio test can also be applied.

k-means Clustering

We are given a data set of items, with certain features, and values for these features (like a vector). The task is to categorize those items into groups. To achieve this, we will use the kMeans algorithm; an unsupervised learning algorithm.

It will help if you think of items as points in an n-dimensional space. The algorithm will categorize the items into k groups of similarity. To calculate that similarity, we will use the euclidean distance as measurement.

The algorithm works as follows:

1. First we initialize k points, called means, randomly.

2. We categorize each item to its closest mean and we update the mean's coordinates, which are the averages of the items categorized in that mean so far.

3. We repeat the process for a given number of iterations and at the end, we have our clusters.

The "points" mentioned above are called means, because they hold the mean values of the items categorized in it. To initialize these means, we have a lot of options. An intuitive method is to initialize the means at random items in the data set. Another method is to initialize the means at random values between the boundaries of the data set (if for a feature x the items have values in [0, 3], we will initialize the means with values for x at [0, 3]).

The above algorithm in pseudocode:

```
Initialize k means with random values

For a given number of iterations:

    Iterate through items:

        Find the mean closest to the item
```

```
    Assign item to mean

    Update mean
```

Read Data

We receive input as a text file ('data.txt'). Each line represents an item, and it contains numerical values (one for each feature) split by commas.

We will read the data from the file, saving it into a list. Each element of the list is another list containing the item values for the features. We do this with the following function:

```python
def ReadData(fileName):

    # Read the file, splitting by lines
    f = open(fileName, 'r');
    lines = f.read().splitlines();
    f.close();

    items = [];

    for i in range(1, len(lines)):
        line = lines[i].split(',');
        itemFeatures = [];

        for j in range(len(line)-1):
            v = float(line[j]); # Convert feature value to float
            itemFeatures.append(v); # Add feature value to dict

        items.append(itemFeatures);

    shuffle(items);

    return items;
```

Initialize Means

We want to initialize each mean's values in the range of the feature values of the items. For that, we need to find the min and max for each feature. We accomplish that with the following function:

```python
def FindColMinMax(items):
    n = len(items[0]);
```

```
minima = [sys.maxint for i in range(n)];

maxima = [-sys.maxint -1 for i in range(n)];


for item in items:

    for f in range(len(item)):

        if (item[f] < minima[f]):

            minima[f] = item[f];


        if (item[f] > maxima[f]):

            maxima[f] = item[f];


return minima,maxima;
```

The variables minima, maxima are lists containing the min and max values of the items respectively. We initialize each mean's feature values randomly between the corresponding minimum and maximum in those above two lists:

```
def InitializeMeans(items, k, cMin, cMax):


    # Initialize means to random numbers between

    # the min and max of each column/feature

    f = len(items[0]); # number of features

    means = [[0 for i in range(f)] for j in range(k)];


    for mean in means:

        for i in range(len(mean)):


            # Set value to a random float

            # (adding +-1 to avoid a wide placement of a mean)

            mean[i] = uniform(cMin[i]+1, cMax[i]-1);


    return means;
```

Euclidean Distance

We will be using the euclidean distance as a metric of similarity for our data set (note: depending on your items, you can use another similarity metric).

```
def EuclideanDistance(x, y):

    S = 0; #  The sum of the squared differences of the elements

    for i in range(len(x)):

        S += math.pow(x[i]-y[i], 2);


    return math.sqrt(S); #The square root of the sum
```

Update Means

To update a mean, we need to find the average value for its feature, for all the items in the mean/cluster. We can do this by adding all the values and then dividing by the number of items, or we can use a more elegant solution. We will calculate the new average without having to re-add all the values, by doing the following:

```
m = (m*(n-1)+x)/n
```

where m is the mean value for a feature, n is the number of items in the cluster and x is the feature value for the added item. We do the above for each feature to get the new mean.

```
def UpdateMean(n,mean,item):

    for i in range(len(mean)):

        m = mean[i];

        m = (m*(n-1)+item[i])/float(n);

        mean[i] = round(m, 3);


    return mean;
```

Classify Items

Now we need to write a function to classify an item to a group/cluster. For the given item, we will find its similarity to each mean, and we will classify the item to the closest one.

```
def Classify(means,item):


    # Classify item to the mean with minimum distance

    minimum = sys.maxint;

    index = -1;


    for i in range(len(means)):


        # Find distance from item to mean

        dis = EuclideanDistance(item, means[i]);
```

```
        if (dis < minimum):

            minimum = dis;

            index = i;


    return index;
```

Find Means

To actually find the means, we will loop through all the items, classify them to their nearest cluster and update the cluster's mean. We will repeat the process for some fixed number of iterations. If between two iterations no item changes classification, we stop the process as the algorithm has found the optimal solution.

The below function takes as input k (the number of desired clusters), the items and the number of maximum iterations, and returns the means and the clusters. The classification of an item is stored in the array belongs to and the number of items in a cluster is stored in clusterSizes.

```python
def CalculateMeans(k,items,maxIterations=100000):


    # Find the minima and maxima for columns
    cMin, cMax = FindColMinMax(items);


    # Initialize means at random points
    means = InitializeMeans(items,k,cMin,cMax);


    # Initialize clusters, the array to hold
    # the number of items in a class
    clusterSizes= [0 for i in range(len(means))];


    # An array to hold the cluster an item is in
    belongsTo = [0 for i in range(len(items))];


    # Calculate means
    for e in range(maxIterations):


        # If no change of cluster occurs, halt
        noChange = True;
        for i in range(len(items)):
```

```
        item = items[i];


        # Classify item into a cluster and update the
        # corresponding means.
        index = Classify(means,item);


        clusterSizes[index] += 1;
        cSize = clusterSizes[index];
        means[index] = UpdateMean(cSize,means[index],item);


        # Item changed cluster
        if(index != belongsTo[i]):
            noChange = False;


        belongsTo[i] = index;


    # Nothing changed, return
    if (noChange):
        break;


return means;
```

Find Clusters

Finally we want to find the clusters, given the means. We will iterate through all the items and we will classify each item to its closest cluster.

```
def FindClusters(means,items):
    clusters = [[] for i in range(len(means))]; # Init clusters


    for item in items:


        # Classify item into a cluster
        index = Classify(means,item);


        # Add item to cluster
        clusters[index].append(item);
```

```
return clusters;
```

The other popularly used similarity measures are:

- Cosine distance: It determines the cosine of the angle between the point vectors of the two points in the n dimensional space:

$$d = \frac{X.Y}{||X|| * ||Y||}$$

- Manhattan distance: It computes the sum of the absolute differences between the co-ordinates of the two data points:

$$d = \sum_n X_i - Y_i$$

- Minkowski distance: It is also known as the generalised distance metric. It can be used for both ordinal and quantitative variables:

$$d = \left(\sum_n |X_i - Y_i|^{\frac{1}{p}} \right) p$$

References

- Polson, nicholas g.; Scott, steven l. (2011). "Data augmentation for support vector machines". Bayesian analysis. 6 (1): 1–23. Doi:10.1214/11-Ba601

- Data-mining-algorithms-analysis-services-data-mining, data-mining, analysis-services: microsoft.Com, retrieved 15 january, 2019

- "1.4. Support vector machines — scikit-learn 0.20.2 Documentation". Archived from the original on 2017-11-08. Retrieved 2017-11-08

- K-means-clustering-introduction: geeksforgeeks.Org, retrieved 16 february, 2019

- Iffey, s. M; smith, a. B; welsh, a. H; cullis, b. R (2017). "A new reml (parameter expanded) em algorithm for linear mixed models". Australian & new zealand journal of statistics. 59 (4): 433. Doi:10.1111/Anzs.12208

- Langville, amy n.; Meyer, carl d. (2006). Google's pagerank and beyond: the science of search engine rankings. Princeton university press. Isbn 978-0-691-12202-1

- Narasimha murty, m.; Susheela devi, v. (2011). Pattern recognition: an algorithmic approach. Isbn 978-0857294944

4
Cluster Analysis Method

Cluster analysis is a multivariate method to classify objects into different groups such that similar objects are placed in the same group. There are numerous methods that can be used to carry out cluster analysis such as consensus clustering, data stream clustering, hierarchical clustering, etc. This chapter discusses in detail these methods related to cluster analysis.

Clustering is the process of making a group of abstract objects into classes of similar objects.

- A cluster of data objects can be treated as one group.

- While doing cluster analysis, we first partition the set of data into groups based on data similarity and then assign the labels to the groups.

- The main advantage of clustering over classification is that, it is adaptable to changes and helps single out useful features that distinguish different groups.

Applications of Cluster Analysis

- Clustering analysis is broadly used in many applications such as market research, pattern recognition, data analysis, and image processing.

- Clustering can also help marketers discover distinct groups in their customer base. And they can characterize their customer groups based on the purchasing patterns.

- In the field of biology, it can be used to derive plant and animal taxonomies, categorize genes with similar functionalities and gain insight into structures inherent to populations.

- Clustering also helps in identification of areas of similar land use in an earth observation database. It also helps in the identification of groups of houses in a city according to house type, value, and geographic location.

- Clustering also helps in classifying documents on the web for information discovery.

- Clustering is also used in outlier detection applications such as detection of credit card fraud.

- As a data mining function, cluster analysis serves as a tool to gain insight into the distribution of data to observe characteristics of each cluster.

Requirements of Clustering in Data Mining

The following points throw light on why clustering is required in data mining:

- Scalability – We need highly scalable clustering algorithms to deal with large databases.

- Ability to deal with different kinds of attributes – Algorithms should be capable to be applied on any kind of data such as interval-based (numerical) data, categorical, and binary data.

- Discovery of clusters with attribute shape – The clustering algorithm should be capable of detecting clusters of arbitrary shape. They should not be bounded to only distance measures that tend to find spherical cluster of small sizes.

- High dimensionality – The clustering algorithm should not only be able to handle low-dimensional data but also the high dimensional space.

- Ability to deal with noisy data – Databases contain noisy, missing or erroneous data. Some algorithms are sensitive to such data and may lead to poor quality clusters.

- Interpretability – The clustering results should be interpretable, comprehensible, and usable.

Clustering Methods

Clustering methods can be classified into the following categories:

- Partitioning Method.

- Hierarchical Method.

- Density-based Method.

- Grid-Based Method.

- Model-Based Method.

- Constraint-based Method.

Partitioning Method

Suppose we are given a database of 'n' objects and the partitioning method constructs 'k' partition of data. Each partition will represent a cluster and k ≤ n. It means that it will classify the data into k groups, which satisfy the following requirements:

- Each group contains at least one object.

- Each object must belong to exactly one group.

- For a given number of partitions (say k), the partitioning method will create an initial partitioning.

- Then it uses the iterative relocation technique to improve the partitioning by moving objects from one group to other.

Hierarchical Methods

This method creates a hierarchical decomposition of the given set of data objects. We can classify hierarchical methods on the basis of how the hierarchical decomposition is formed. There are two approaches here:

- Agglomerative Approach.
- Divisive Approach.

Agglomerative Approach

This approach is also known as the bottom-up approach. In this, we start with each object forming a separate group. It keeps on merging the objects or groups that are close to one another. It keep on doing so until all of the groups are merged into one or until the termination condition holds.

Divisive Approach

This approach is also known as the top-down approach. In this, we start with all of the objects in the same cluster. In the continuous iteration, a cluster is split up into smaller clusters. It is down until each object in one cluster or the termination condition holds. This method is rigid, i.e., once a merging or splitting is done, it can never be undone.

Approaches to Improve Quality of Hierarchical Clustering

Here are the two approaches that are used to improve the quality of hierarchical clustering:

- Perform careful analysis of object linkages at each hierarchical partitioning.
- Integrate hierarchical agglomeration by first using a hierarchical agglomerative algorithm to group objects into micro-clusters, and then performing macro-clustering on the micro-clusters.

Density-based Method

This method is based on the notion of density. The basic idea is to continue growing the given cluster as long as the density in the neighborhood exceeds some threshold, i.e., for each data point within a given cluster, the radius of a given cluster has to contain at least a minimum number of points.

Grid-based Method

In this, the objects together form a grid. The object space is quantized into finite number of cells that form a grid structure.

Advantages

- The major advantage of this method is fast processing time.
- It is dependent only on the number of cells in each dimension in the quantized space.

Model-based Methods

In this method, a model is hypothesized for each cluster to find the best fit of data for a given model. This method locates the clusters by clustering the density function. It reflects spatial distribution of the data points.

This method also provides a way to automatically determine the number of clusters based on standard statistics, taking outlier or noise into account. It therefore yields robust clustering methods.

Constraint-based Method

In this method, the clustering is performed by the incorporation of user or application-oriented constraints. A constraint refers to the user expectation or the properties of desired clustering results. Constraints provide us with an interactive way of communication with the clustering process. Constraints can be specified by the user or the application requirement.

Automatic Clustering Algorithms

Automatic clustering algorithms are algorithms that can perform clustering without prior knowledge of data sets. In contrast with other cluster analysis techniques, automatic clustering algorithms can determine the optimal number of clusters even in the presence of noise and outlier points.

Centroid-based

Given a set of n objects, centroid-based algorithms create k partitions based on a dissimilarity function, such that $k \leq n$. A major problem in applying this type of algorithm is determining the appropriate number of clusters for unlabeled data. Therefore, most research in clustering analysis has been focused on the automation of the process.

Automated selection of k in a K-means clustering algorithm, one of the most used centroid-based clustering algorithms, is still a major problem in machine learning. The most accepted solution to this problem is the elbow method. It consists of running k-means clustering to the data set with a range of values, calculating the sum of squared errors for each, and plotting them in a line chart. If the chart looks like an arm, the best value of k will be on the "elbow".

Another method that modifies the k-means algorithm for automatically choosing the optimal number of clusters is the G-means algorithm. It was developed from the hypothesis that a subset of the data follows a Gaussian distribution. Thus, k is increased until each k-means center's data is Gaussian. This algorithm only requires the standard statistical significance level as a parameter and does not set limits for the covariance of the data.

Connectivity-based Hierarchical Clustering

Connectivity-based clustering or hierarchical clustering is based on the idea that objects have more similarities to other nearby objects than to those further away. Therefore, the generated clusters from this type of algorithm will be the result of the distance between the analyzed objects.

Hierarchical models can either be divisive, where partitions are built from the entire data set available, or agglomerating, where each partition begins with a single object and additional objects are added to the set. Although hierarchical clustering has the advantage of allowing any valid metric to be used as the defined distance, it is sensitive to noise and fluctuations in the data set and is more difficult to automate.

Methods have been developed to improve and automate existing hierarchical clustering algorithms such as an automated version of single linkage hierarchical cluster analysis (HCA). This computerized method bases its success on a self-consistent outlier reduction approach followed by the building of a descriptive function which permits defining natural clusters. Discarded objects can also be assigned to these clusters. Essentially, one needs not to resort to external parameters to identify natural clusters. Information gathered from HCA, automated and reliable, can be resumed in a dendrogram with the number of natural clusters and the corresponding separation, an option not found in classical HCA. This method includes the two following steps: outliers being removed (this is applied in many filtering applications) and an optional classification allowing expanding clusters with the whole set of objects.

BIRCH (balanced iterative reducing and clustering using hierarchies) is an algorithm used to perform connectivity-based clustering for large data-sets. It is regarded as one of the fastest clustering algorithms, but it is limited its requirement of the number of clusters as input. Therefore, new algorithms based on BIRCH have been developed in which there is no need to provide the cluster count from the beginning, but that preserves the quality and speed of the clusters. The main modification is to remove the final step of BIRCH, where the user had to input the cluster count, and to improve the rest of the algorithm, referred to as tree-BIRCH, by optimizing a threshold parameter from the data. In this resulting algorithm, the threshold parameter is calculated from the maximum cluster radius and the minimum distance between clusters, which are often known. This method proved to be efficient for data sets of tens of thousands of clusters. If going beyond that amount, a supercluster splitting problem is introduced. For this, other algorithms have been developed, like MDB-BIRCH, which reduces super cluster splitting with relatively high speed.

Density-based

Unlike partitioning and hierarchical methods, density-based clustering algorithms are able to find clusters of any arbitrary shape, not only spheres.

The density-based clustering algorithm uses autonomous machine learning that identifies patterns regarding geographical location and distance to a particular number of neighbors. It is considered autonomous because a priori knowledge on what is a cluster is not required. This type of algorithm provides different methods to find clusters in the data. The fastest method is DBSCAN, which uses a defined distance to differentiate between dense groups of information and sparser noise. Moreover, HDBSCAN can self-adjust by using a range of distances instead of a specified one. Lastly, the method OPTICS creates a reachability plot based on the distance from neighboring features to separate noise from clusters of varying density.

These methods still require the user to provide the cluster center and cannot be considered automatic. The Automatic Local Density Clustering Algorithm (ALDC) is an example of the new research focused on developing automatic density-based clustering. ALDC works out local density and distance deviation of every point, thus expanding the difference between the potential cluster center and other points. This expansion allows the machine to work automatically. The machine identifies cluster centers and assigns the points that are left by their closest neighbor of higher density.

In the automation of data density to identify clusters, research has also been focused on artificially generating the algorithms. For instance, the Estimation of Distribution Algorithms guarantees the generation of valid algorithms by the directed acyclic graph (DAG), in which nodes represent procedures (building block) and edges represent possible execution sequences between two nodes. Building Blocks determine the EDA's alphabet or, in other words, any generated algorithm. Clustering algorithms artificially generated are compared to DBSCAN, a manual algorithm, in experimental results.

Clustering High-dimensional Data

Clustering high-dimensional data is the cluster analysis of data with anywhere from a few dozen to many thousands of dimensions. Such high-dimensional spaces of data are often encountered in areas such as medicine, where DNA microarray technology can produce many measurements at once, and the clustering of text documents, where, if a word-frequency vector is used, the number of dimensions equals the size of the vocabulary.

Problems

Four problems need to be overcome for clustering in high-dimensional data:

- Multiple dimensions are hard to think in, impossible to visualize, and due to the exponential growth of the number of possible values with each dimension, complete enumeration of all subspaces becomes intractable with increasing dimensionality. This problem is known as the curse of dimensionality.

- The concept of distance becomes less precise as the number of dimensions grows, since the distance between any two points in a given dataset converges. The discrimination of the nearest and farthest point in particular becomes meaningless:

$$\lim_{d \to \infty} \frac{dist_{\max} - dist_{\min}}{dist_{\min}} = 0$$

- A cluster is intended to group objects that are related, based on observations of their attribute's values. However, given a large number of attributes some of the attributes will usually not be meaningful for a given cluster. For example, in newborn screening a cluster of samples might identify newborns that share similar blood values, which might lead to insights about the relevance of certain blood values for a disease. But for different diseases, different blood values might form a cluster, and other values might be uncorrelated. This is known as the *local feature relevance* problem: different clusters might be found in different subspaces, so a global filtering of attributes is not sufficient.

- Given a large number of attributes, it is likely that some attributes are correlated. Hence, clusters might exist in arbitrarily oriented affine subspaces.

Recent research indicates that the discrimination problems only occur when there is a high number of irrelevant dimensions, and that shared-nearest-neighbor approaches can improve results.

Approaches

Approaches towards clustering in axis-parallel or arbitrarily oriented affine subspaces differ in how they interpret the overall goal, which is finding clusters in data with high dimensionality. An overall different approach is to find clusters based on pattern in the data matrix, often referred to as biclustering, which is a technique frequently utilized in bioinformatics.

Subspace Clustering

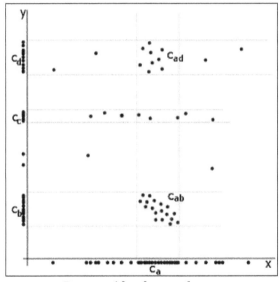

2D space with subspace clusters.

The adjacent image shows a mere two-dimensional space where a number of clusters can be identified. In the one-dimensional subspaces, the clusters c_a (in subspace $\{x\}$) and c_b, c_c, c_d (in subspace $\{y\}$) can be found. The c_c cannot be considered a cluster in a two-dimensional (sub-)space, since it is too sparsely distributed in the x axis. In two dimensions, the two clusters c_{ab} and c_{ab} can be identified.

The problem of subspace clustering is given by the fact that there are 2^d different subspaces of a space with d dimensions. If the subspaces are not axis-parallel, an infinite number of subspaces is possible. Hence, subspace clustering algorithms utilize some kind of heuristic to remain computationally feasible, at the risk of producing inferior results. For example, the *downward-closure property* can be used to build higher-dimensional subspaces only by combining lower-dimensional ones, as any subspace T containing a cluster, will result in a full space S also to contain that cluster (i.e. $S \subseteq T$), an approach taken by most of the traditional algorithms such as CLIQUE, SUBCLU. It is also possible to define a subspace using different degrees of relevance for each dimension, an approach taken by iMWK-Means, EBK-Modes and CBK-Modes.

Projected Clustering

Projected clustering seeks to assign each point to a unique cluster, but clusters may exist in different subspaces. The general approach is to use a special distance function together with a regular clustering algorithm.

For example, the PreDeCon algorithm checks which attributes seem to support a clustering for each point, and adjusts the distance function such that dimensions with low variance are amplified in the distance function. In the figure, the cluster c_c might be found using DBSCAN with a distance function that places less emphasis on the x-axis and thus exaggerates the low difference in the y-axis sufficiently enough to group the points into a cluster.

PROCLUS uses a similar approach with a k-medoid clustering. Initial medoids are guessed, and for each medoid the subspace spanned by attributes with low variance is determined. Points are assigned to the medoid closest, considering only the subspace of that medoid in determining the distance. The algorithm then proceeds as the regular PAM algorithm.

If the distance function weights attributes differently, but never with 0 (and hence never drops irrelevant attributes), the algorithm is called a "soft"-projected clustering algorithm.

Hybrid Approaches

Not all algorithms try to either find a unique cluster assignment for each point or all clusters in all subspaces; many settle for a result in between, where a number of possibly overlapping, but not necessarily exhaustive set of clusters are found. An example is FIRES, which is from its basic approach a subspace clustering algorithm, but uses a heuristic too aggressive to credibly produce all subspace clusters. Another hybrid approach is to include a human into the algorithmic loop. Human domain expertise can help to reduce an exponential search space through heuristic selection of samples. This can be beneficial in the health domain where, e.g., medical doctors are confronted with high-dimensional descriptions of patient conditions and measurements on the success of certain therapies. An important question in such data is to compare and correlate patient conditions and therapy results along with combinations of dimensions. The number of dimensions is often very large, consequently one needs to map them to a smaller number of relevant dimensions to be more amenable for expert analysis. This is because irrelevant, redundant, and conflicting dimensions can negatively affect effectiveness and efficiency of the whole analytic process.

Consensus Clustering

Consensus clustering is an important elaboration of traditional cluster analysis. Consensus clustering, also called cluster ensembles or aggregation of clustering (or partitions), refers to the situation in which a number of different (input) clusterings have been obtained for a particular dataset and it is desired to find a single (consensus) clustering which is a better fit in some sense than the existing clusterings. Consensus clustering is thus the problem of reconciling clustering information about the same data set coming from different sources or from different runs of the same algorithm. When cast as an optimization problem, consensus clustering is known as median partition, and has been shown to be NP-complete, even when the number of input clusterings is three. Consensus clustering for unsupervised learning is analogous to ensemble learning in supervised learning.

Issues with Existing Clustering Techniques

- Current clustering techniques do not address all the requirements adequately.

- Dealing with large number of dimensions and large number of data items can be problematic because of time complexity;

- Effectiveness of the method depends on the definition of "distance" (for distance-based clustering);

- If an obvious distance measure doesn't exist, we must "define" it, which is not always easy, especially in multidimensional spaces;

- The result of the clustering algorithm (that, in many cases, can be arbitrary itself) can be interpreted in different ways.

Justification for using Consensus Clustering

There are potential shortcomings for all existing clustering techniques. This may cause interpretation of results to become difficult, especially when there is no knowledge about the number of clusters. Clustering methods are also very sensitive to the initial clustering settings, which can cause non-significant data to be amplified in non-reiterative methods. An extremely important issue in cluster analysis is the validation of the clustering results, that is, how to gain confidence about the significance of the clusters provided by the clustering technique (cluster numbers and cluster assignments). Lacking an external objective criterion (the equivalent of a known class label in supervised analysis), this validation becomes somewhat elusive. Iterative descent clustering methods, such as the SOM and k-means clustering circumvent some of the shortcomings of hierarchical clustering by providing for univocally defined clusters and cluster boundaries. Consensus clustering provides a method that represents the consensus across multiple runs of a clustering algorithm, to determine the number of clusters in the data, and to assess the stability of the discovered clusters. The method can also be used to represent the consensus over multiple runs of a clustering algorithm with random restart (such as K-means, model-based Bayesian clustering, SOM, etc.), so as to account for its sensitivity to the initial conditions. It can provide data for a visualization tool to inspect cluster number, membership, and boundaries. However, they lack the intuitive and visual appeal of hierarchical clustering dendrograms, and the number of clusters must be chosen a priori.

Over-interpretation Potential of Consensus Clustering

Consensus clustering can be a powerful tool for identifying clusters, but it needs to be applied with caution. It has been shown that consensus clustering is able to claim apparent stability of chance partitioning of null datasets drawn from a unimodal distribution, and thus has the potential to lead to over-interpretation of cluster stability in a real study. If clusters are not well separated, consensus clustering could lead one to conclude apparent structure when there is none, or declare cluster stability when it is subtle. To reduce the false positive potential in clustering samples (observations), Şenbabaoğlu *et al* recommends: (1) doing a formal test of cluster strength using simulated unimodal data with the same feature space correlation structure as in the empirical data, (2) not relying solely on the consensus matrix heatmap to declare the existence of clusters, or to estimate optimal K, (3) applying the proportion of ambiguous clustering (PAC) as a simple yet powerful method to infer optimal K.

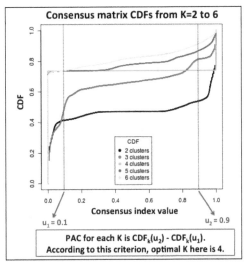

PAC measure (proportion of ambiguous clustering). Optimal K is the K with lowest PAC value.

PAC: In the CDF curve of a consensus matrix, the lower left portion represents sample pairs rarely clustered together, the upper right portion represents those almost always clustered together, whereas the middle segment represent those with ambiguous assignments in different clustering runs. The "proportion of ambiguous clustering" (PAC) measure quantifies this middle segment; and is defined as the fraction of sample pairs with consensus indices falling in the interval $(u_1, u_2) \in [0, 1]$ where u_1 is a value close to 0 and u_2 is a value close to 1 (for instance $u_1=0.1$ and $u_2=0.9$). A low value of PAC indicates a flat middle segment, and a low rate of discordant assignments across permuted clustering runs. We can therefore infer the optimal number of clusters by the K value having the lowest PAC.

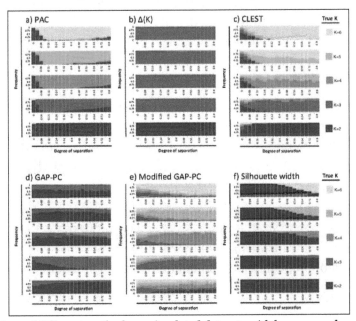

Inferred optimal K values of different methods on simulated datasets with known number of clusters and known degree of separation between clusters. Consensus clustering followed by PAC outperforms other methods.

In simulated datasets with known number of clusters, consensus clustering+PAC has been shown to perform better than several other commonly used methods such as consensus clustering+Δ(K), CLEST, GAP, and silhouette width.

Hard Ensemble Clustering

This approach by Strehl and Ghosh introduces the problem of combining multiple partitionings of a set of objects into a single consolidated clustering without accessing the features or algorithms that determined these partitionings. They discuss three approaches towards solving this problem to obtain high quality consensus functions. Their techniques have low computational costs and this makes it feasible to evaluate each of the techniques discussed below and arrive at the best solution by comparing the results against the objective function.

Efficient Consensus Functions

1. Cluster-based similarity partitioning algorithm (CSPA): In CSPA the similarity between two data-points is defined to be directly proportional to number of constituent clusterings of the ensemble in which they are clustered together. The intuition is that the more similar two data-points are the higher is the chance that constituent clusterings will place them in the same cluster. CSPA is the simplest heuristic, but its computational and storage complexity are both quadratic in n.

2. Hyper-graph partitioning algorithm (HGPA): The HGPA algorithm takes a very different approach to finding the consensus clustering than the previous method. The cluster ensemble problem is formulated as partitioning the hypergraph by cutting a minimal number of hyperedges. They make use of hMETIS which is a hypergraph partitioning package system.

3. Meta-clustering algorithm (MCLA): The meta-cLustering algorithm (MCLA) is based on clustering clusters. First, it tries to solve the cluster correspondence problem and then uses voting to place data-points into the final consensus clusters. The cluster correspondence problem is solved by grouping the clusters identified in the individual clusterings of the ensemble. The clustering is performed using METIS and Spectral clustering.

Soft Clustering Ensembles

Punera and Ghosh extended the idea of hard clustering ensembles to the soft clustering scenario. Each instance in a soft ensemble is represented by a concatenation of r posterior membership probability distributions obtained from the constituent clustering algorithms. We can define a distance measure between two instances using the Kullback–Leibler (KL) divergence, which calculates the "distance" between two probability distributions.

1. sCSPA: sCSPA extends CSPA by calculating a similarity matrix. Each object is visualized as a point in dimensional space, with each dimension corresponding to probability of its belonging to a cluster. This technique first transforms the objects into a label-space and then interprets the dot product between the vectors representing the objects as their similarity.

2. sMCLA: sMCLA extends MCLA by accepting soft clusterings as input. sMCLA's working can be divided into the following steps:

- Construct soft meta-graph of clusters.

- Group the clusters into meta-clusters.

- Collapse meta-clusters using weighting.

- Compete for objects.

3. sHBGF: HBGF represents the ensemble as a bipartite graph with clusters and instances as nodes, and edges between the instances and the clusters they belong to. This approach can be trivially adapted to consider soft ensembles since the graph partitioning algorithm METIS accepts weights on the edges of the graph to be partitioned. In sHBGF, the graph has $n + t$ vertices, where t is the total number of underlying clusters.

4. Bayesian consensus clustering (BCC): BCC defines a fully Bayesian model for soft consensus clustering in which multiple source clusterings, defined by different input data or different probability models, are assumed to adhere loosely to a consensus clustering. The full posterior for the separate clusterings, and the consensus clustering, are inferred simultaneously via Gibbs sampling.

Data Stream Clustering

In computer science, data stream clustering is defined as the clustering of data that arrive continuously such as telephone records, multimedia data, financial transactions etc. Data stream clustering is usually studied as a streaming algorithm and the objective is, given a sequence of points, to construct a good clustering of the stream, using a small amount of memory and time.

The problem of data stream clustering is defined as:

- Input: A sequence of n points in metric space and an integer k.

- Output: k centers in the set of the n points so as to minimize the sum of distances from data points to their closest cluster centers.

This is the streaming version of the k-median problem.

Algorithms

STREAM

STREAM is an algorithm for clustering data streams described by Guha, Mishra, Motwani and O'Callaghan which achieves a constant factor approximation for the k-Median problem in a single pass and using small space.

Theorem — STREAM can solve the k-Median problem on a data stream in a single pass, with time $O(n^{1+e})$ and space $\theta(n^{\varepsilon})$ up to a factor $2^{O(1/e)}$, where n the number of points and $e < 1/2$.

To understand STREAM, the first step is to show that clustering can take place in small space (not caring about the number of passes). Small-space is a divide-and-conquer algorithm that divides the data, S, into ℓ pieces, clusters each one of them (using k-means) and then clusters the centers obtained.

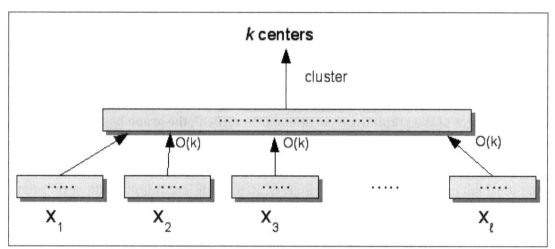

Small-space Algorithm representation.

Algorithm Small-space

- Divide S into ℓ disjoint pieces $X_1, \ldots, X_\ell$.

- For each i, find $O(k)$ centers in X_i. Assign each point in X_i to its closest center.

- Let X' be the $O(\ell k)$ centers, where each center c is weighted by the number of points assigned to it.

- Cluster X' to find k centers.

Where, we run a bicriteria (a,b)-approximation algorithm which outputs at most ak medians with cost at most b times the optimum k-Median solution and in Step 4 we run a c-approximation algorithm then the approximation factor of small-space() algorithm is $2c(1+2b)+2b$. We can also generalize Small-space so that it recursively calls itself i times on a successively smaller set of weighted centers and achieves a constant factor approximation to the k-median problem.

The problem with the Small-space is that the number of subsets ℓ that we partition S into is limited, since it has to store in memory the intermediate medians in X. So, if M is the size of memory, we need to partition S into ℓ subsets such that each subset fits in memory, (n/ℓ) and so that the weighted ℓk centers also fit in memory, $\ell k < M$. But such an ℓ may not always exist.

The STREAM algorithm solves the problem of storing intermediate medians and achieves better running time and space requirements. The algorithm works as follows:

- Input the first m points; using the randomized algorithm presented in reduce these to $O(k)$ (say $2k$) points.

- Repeat the above till we have seen $m^2/(2k)$ of the original data points. We now have m intermediate medians.

- Using a local search algorithm, cluster these m first-level medians into $2k$ second-level medians and proceed.

- In general, maintain at most m level-i medians, and on seeing m, generate $2k$ level-$i+1$ medians, with the weight of a new median as the sum of the weights of the intermediate medians assigned to it.

- When we have seen all the original data points, we cluster all the intermediate medians into k final medians, using the primal dual algorithm.

Other Algorithms

Other well-known algorithms used for data stream clustering are:

- BIRCH: It builds a hierarchical data structure to incrementally cluster the incoming points using the available memory and minimizing the amount of I/O required. The complexity of the algorithm is $O(N)$ since one pass suffices to get a good clustering (though, results can be improved by allowing several passes).

- COBWEB: It is an incremental clustering technique that keeps a hierarchical clustering model in the form of a classification tree. For each new point COBWEB descends the tree, updates the nodes along the way and looks for the best node to put the point on (using a category utility function).

- C2ICM: It builds a flat partitioning clustering structure by selecting some objects as cluster seeds/initiators and a non-seed is assigned to the seed that provides the highest coverage, addition of new objects can introduce new seeds and falsify some existing old seeds, during incremental clustering new objects and the members of the falsified clusters are assigned to one of the existing new/old seeds.

Mean-shift Clustering

Mean-shift is falling under the category of a clustering algorithm in contrast of unsupervised learning that assigns the data points to the clusters iteratively by shifting points towards the mode (mode is the highest density of data points in the region, in the context of the Mean-shift). As such, it is also known as the Mode-seeking algorithm. Mean-shift algorithm has applications in the field of image processing and computer vision.

Given a set of data points, the algorithm iteratively assigns each data point towards the closest cluster centroid and direction to the closest cluster centroid is determined by where most of the points near-by are at. So each iteration each data point will move closer to where the most points are at, which is or will lead to the cluster center. When the algorithm stops, each point is assigned to a cluster.

Unlike the popular K-means cluster algorithm, mean-shift does not require specifying the number of clusters in advance. The number of clusters is determined by the algorithm with respect to the data.

Kernel Density Estimation

The first step when applying mean shift clustering algorithms is representing your data in a mathematical manner this means representing your data as points such as the set below.

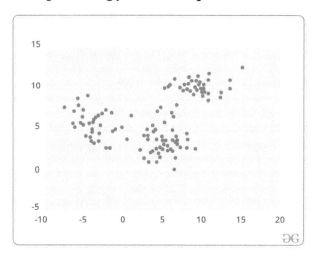

Mean-shift builds upon the concept of kernel density estimation is sort KDE. Imagine that the above data was sampled from a probability distribution. KDE is a method to estimate the underlying distribution also called the probability density function for a set of data.

It works by placing a kernel on each point in the data set. A kernel is a fancy mathematical word for a weighting function generally used in convolution. There are many different types of kernels, but the most popular one is the Gaussian kernel. Adding up all of the individual kernels generates a probability surface example density function. Depending on the kernel bandwidth parameter used, the resultant density function will vary.

Below is the KDE surface for our points above using a Gaussian kernel with a kernel bandwidth of 2.

Surface Plot

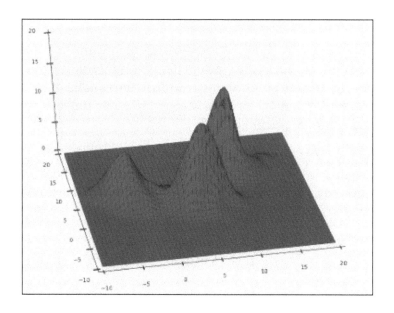

Contour Plot

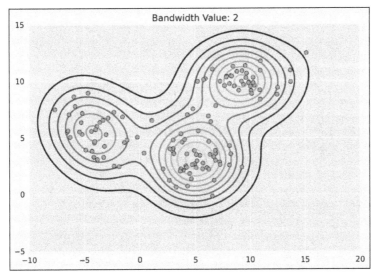

Bandwidth Value.

Below is the Python implementation:

```
import numpy as np
import pandas as pd
from sklearn.cluster import MeanShift
from sklearn.datasets.samples_generator import make_blobs
from matplotlib import pyplot as plt
from mpl_toolkits.mplot3d import Axes3D


# We will be using the make_blobs method
# in order to generate our own data.

clusters = [[2, 2, 2], [7, 7, 7], [5, 13, 13]]


X, _ = make_blobs(n_samples = 150, centers = clusters,
                                    cluster_std = 0.60)


# After training the model, We store the
# coordinates for the cluster centers
ms = MeanShift()
ms.fit(X)
cluster_centers = ms.cluster_centers_
```

```
# Finally We plot the data points
# and centroids in a 3D graph.
fig = plt.figure()


ax = fig.add_subplot(111, projection ='3d')


ax.scatter(X[:, 0], X[:, 1], X[:, 2], marker ='o')


ax.scatter(cluster_centers[:, 0], cluster_centers[:, 1],
          cluster_centers[:, 2], marker = >x>, color = >red>,
          s = 300, linewidth = 5, zorder = 10)


plt.show()
```

Output

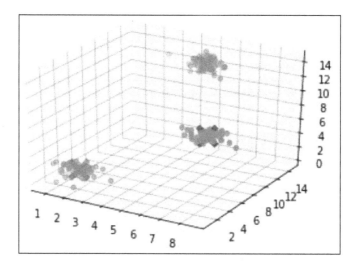

To illustrate, suppose we are given a data set {ui} of points in d-dimensional space, sampled from some larger population, and that we have chosen a kernel K having bandwidth parameter h. Together, these data and kernel function returns the following kernel density estimator for the full population's density function.

$$f_K(u) = \frac{1}{nh^d} \sum_{i=1}^{n} K(\frac{u-u_i}{h})$$

The kernel function here is required to satisfy the following two conditions:

1. $\int K(u)du = 1.$

2. $K(u) = K(|u|)$ for all values of u.

Two popular kernel functions that satisfy these conditions are given by:

1. Flat/Uniform $K(\mathrm{u}) = \dfrac{1}{2} \begin{cases} 1 & -1 \le |\mathrm{u}| \le 1 \\ 0 & \text{else} \end{cases}$.

2. Gaussian$= K(\mathrm{u}) = \dfrac{1}{2(\pi)^{d/2}} e^{-\frac{1}{2}|\mathrm{u}|^2}$.

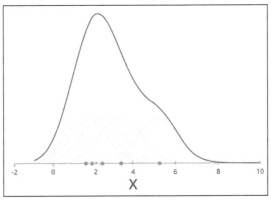

Kernel density estimation using a gussain kernel for each data point:
Adding up small Gauggians about each example returns our net
estimate for the total density, the black curve.

We have plotted an example in one dimension using the Gaussian kernel to estimate the density of some population along the x-axis. We can see that each sample point adds a small Gaussian to our estimate, centered about it and equations above may look a bit intimidating, but the graphic here should clarify that the concept is pretty straightforward.

Iterative Mode Search

1. Initialize random seed and window W.

2. Calculate the center of gravity (mean) of W.

3. Shift the search window to the mean.

4. Repeat Step 2 until convergence.

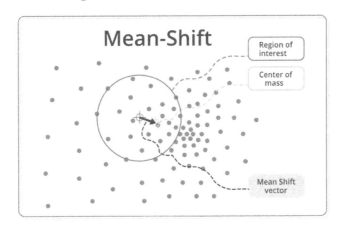

General algorithm outline:

```
for p in copied_points:
    while not at_kde_peak:
        p = shift(p, original_points)
```

Shift function looks like this:

```
def shift(p, original_points):
    shift_x = float(0)
    shift_y = float(0)
    scale_factor = float(0)

    for p_temp in original_points:
        # numerator
        dist = euclidean_dist(p, p_temp)
        weight = kernel(dist, kernel_bandwidth)
        shift_x += p_temp[0] * weight
        shift_y += p_temp[1] * weight
        # denominator
        scale_factor += weight

    shift_x = shift_x / scale_factor
    shift_y = shift_y / scale_factor
    return [shift_x, shift_y]
```

Pros

- Finds variable number of modes.

- Robust to outliers.

- General, application-independent tool.

- Model-free, doesn't assume any prior shape like spherical, elliptical, etc. on data clusters.

- Just a single parameter (window size h) where h has a physical meaning (unlike k-means).

Cons

- Output depends on window size.

- Window size (bandwidth) selecHon is not trivial.

- Computationally (relatively) expensive (approx 2s/image).

- Doesn't scale well with dimension of feature space.

DBSCAN

Density-based spatial clustering of applications with noise (DBSCAN) is a data clustering algorithm proposed by Martin Ester, Hans-Peter Kriegel, Jörg Sander and Xiaowei Xu in 1996. It is a density-based clustering non-parametric algorithm: given a set of points in some space, it groups together points that are closely packed together (points with many nearby neighbors), marking as outliers points that lie alone in low-density regions (whose nearest neighbors are too far away). DBSCAN is one of the most common clustering algorithms and also most cited in scientific literature.

In 2014, the algorithm was awarded the test of time award (an award given to algorithms which have received substantial attention in theory and practice) at the leading data mining conference, KDD.

Preliminary

Consider a set of points in some space to be clustered. Let ε be a parameter specifying the radius of a neighborhood with respect to some point. For the purpose of DBSCAN clustering, the points are classified as *core points*, *(density)reachable points* and *outliers*, as follows:

- A point p is a *core point* if at least minPts points are within distance ε of it (including p).

- A point q is *directly reachable* from p if point q is within distance ε from core point p. Points are only said to be directly reachable from core points.

- A point q is *reachable* from p if there is a path $p_1, ..., p_n$ with $p_1 = p$ and $p_n = q$, where each p_{i+1} is directly reachable from p_i. Note that this implies that all points on the path must be core points, with the possible exception of q.

- All points not reachable from any other point are outliers or noise points.

Now if p is a core point, then it forms a *cluster* together with all points (core or non-core) that are reachable from it. Each cluster contains at least one core point; non-core points can be part of a cluster, but they form its "edge", since they cannot be used to reach more points.

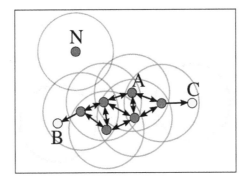

In this diagram, minPts = 4. Point A and the other red points are core points, because the area surrounding these points in an ε radius contain at least 4 points (including the point itself). Because they are all reachable from one another, they form a single cluster. Points B and C are not core points, but are reachable from A (via other core points) and thus belong to the cluster as well. Point N is a noise point that is neither a core point nor directly-reachable.

Reachability is not a symmetric relation since, by definition, no point may be reachable from a non-core point, regardless of distance (so a non-core point may be reachable, but nothing can be reached from it). Therefore, a further notion of *connectedness* is needed to formally define the extent of the clusters found by DBSCAN. Two points p and q are density-connected if there is a point o such that both p and q are reachable from o. Density-connectedness *is* symmetric.

A cluster then satisfies two properties:

- All points within the cluster are mutually density-connected.

- If a point is density-reachable from any point of the cluster, it is part of the cluster as well.

Algorithm

Original Query-based Algorithm

DBSCAN requires two parameters: ε (eps) and the minimum number of points required to form a dense region (minPts). It starts with an arbitrary starting point that has not been visited. This point's ε-neighborhood is retrieved, and if it contains sufficiently many points, a cluster is started. Otherwise, the point is labeled as noise. Note that this point might later be found in a sufficiently sized ε-environment of a different point and hence be made part of a cluster.

If a point is found to be a dense part of a cluster, its ε-neighborhood is also part of that cluster. Hence, all points that are found within the ε-neighborhood are added, as is their own ε-neighborhood when they are also dense. This process continues until the density-connected cluster is completely found. Then, a new unvisited point is retrieved and processed, leading to the discovery of a further cluster or noise.

DBSCAN can be used with any distance function (as well as similarity functions or other predicates). The distance function (dist) can therefore be seen as an additional parameter.

The algorithm can be expressed in pseudocode as follows:

```
DBSCAN(DB, distFunc, eps, minPts) {
  C = 0                                               /* Cluster counter */
  for each point P in database DB {
    if label(P) ≠ undefined then continue       /* Previously processed in inner loop */
      Neighbors N = RangeQuery(DB, distFunc, P, eps)     /* Find neighbors */
    if |N| < minPts then {                          /* Density check */
      label(P) = Noise                              /* Label as Noise */
      continue
    }
```

```
    C = C + 1                                          /* next cluster label */
    label(P) = C                                       /* Label initial point */
    Seed set S = N \ {P}                               /* Neighbors to expand */
    for each point Q in S {                            /* Process every seed point */
      if label(Q) = Noise then label(Q) = C        /* Change Noise to border point */
      if label(Q) ≠ undefined then continue          /* Previously processed */
      label(Q) = C                                     /* Label neighbor */
      Neighbors N = RangeQuery(DB, distFunc, Q, eps)   /* Find neighbors */
      if |N| ≥ minPts then {                           /* Density check */
        S = S ∪ N                                  /* Add new neighbors to seed set */
      }
    }
  }
}
```

where RangeQuery can be implemented using a database index for better performance, or using a slow linear scan:

```
RangeQuery(DB, distFunc, Q, eps) {

  Neighbors = empty list

  for each point P in database DB {            /* Scan all points in the database */

    if distFunc(Q, P) ≤ eps then {             /* Compute distance and check epsilon */

      Neighbors = Neighbors ∪ {P}              /* Add to result */

    }

  }

  return Neighbors

}
```

Abstract Algorithm

The DBSCAN algorithm can be abstracted into the following steps:

1. Find the points in the ε (eps) neighborhood of every point, and identify the core points with more than minPts neighbors.

2. Find the connected components of *core* points on the neighbor graph, ignoring all non-core points.

3. Assign each non-core point to a nearby cluster if the cluster is an ε (eps) neighbor, otherwise assign it to noise.

A naive implementation of this requires storing the neighborhoods in step 1, thus requiring substantial memory. The original DBSCAN algorithm does not require this by performing these steps for one point at a time.

Complexity

DBSCAN visits each point of the database, possibly multiple times (e.g., as candidates to different clusters). For practical considerations, however, the time complexity is mostly governed by the number of regionQuery invocations. DBSCAN executes exactly one such query for each point, and if an indexing structure is used that executes a neighborhood query in $O(\log n)$, an overall average runtime complexity of $O(n \log n)$ is obtained (if parameter ε is chosen in a meaningful way, i.e. such that on average only $O(\log n)$ points are returned). Without the use of an accelerating index structure, or on degenerated data (e.g. all points within a distance less than ε), the worst case run time complexity remains $O(n^2)$. The distance matrix of size $(n^2-n)/2$ can be materialized to avoid distance recomputations, but this needs $O(n^2)$ memory, whereas a non-matrix based implementation of DBSCAN only needs $O(n)$ memory.

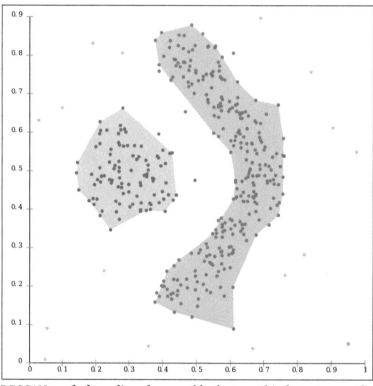

DBSCAN can find non-linearly separable clusters. This dataset cannot be adequately clustered with k-means or Gaussian Mixture EM clustering.

Advantages

- DBSCAN does not require one to specify the number of clusters in the data a priori, as opposed to k-means.

- DBSCAN can find arbitrarily shaped clusters. It can even find a cluster completely surrounded by (but not connected to) a different cluster. Due to the MinPts parameter, the so-called single-link effect (different clusters being connected by a thin line of points) is reduced.

- DBSCAN has a notion of noise, and is robust to outliers.

- DBSCAN requires just two parameters and is mostly insensitive to the ordering of the points in the database. However, points sitting on the edge of two different clusters might swap cluster membership if the ordering of the points is changed, and the cluster assignment is unique only up to isomorphism.

- DBSCAN is designed for use with databases that can accelerate region queries, e.g. using an R* tree.

- The parameters minPts and ε can be set by a domain expert, if the data is well understood.

Disadvantages

1. DBSCAN is not entirely deterministic: border points that are reachable from more than one cluster can be part of either cluster, depending on the order the data are processed. For most data sets and domains, this situation does not arise often and has little impact on the clustering result: both on core points and noise points, DBSCAN is deterministic. DBSCAN* is a variation that treats border points as noise, and this way achieves a fully deterministic result as well as a more consistent statistical interpretation of density-connected components.

2. The quality of DBSCAN depends on the distance measure used in the function region-Query(P, ε). The most common distance metric used is Euclidean distance. Especially for high-dimensional data, this metric can be rendered almost useless due to the so-called "Curse of dimensionality", making it difficult to find an appropriate value for ε. This effect, however, is also present in any other algorithm based on Euclidean distance.

- DBSCAN cannot cluster data sets well with large differences in densities, since the minPts-ε combination cannot then be chosen appropriately for all clusters.

- If the data and scale are not well understood, choosing a meaningful distance threshold ε can be difficult.

Parameter Estimation

Every data mining task has the problem of parameters. Every parameter influences the algorithm in specific ways. For DBSCAN, the parameters ε and *minPts* are needed. The parameters must be specified by the user. Ideally, the value of ε is given by the problem to solve (e.g. a physical distance), and *minPts* is then the desired minimum cluster size.

- MinPts: As a rule of thumb, a minimum *minPts* can be derived from the number of dimensions D in the data set, as $minPts \geq D + 1$. The low value of $minPts = 1$ does not make sense, as then every point on its own will already be a cluster. With $minPts \leq 2$, the result will be the same as of hierarchical clustering with the single link metric, with the dendrogram cut at height ε. Therefore, *minPts* must be chosen at least 3. However, larger values are usually better for data sets with noise and will yield more significant clusters. As a rule of thumb, $minPts = 2 \cdot dim$ can be used, but it may be necessary to choose larger values for very large data, for noisy data or for data that contains many duplicates.

- ε: The value for ε can then be chosen by using a k-distance graph, plotting the distance to the $k = minPts\text{-}1$ nearest neighbor ordered from the largest to the smallest value. Good values of ε are where this plot shows an "elbow": if ε is chosen much too small, a large part of the data will not be clustered; whereas for a too high value of ε, clusters will merge and the majority of objects will be in the same cluster. In general, small values of ε are preferable, and as a rule of thumb only a small fraction of points should be within this distance of each other. Alternatively, an OPTICS plot can be used to choose ε, but then the OPTICS algorithm itself can be used to cluster the data.

- Distance function: The choice of distance function is tightly coupled to the choice of ε, and has a major impact on the results. In general, it will be necessary to first identify a reasonable measure of similarity for the data set, before the parameter ε can be chosen. There is no estimation for this parameter, but the distance functions needs to be chosen appropriately for the data set. For example, on geographic data, the great-circle distance is often a good choice.

OPTICS can be seen as a generalization of DBSCAN that replaces the ε parameter with a maximum value that mostly affects performance. *MinPts* then essentially becomes the minimum cluster size to find. While the algorithm is much easier to parameterize than DBSCAN, the results are a bit more difficult to use, as it will usually produce a hierarchical clustering instead of the simple data partitioning that DBSCAN produces.

Recently, one of the original authors of DBSCAN has revisited DBSCAN and OPTICS, and published a refined version of hierarchical DBSCAN (HDBSCAN*), which no longer has the notion of border points. Instead, only the core points form the cluster.

Relationship to Spectral Clustering

DBSCAN can be seen as special (efficient) variant of spectral clustering: Connected components correspond to optimal spectral clusters (no edges cut – spectral clustering tries to partition the data with a minimum cut); DBSCAN finds connected components on the (asymmetric) reachability graph. However, spectral clustering can be computationally intensive (up to $O(n^3)$ without approximation and further assumptions), and one has to choose the number of clusters k for both the number of eigenvectors to choose and the number of clusters to produce with k-means on the spectral embedding. Thus, for performance reasons, the original DBSCAN algorithm remains preferable to a spectral implementation, and this relationship is so far only of theoretical interest.

Extensions

Generalized DBSCAN (GDBSCAN) is a generalization by the same authors to arbitrary "neighborhood" and "dense" predicates. The ε and *minPts* parameters are removed from the original algorithm and moved to the predicates. For example, on polygon data, the "neighborhood" could be any intersecting polygon, whereas the density predicate uses the polygon areas instead of just the object count.

Various extensions to the DBSCAN algorithm have been proposed, including methods for parallelization, parameter estimation, and support for uncertain data. The basic idea has been extended to hierarchical clustering by the OPTICS algorithm. DBSCAN is also used as part of subspace clustering algorithms like PreDeCon and SUBCLU. HDBSCAN is a hierarchical version of DBSCAN which is also faster than OPTICS, from which a flat partition consisting of the most prominent clusters can be extracted from the hierarchy.

Availability

Different implementations of the same algorithm were found to exhibit enormous performance differences, with the fastest on a test data set finishing in 1.4 seconds, the slowest taking 13803 seconds. The differences can be attributed to implementation quality, language and compiler differences, and the use of indexes for acceleration.

- Apache Commons Math contains a Java implementation of the algorithm running in quadratic time.

- ELKI offers an implementation of DBSCAN as well as GDBSCAN and other variants. This implementation can use various index structures for sub-quadratic runtime and supports arbitrary distance functions and arbitrary data types, but it may be outperformed by low-level optimized (and specialized) implementations on small data sets.

- PostGIS includes ST_ClusterDBSCAN: A 2D implementation of DBSCAN that uses R-tree index. Any geometry type is supported, e.g. Point, LineString, Polygon, etc.

- R contains implementations of DBSCAN in the packages dbscan and fpc. Both packages support arbitrary distance functions via distance matrices. The package fpc does not have index support (and thus has quadratic runtime and memory complexity) and is rather slow due to the R interpreter. The package dbscan provides a fast C++ implementation using k-d trees (for Euclidean distance only) and also includes implementations of DBSCAN*, HDBSCAN*, OPTICS, OPTICSXi, and other related methods.

- Scikit-learn includes a Python implementation of DBSCAN for arbitrary Minkowski metrics, which can be accelerated using k-d trees and ball trees but which uses worst-case quadratic memory. A contribution to scikit-learn provides an implementation of the HDBSCAN* algorithm.

- Pyclustering library includes a Python and C++ implementation of DBSCAN for Euclidean distance only as well as OPTICS algorithm.

- SPMF includes an implementation of the DBSCAN algorithm with k-d tree support for Euclidean distance only.

- Weka contains (as an optional package in latest versions) a basic implementation of DBSCAN that runs in quadratic time and linear memory.

Hierarchical Clustering

In data mining and statistics, hierarchical clustering (also called hierarchical cluster analysis or HCA) is a method of cluster analysis which seeks to build a hierarchy of clusters. Strategies for hierarchical clustering generally fall into two types:

- Agglomerative: This is a "bottom-up" approach - each observation starts in its own cluster, and pairs of clusters are merged as one moves up the hierarchy.

- Divisive: This is a "top-down" approach - all observations start in one cluster, and splits are performed recursively as one moves down the hierarchy.

In general, the merges and splits are determined in a greedy manner. The results of hierarchical clustering are usually presented in a dendrogram.

The standard algorithm for hierarchical agglomerative clustering (HAC) has a time complexity of $\mathcal{O}(n^3)$ and requires $\mathcal{O}(n^2)$ memory, which makes it too slow for even medium data sets. However, for some special cases, optimal efficient agglomerative methods (of complexity $\mathcal{O}(n^2)$) are known: SLINK for single-linkage and CLINK for complete-linkage clustering. With a heap the runtime of the general case can be reduced to $\mathcal{O}(n^2 \log n)$ at the cost of further increasing the memory requirements. In many programming languages, the memory overheads of this approach are too large to make it practically usable.

Except for the special case of single-linkage, none of the algorithms (except exhaustive search in $\mathcal{O}(n^2)$) can be guaranteed to find the optimum solution.

Divisive clustering with an exhaustive search is $\mathcal{O}(n^2)$, but it is common to use faster heuristics to choose splits, such as k-means.

Cluster Dissimilarity

In order to decide which clusters should be combined (for agglomerative), or where a cluster should be split (for divisive), a measure of dissimilarity between sets of observations is required. In most methods of hierarchical clustering, this is achieved by use of an appropriate metric (a measure of distance between pairs of observations), and a linkage criterion which specifies the dissimilarity of sets as a function of the pairwise distances of observations in the sets.

Metric

The choice of an appropriate metric will influence the shape of the clusters, as some elements may be close to one another according to one distance and farther away according to another. For example, in a 2-dimensional space, the distance between the point (1,0) and the origin (0,0) is always 1 according to the usual norms, but the distance between the point (1,1) and the origin (0,0) can be 2 under Manhattan distance, $\sqrt{2}$ under Euclidean distance, or 1 under maximum distance.

Some commonly used metrics for hierarchical clustering are:

Names	Formula
Euclidean distance	$\|a-b\|_2 = \sqrt{\sum_i (a_i - b_i)^2}$
Squared Euclidean distance	$\|a-b\|_2^2 = \sum_i (a_i - b_i)^2$
Manhattan distance	$\|a-b\|_1 = \sum_i |a_i - b_i|$

Maximum distance	$\| a-b \|_{\infty} = \max_i |a_i - b_i|$
Mahalanobis distance	$\sqrt{(a-b)^{\top} S^{-1}(a-b)}$ where S is the Covariance matrix

For text or other non-numeric data, metrics such as the Hamming distance or Levenshtein distance are often used.

A review of cluster analysis in health psychology research found that the most common distance measure in published studies in that research area is the Euclidean distance or the squared Euclidean distance.

Linkage Criteria

The linkage criterion determines the distance between sets of observations as a function of the pairwise distances between observations.

Some commonly used linkage criteria between two sets of observations A and B are:

Names	Formula
Maximum or complete-linkage clustering	$\max\{d(a,b) : a \in A, b \in B\}$.
Minimum or single-linkage clustering	$\min\{d(a,b) : a \in A, b \in B\}$.
Unweighted average linkage clustering (or UPGMA)	$\dfrac{1}{|A| \cdot |B|} \sum_{a \in A} \sum_{b \in B} d(a,b)$.
Weighted average linkage clustering (or WPGMA)	$d(i \cup j, k) = \dfrac{d(i,k) + d(j,k)}{2}$.
Centroid linkage clustering, or UPGMC	$\| c_s - c_t \|$ where c_s and c_t are the centroids of clusters s and t, respectively.
Minimum energy clustering	$\dfrac{2}{nm} \sum_{i,j=1}^{n,m} \| a_i - b_j \|_2 - \dfrac{1}{n^2} \sum_{i,j=1}^{n} \| a_i - a_j \|_2 - \dfrac{1}{m^2} \sum_{i,j=1}^{m} \| b_i - b_j \|_2$

where d is the chosen metric. Other linkage criteria include:

- The sum of all intra-cluster variance.

- The increase in variance for the cluster being merged (Ward's criterion).

- The probability that candidate clusters spawn from the same distribution function (V-linkage).

- The product of in-degree and out-degree on a k-nearest-neighbor graph (graph degree linkage).

- The increment of some cluster descriptor (i.e., a quantity defined for measuring the quality of a cluster) after merging two clusters.

Agglomerative Clustering Example

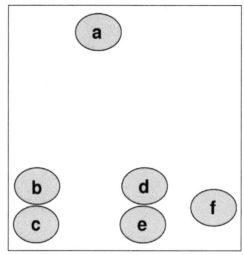

Raw data.

For example, suppose this data is to be clustered, and the Euclidean distance is the distance metric.

The hierarchical clustering dendrogram would be as such:

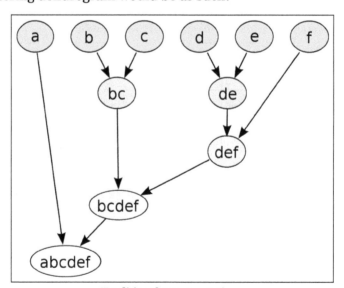

Traditional representation.

Cutting the tree at a given height will give a partitioning clustering at a selected precision. In this example, cutting after the second row (from the top) of the dendrogram will yield clusters {a} {b c} {d e} {f}. Cutting after the third row will yield clusters {a} {b c} {d e f}, which is a coarser clustering, with a smaller number but larger clusters.

This method builds the hierarchy from the individual elements by progressively merging clusters. In our example, we have six elements {a} {b} {c} {d} {e} and {f}. The first step is to determine which elements to merge in a cluster. Usually, we want to take the two closest elements, according to the chosen distance.

Optionally, one can also construct a distance matrix at this stage, where the number in the i-th row j-th column is the distance between the i-th and j-th elements. Then, as clustering progresses, rows and columns are merged as the clusters are merged and the distances updated. This is a common way to implement this type of clustering, and has the benefit of caching distances between clusters.

Suppose we have merged the two closest elements b and c, we now have the following clusters $\{a\}$, $\{b, c\}$, $\{d\}$, $\{e\}$ and $\{f\}$, and want to merge them further. To do that, we need to take the distance between $\{a\}$ and $\{b\ c\}$, and therefore define the distance between two clusters. Usually the distance between two clusters $\mathcal{A}$ and $\mathcal{B}$ is one of the following:

- The maximum distance between elements of each cluster (also called complete-linkage clustering):
$$\max\{d(x,y) : x \in \mathcal{A}, y \in \mathcal{B}\}.$$

- The minimum distance between elements of each cluster (also called single-linkage clustering):
$$\min\{d(x,y) : x \in \mathcal{A}, y \in \mathcal{B}\}.$$

- The mean distance between elements of each cluster (also called average linkage clustering, used e.g. in UPGMA):
$$\frac{1}{|\mathcal{A}| \cdot |\mathcal{B}|} \sum_{x \in \mathcal{A}} \sum_{y \in \mathcal{B}} d(x,y).$$

- The sum of all intra-cluster variance.

- The increase in variance for the cluster being merged (Ward's method)

- The probability that candidate clusters spawn from the same distribution function (V-linkage).

In case of tied minimum distances, a pair is randomly chosen, thus being able to generate several structurally different dendrograms. Alternatively, all tied pairs may be joined at the same time, generating a unique dendrogram.

One can always decide to stop clustering when there is a sufficiently small number of clusters (number criterion). Some linkages may also guarantee that agglomeration occurs at a greater distance between clusters than the previous agglomeration, and then one can stop clustering when the clusters are too far apart to be merged (distance criterion). However, this is not the case of, e.g., the centroid linkage where the so-called reversals (inversions, departures from ultrametricity) may occur.

Divisive Clustering

The basic principle of divisive clustering was published as the DIANA (DIvisive ANAlysis Clustering) algorithm. Initially, all data is in the same cluster, and the largest cluster is split until every object is separate. Because there exist $O(2^n)$ ways of splitting each cluster, heuristics are needed. DIANA chooses the object with the maximum average dissimilarity and then moves all objects to this cluster that are more similar to the new cluster than to the remainder.

Open Source Implementations

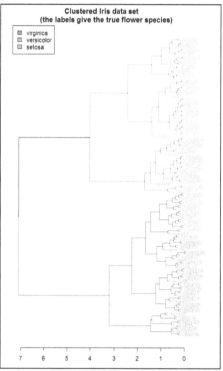

Hierarchical clustering dendrogram of the Iris dataset (using R).

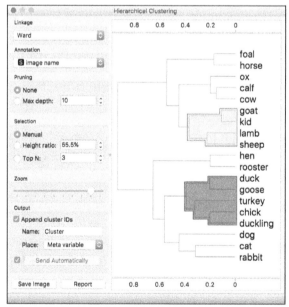

Hierarchical clustering and interactive dendrogram visualization in Orange data mining suite.

- ALGLIB implements several hierarchical clustering algorithms (single-link, complete-link, Ward) in C++ and C# with $O(n^2)$ memory and $O(n^3)$ run time.

- ELKI includes multiple hierarchical clustering algorithms, various linkage strategies and also includes the efficient SLINK, CLINK and Anderberg algorithms, flexible cluster extraction from dendrograms and various other cluster analysis algorithms.

- Octave, the GNU analog to MATLAB implements hierarchical clustering in function "linkage".

- Orange, a data mining software suite, includes hierarchical clustering with interactive dendrogram visualisation.

- R has many packages that provide functions for hierarchical clustering.

- SciPy implements hierarchical clustering in Python, including the efficient SLINK algorithm.

- Scikit-learn also implements hierarchical clustering in Python.

- Weka includes hierarchical cluster analysis.

Commercial Implementations

- MATLAB includes hierarchical cluster analysis.

- SAS includes hierarchical cluster analysis in PROC CLUSTER.

- Mathematica includes a Hierarchical Clustering Package.

- NCSS includes hierarchical cluster analysis.

- SPSS includes hierarchical cluster analysis.

- Qlucore Omics Explorer includes hierarchical cluster analysis.

- Stata includes hierarchical cluster analysis.

- CrimeStat includes a nearest neighbor hierarchical cluster algorithm with a graphical output for a Geographic Information System.

Affinity Propagation

Affinity Propagation is a clustering method that next to qualitative cluster, also determines the number of clusters, k, for you. Let's walk through the implementation of this algorithm, to see how it works.

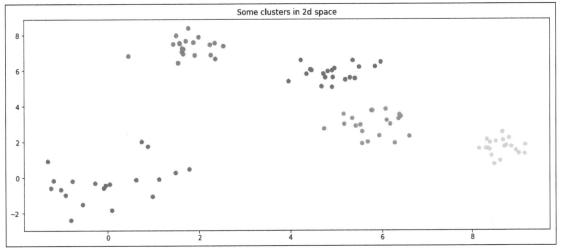

Some clusters in 2d space.

As it is a clustering algorithm, we also give it random data to cluster so it can go crazy with its OCD.

```
# all the imports needed for this blog
import numpy as np
import matplotlib.pyplot as plt
from itertools import cycle
n = 20
size = (n, 2)
np.random.seed(3)
x = np.random.normal(0, 1, size)
for i in range(4):
    center = np.random.rand(2) * 10
        x = np.append(x, np.random.normal(center, .5, size), axis=0)


        c = [c for s in [v * n for v in 'bgrcmyk'] for c in list(s)]
        plt.figure(figsize=(15, 6))
        plt.title('Some clusters in 2d space')
        plt.scatter(x[:, 0], x[:, 1], c=c)
        plt.show()
```

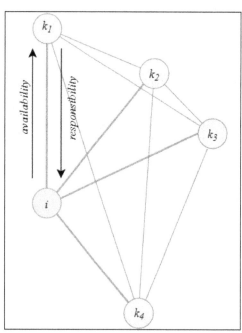

Graph of five data points.

In Affinity Propagation the data points can be seen as a network where all the data points send messages to all other points. The subject of these messages are the willingness of the points being exemplars. Exemplars are points that explain the other data points 'best' and are the most significant of their cluster. A cluster only has one exemplar. All the data points want to collectively determine which data points are an exemplar for them. These messages are stored in two matrices.

- The 'responsibility' matrix R: In this matrix, $r(i,k)$ reflects how well-suited point k is to be an exemplar for point i.

- The 'availability' matrix A: $a(i,k)$ eflects how appropriate it would be for point i to choose point k as its exemplar.

Both matrices can be interpreted as log probabilities and are thus negative valued.

Those two matrices actually represent a graph where every data point is connected with all other points. For five data points we could imagine a graph as seen in figure.

This network can be encoded in a matrix where every index i, k is a connection between two points.

$$\text{Message graph} = \begin{bmatrix} i,i & i,k_1 & \cdots & i,k_4 \\ \vdots & & \ddots & \\ k_4,i & k_4,k_1 & \cdots & k_4,k_4 \end{bmatrix}$$

Similarity

The algorithm converts through iteration. The first messages sent per iteration, are the responsibilities. These responsibility values are based on a similarity function s.

The similarity function used by the authors is the negative euclidian distance squared.

$$s(i, k) = -\left\| x_i - x_k \right\|^2$$

We can simply implement this similarity function and define a similarity matrix S, which is a graph of the similarities between all the points. We also initialize the R and A matrix to zeros.

```python
def similarity(xi, xj):

    return -((xi - xj)**2).sum()

def create_matrices():

    S = np.zeros((x.shape[0], x.shape[0]))

    R = np.array(S)

    A = np.array(S)


    # compute similarity for every data point.

    for i in range(x.shape[0]):

        for k in range(x.shape[0]):

            S[i, k] = similarity(x[i], x[k])


    return A, R, S
```

Responsibility

The responsibility messages are defined by:

$$r(i,k) \leftarrow s(i,k) - \max_{k' s.t. k' \neq k} \{a(i,k') + s(i,k')\}$$

We could implement this with a nested for loop where we iterate over every row i and then determine the $\max(A + S)$ (of that row) for every index not equal to k or i (The index should not be equal to i as it would be sending messages to itself). The damping factor is just there for nummerical stabilization and can be regarded as a slowly converging learning rate. The authors advised to choose a damping factor within the range of 0.5 to 1.

Nested implementation

```
def update_r(damping=0.9):

    global R

    for i in range(x.shape[0]):

        for k in range(x.shape[0]):

            v = S[i, :] + A[i, :]

            v[k] = -np.inf

            v[i]= -np.inf

            R[i, k] = R[i, k] * damping + (1 - damping) * (S[i, k] - np.max(v))
```

Iterating over every index with a nested for loop is of course a heavy operation. Let's profile (time) the function and see if we can optimize it by vectorizing the loops.

```
A, R, S = create_matrices()

%timeit update_r()

>>> 41 ms ± 1.36 ms per loop (mean ± std. dev. of 7 runs, 10 loops each)
```

41 ms is our baseline. That shouldn't be too hard to beat. Note that $s(i,k)$ in $r(i,k) \leftarrow s(i,k) - \max_{k' s.t. k' \neq k} \{a(i,k') + s(i,k')\}$ is already defined and is equal to our matrix S. The harder part is $\max_{k' s.t. k' \neq k} \{a(i,k') + s(i,k')\}$ but we can make this easier by ignoring the limitations on the max function for a while. Let's first focus on the inner part of the max function.

$$v = a(i,k) + s(i,k)$$

```
v = S + A

rows = np.arange(x.shape[0])
```

As data points shouldn't send messages to itself, fill the diagonal with negative infinity so it will never be identified as the maximum value.

```
np.fill_diagonal(v, -np.inf)
```

Then we can determine the maximum value for all rows.

```
idx_max = np.argmax(v, axis=1)

first_max = v[rows, idx_max]
```

Note that allmost all columns in a row have the same maximum row value. This is true for all but the maximum value itself. As the max function iterates over k' where k' is chosen so that $k' \neq k$. The maximum value in a row may point to itself, but must choose the second maximum value. We can implement that by setting the indices where $k' = k$ to negative infinity and determine the new maximum value per row.

```
v[rows, idx_max] = -np.inf

second_max = v[rows, np.argmax(v, axis=1)]
```

The final result for $\max\limits_{k's.t.k'\neq k} \{a(i,k') + s(i,k')\}$ can now be determined by broadcasting the maximum value per row to a symmetrical square matrix and replacing the indices holding the maximum value of the matrix v ($v = a(i,k) + s(i,k)$) with the second maximum value.

```
max_matrix = np.zeros_like(R) + first_max[:, None]

max_matrix[rows, idx_max] = second_max

new_val = S - max_matrix
```

Putting it together in one function results in:

Vectorized Implementation

```
def update_r(damping=0.9):

    global R

    # For every column k, except for the column with the maximum value the max is the same.

    # So we can subtract the maximum for every row,

    # and only need to do something different for k == argmax


    v = S + A

    rows = np.arange(x.shape[0])

    # We only compare the current point to all other points,

    # so the diagonal can be filled with -infinity

    np.fill_diagonal(v, -np.inf)


    # max values

    idx_max = np.argmax(v, axis=1)

    first_max = v[rows, idx_max]


    # Second max values. For every column where k is the max value.

    v[rows, idx_max] = -np.inf
```

```
second_max = v[rows, np.argmax(v, axis=1)]


# Broadcast the maximum value per row over all the columns per row.

max_matrix = np.zeros_like(R) + first_max[:, None]

max_matrix[rows, idx_max] = second_max


new_val = S - max_matrix


R = R * damping + (1 - damping) * new_val
```

If we time this new function implementation we find an average execution time of 76 microseconds, which is more than 500x faster than our original implementation.

```
A, R, S = create_matrices()

%timeit update_r()

75.7 µs ± 674 ns per loop (mean ± std. dev. of 7 runs, 10000 loops each)
```

Availability

The availability messages are defined by the following formulas. For all points not on the diagonal of A (all the messages going from one data point to all other points), the update is equal to the responsibility that point k assigns to itself and the sum of the responsibilities that other data points (except the current point) assign to k. Note that, due to the min function, this holds only true for negative values.

$$a(i,k) \leftarrow \min(0, r(k,k) + \sum_{i' s.t. i' \notin \{i,k\}} \max\{0, r(i',k)\}$$

For points on the diagonal of A (the availability value that a data point sends to itself), the message value is equal to the sum of all positive responsibility values send to the current data point.

$$a(k,k) \leftarrow \sum_{i' \neq k} \max(0, r(i',k))$$

These two formulas are implemented in the following function.

Nested implementation

```
def update_a(damping=0.9):
    global A
    for i in range(x.shape[0]):
        for k in range(x.shape[0]):
            a = np.array(R[:, k]) # Select column k
            # All indices but the diagonal
            if i != k:
```

```
        a[i] = -np.inf

        a[k] = - np.inf

        a[a < 0] = 0

        A[i, k] = A[i, k] * damping + (1 - damping) * min(0, R[k, k] + a.sum())
    # The diagonal

    else:

        a[k] = -np.inf

        a[a < 0] = 0

        A[k, k] = A[k, k] * damping + (1 - damping) * a.sum()
```

This function works and is pretty readable. However let's go through the optimization process again and try to vectorize the logic above, exchanging readability for performance in doing so.

The current execution time is 53 milliseconds.

```
A, R, S = create_matrices()

%timeit update_a()

>>> 52.5 ms ± 375 µs per loop (mean ± std. dev. of 7 runs, 10 loops each)
```

Let's focus on $\sum_{i's.t.i'\notin\{i,k\}} \max\{0, r(i',k)\}$ part of, $a(i,k) \leftarrow \min(0, r(k,k) + \sum_{i's.t.i'\notin\{i,k\}} \max\{0, r(i',k)\})$.

We first copy matrix R as we will be modifying this to determine the sum we just mentioned. The sum is only over the positive values, so we can clip the negative values and change them to zero. If we later sum over the whole array, these zero valued indices won't influence the result.

```
a = np.array(R)

a[v < 0] = 0
```

The sum is over all indices i' such that $i' \notin \{i,k\}$.

The part $i' \neq k$ is easy. This means that the diagonal $r(i,k)$ is not included in the sum.

```
 np.fill_diagonal(a, 0)
```

The part $i' \neq i$ is harder, as i is the index the sum iterates over. This means that for every index i the same index is excluded. This is harder to vectorize. However, we can get around this by first including it in the sum, and finally subtracting the value for every index $r(i,k)$. In the code below we also add the $r(i,k)$. We will have defined the $r(k,k) + \sum_{i's.t.i'\notin\{i,k\}} \max\{0, r(i',k)\}$ part of equation, $a(i,k) \leftarrow \min(0, r(k,k) + \sum_{i's.t.i'\notin\{i,k\}} \max\{0, r(i',k)\})$.

These sums are the same for every row in the matrix. The 1D sum vector can be broadcasted to a matrix with the shape of A. Once we have reshaped by broadcasting we subtract positive values we unjustly included in the sum.

```
# diagonal k, k
```

```
k_k_idx = np.arange(x.shape[0])

a = a.sum(axis=0)

a = a + R[k_k_idx, k_k_idx]

a = np.ones(A.shape) * a # reshape to a square matrix

a -= np.clip(R, 0, np.inf) # subtract the values that should not be included in the sum
```

In equation, $a(i,k) \leftarrow \min(0, r(k,k) + \sum\limits_{i's.t.i' \notin \{i,k\}} \max\{0, r(i',k)\}$ the final result is the minimum of
0 and what we've just computed. So we can clip the values larger than 0.

```
# a(i, k)

a[a < 0] = 0
```

For equation, $a(k,k) \leftarrow \sum\limits_{i' \neq k} \max(0, r(i',k))$ vectorizing is slightly easier. We make another copy of
R and we note that we again should include only positive values in our sum where $i' \neq k$. We can

set the diagonal of our copy to zero so it has no influence on the sum and we can clip the negative
values to zero.

```
np.fill_diagonal(w, 0)

w[w < 0] = 0
```

With all the zeros on the right places we can now compute the sum and add it to the diagonal of a
(this is $a(k,k)$).

```
a[k_k_idx, k_k_idx] = w.sum(axis=0)
```

Combining it all in one function we'll get:

Vectorized implementation

```
def update_a(damping=0.9):
    global A

    k_k_idx = np.arange(x.shape[0])
    # set a(i, k)
    a = np.array(R)
    a[a < 0] = 0
    np.fill_diagonal(a, 0)
    a = a.sum(axis=0) # columnwise sum
    a = a + R[k_k_idx, k_k_idx]


    # broadcasting of columns 'r(k, k) + sum(max(0, r(i', k))) to rows.
```

```
a = np.ones(A.shape) * a


# For every column k, subtract the positive value of k.
# This value is included in the sum and shouldn't be
a -= np.clip(R, 0, np.inf)
a[a > 0] = 0


# set(a(k, k))
w = np.array(R)
np.fill_diagonal(w, 0)


w[w < 0] = 0


a[k_k_idx, k_k_idx] = w.sum(axis=0) # column wise sum
A = A * damping + (1 - damping) * a
```

This vectorized function has an average execution time of 70 microseconds. This is approximately 590x faster than the nested implementation. Affinity Propagation has a complexity of $O(n^2)$. So with increasing data points the optimization isn't a luxury.

Exemplars:

The final examplars are chosen by the maximum value of $A + B$.

$$exemplar(i,k) = \max\{a(i',k) + b)i',k)\}$$

We implement this in a function where we immediatly plot the final clustering result.

```
def plot_iteration(A, R):
    fig = plt.figure(figsize=(12, 6))
    sol = A + R
    # every data point i chooses the maximum index k
    labels = np.argmax(sol, axis=1)
    exemplars = np.unique(labels)
    colors = dict(zip(exemplars, cycle('bgrcmyk')))


    for i in range(len(labels)):
        X = x[i][0]
        Y = x[i][1]
```

```
    if i in exemplars:
        exemplar = i
        edge = 'k'
        ms = 10
    else:
        exemplar = labels[i]
        ms = 3
        edge = None
        plt.plot([X, x[exemplar][0]], [Y, x[exemplar][1]], c=colors[exemplar])
    plt.plot(X, Y, 'o', markersize=ms,  markeredgecolor=edge, c=colors[exemplar])a


plt.title('Number of exemplars: %s' % len(exemplars))
return fig, labels, exemplars
```

Clustering

Now we have got all set. We can execute this algorithm on our data that we generated earlier. The inputs for this algorithm are:

- The number of iterations. Which should be choosen so that the exemplars don't change, i.e. convergence is reached.

- The damping factor. Could be changed for faster iterations or more nummerical stability.

- The preference.

The last input, the preference, is set to the diagonal of the S matrix. This preference value indicates how strongly a data point thinks itself should be an exemplar. In our case, the maximum similarity value is an euclidian distance of 0, which already is the value of the diagonal of S. If we choose the leave this value unmodified. We will see almost no clustering as most data points choose to be an exemplar for themselves.

Clustering if a preference of 0 is chosen for all the data points.

Just as in the real world, when everybody is just thinking about themselves it doesn't result in all too much concencus. If you haven't got a priori knowledge of the data points it is advised to start with a preference equal to the median of S (approximately -25 in our case). And let's see how we set this preference input and actually do the clustering iterations:

```
A, R, S = create_matrices()
preference = np.median(S)
np.fill_diagonal(S, preference)
damping = 0.5
```

```
figures = []

last_sol = np.ones(A.shape)

last_exemplars = np.array([])


c = 0

for i in range(200):

    update_r(damping)

    update_a(damping)


    sol = A + R

    exemplars = np.unique(np.argmax(sol, axis=1))


    if last_exemplars.size != exemplars.size or np.all(last_exemplars != exemplars):

        fig, labels, exemplars = plot_iteration(A, R, i)

        figures.append(fig)


    if np.allclose(last_sol, sol):

        print(exemplars, i)

        break


    last_sol = sol

    last_exemplars = exemplars
```

References

- "Using the elbow method to determine the optimal number of clusters for k-means clustering". Bl.ocks.org. Retrieved 2018-11-12

- Dm-cluster-analysis, data-mining: tutorialspoint.com, Retrieved 19 February, 2019

- Lorbeer, Boris; Kosareva, Ana; Deva, Bersant; Softić, Dženan; Ruppel, Peter; Küpper, Axel (2018-03-01). "Variations on the Clustering Algorithm BIRCH". Big Data Research. 11: 44–53. Doi:10.1016/j.bdr.2017.09.002. ISSN 2214-5796

- Algorithm-breakdown-affinity-propagation: ritchievink.com, Retrieved 17 March, 2019

- Filkov, Vladimir (2003). Integrating microarray data by consensus clustering. In Proceedings of the 15th IEEE International Conference on Tools with Artificial Intelligence. Pp. 418–426. Citeseerx 10.1.1.116.8271. Doi:10.1109/TAI.2003.1250220. ISBN 978-0-7695-2038-4

- Ml-mean-shift-clustering: geeksforgeeks.org, Retrieved 18 April, 2019

- Bonizzoni, Paola; Della Vedova, Gianluca; Dondi, Riccardo; Jiang, Tao (2008). "On the Approximation of Correlation Clustering and Consensus Clustering". Journal of Computer and System Sciences. 74 (5): 671–696. Doi:10.1016/j.jcss.2007.06.024

5
Applications of Data Mining

Data Mining is widely used in various areas such as agriculture, fraud detection, healthcare sector, marketing intelligence and bioinformatics. This chapter has been carefully written to provide an easy understanding of these applications of data mining.

Data mining is primarily used today by companies with a strong consumer focus — retail, financial, communication, and marketing organizations, to "drill down" into their transactional data and determine pricing, customer preferences and product positioning, impact on sales, customer satisfaction and corporate profits. With data mining, a retailer can use point-of-sale records of customer purchases to develop products and promotions to appeal to specific customer segments.

Market Basket Analysis

Market basket analysis is a modeling technique based upon a theory that if you buy a certain group of items you are more likely to buy another group of items. This technique may allow the retailer to understand the purchase behavior of a buyer. This information may help the retailer to know the buyer's needs and change the store's layout accordingly. Using differential analysis comparison of results between different stores, between customers in different demographic groups can be done.

Manufacturing Engineering

Knowledge is the best asset a manufacturing enterprise would possess. Data mining tools can be very useful to discover patterns in complex manufacturing process. Data mining can be used in system-level designing to extract the relationships between product architecture, product portfolio, and customer needs data. It can also be used to predict the product development span time, cost, and dependencies among other tasks.

Customer Relationship Management

Customer Relationship Management is all about acquiring and retaining customers, also improving customers' loyalty and implementing customer focused strategies. To maintain a proper relationship with a customer a business need to collect data and analyse the information. This is where data mining plays its part. With data mining technologies the collected data can be used for analysis. Instead of being confused where to focus to retain customer, the seekers for the solution get filtered results.

Fraud Detection

Billions of dollars have been lost to the action of frauds. Traditional methods of fraud detection are time consuming and complex. Data mining aids in providing meaningful patterns and turning data into information. Any information that is valid and useful is knowledge. A perfect fraud detection system should protect information of all the users. A supervised method includes collection of sample records. These records are classified fraudulent or non-fraudulent. A model is built using this data and the algorithm is made to identify whether the record is fraudulent or not.

Intrusion Detection

Any action that will compromise the integrity and confidentiality of a resource is an intrusion. The defensive measures to avoid an intrusion includes user authentication, avoid programming errors, and information protection. Data mining can help improve intrusion detection by adding a level of focus to anomaly detection. It helps an analyst to distinguish an activity from common everyday network activity. Data mining also helps extract data which is more relevant to the problem.

Lie Detection

Apprehending a criminal is easy whereas bringing out the truth from him is difficult. Law enforcement can use mining techniques to investigate crimes, monitor communication of suspected terrorists. This filed includes text mining also. This process seeks to find meaningful patterns in data which is usually unstructured text. The data sample collected from previous investigations are compared and a model for lie detection is created. With this model processes can be created according to the necessity.

Customer Segmentation

Traditional market research may help us to segment customers but data mining goes in deep and increases market effectiveness. Data mining aids in aligning the customers into a distinct segment and can tailor the needs according to the customers. Market is always about retaining the customers. Data mining allows to find a segment of customers based on vulnerability and the business could offer them with special offers and enhance satisfaction.

Financial Banking

With computerised banking everywhere huge amount of data is supposed to be generated with new transactions. Data mining can contribute to solving business problems in banking and finance by finding patterns, causalities, and correlations in business information and market prices that are not immediately apparent to managers because the volume data is too large or is generated too quickly to screen by experts. The managers may find these information for better segmenting,targeting, acquiring, retaining and maintaining a profitable customer.

Corporate Surveillance

Corporate surveillance is the monitoring of a person or group's behavior by a corporation. The data collected is most often used for marketing purposes or sold to other corporations, but is also regularly shared with government agencies. It can be used by the business to tailor their products desirable by their customers. The data can be used for direct marketing purposes, such as the targeted advertisements on Google and Yahoo, where ads are targeted to the user of the search engine by analyzing their search history and emails.

Research Analysis

History shows that we have witnessed revolutionary changes in research. Data mining is helpful in data cleaning, data pre-processing and integration of databases. The researchers can find any similar data from the database that might bring any change in the research. Identification of any co-occurring sequences and the correlation between any activities can be known. Data visualisation and visual data mining provide us with a clear view of the data.

Criminal Investigation

Criminology is a process that aims to identify crime characteristics. Actually crime analysis includes exploring and detecting crimes and their relationships with criminals. The high volume of crime datasets and also the complexity of relationships between these kinds of data have made criminology an appropriate field for applying data mining techniques. Text based crime reports can be converted into word processing files. These information can be used to perform crime matching process.

Educational Data Mining

Educational data mining (EDM) describes a research field concerned with the application of data mining, machine learning and statistics to information generated from educational settings (e.g., universities and intelligent tutoring systems). At a high level, the field seeks to develop and improve methods for exploring this data, which often has multiple levels of meaningful hierarchy, in order to discover new insights about how people learn in the context of such settings. In doing so, EDM has contributed to theories of learning investigated by researchers in educational psychology and the learning sciences. The field is closely tied to that of learning analytics, and the two have been compared and contrasted.

Educational data mining refers to techniques, tools, and research designed for automatically extracting meaning from large repositories of data generated by or related to people's learning activities in educational settings. Quite often, this data is extensive, fine-grained, and precise. For example, several learning management systems (LMSs) track information such as when each student accessed each learning object, how many times they accessed it, and how many minutes the learning object was displayed on the user's computer screen. As another example, intelligent tutoring systems record data every time a learner submits a solution to a problem; they may collect the time of the submission, whether or not the solution matches the expected solution, the amount of time that has passed since the last submission, the order in which solution components were entered into the interface, etc. The precision of this data is such that even a fairly short session with a computer-based learning environment (*e.g.*, 30 minutes) may produce a large amount of process data for analysis.

In other cases, the data is less fine-grained. For example, a student's university transcript may contain a temporally ordered list of courses taken by the student, the grade that the student earned in each course, and when the student selected or changed his or her academic major. EDM leverages both types of data to discover meaningful information about different types of learners and how they learn, the structure of domain knowledge, and the effect of instructional strategies embedded within various learning environments. These analyses provide new information that would be difficult to discern by looking at the raw data. For example, analyzing data from an LMS may reveal a relationship between the learning objects that a student accessed during the course and their final course grade. Similarly, analyzing student transcript data may reveal a relationship between a student's grade in a particular course and their decision to change their academic major. Such information provides insight into the design of learning environments, which allows students, teachers, school administrators, and educational policy makers to make informed decisions about how to interact with, provide, and manage educational resources.

While the analysis of educational data is not itself a new practice, recent advances in educational technology, including the increase in computing power and the ability to log fine-grained data about students' use of a computer-based learning environment, have led to an increased interest in developing techniques for analyzing the large amounts of data generated in educational settings. This interest translated into a series of EDM workshops held from 2000 to 2007 as part of several international research conferences. In 2008, a group of researchers established what has become an annual international research conference on EDM, the first of which took place in Montreal, Quebec, Canada.

As interest in EDM continued to increase, EDM researchers established an academic journal in 2009, the *Journal of Educational Data Mining*, for sharing and disseminating research results. In 2011, EDM researchers established the International Educational Data Mining Society to connect EDM researchers and continue to grow the field.

With the introduction of public educational data repositories in 2008, such as the Pittsburgh Science of Learning Centre's (PSLC) DataShop and the National Center for Education Statistics (NCES), public data sets have made educational data mining more accessible and feasible, contributing to its growth.

Goals

Ryan S. Baker and Kalina Yacef identified the following four goals of EDM:

- Predicting students' future learning behavior – With the use of student modeling, this goal can be achieved by creating student models that incorporate the learner's characteristics, including detailed information such as their knowledge, behaviors and motivation to learn. The user experience of the learner and their overall satisfaction with learning are also measured.

- Discovering or improving domain models – Through the various methods and applications of EDM, discovery of new and improvements to existing models is possible. Examples include illustrating the educational content to engage learners and determining optimal instructional sequences to support the student's learning style.

- Studying the effects of educational support that can be achieved through learning systems.

- Advancing scientific knowledge about learning and learners by building and incorporating student models, the field of EDM research and the technology and software used.

Users and Stakeholders

There are four main users and stakeholders involved with educational data mining. These include:

- Learners – Learners are interested in understanding student needs and methods to improve the learner's experience and performance. For example, learners can also benefit from the discovered knowledge by using the EDM tools to suggest activities and resources that they can use based on their interactions with the online learning tool and insights from past or similar learners. For younger learners, educational data mining can also inform parents about their child's learning progress. It is also necessary to effectively group learners in an online environment. The challenge is to learn these groups based on the complex data as well as develop actionable models to interpret these groups.

- Educators – Educators attempt to understand the learning process and the methods they can use to improve their teaching methods. Educators can use the applications of EDM to determine how to organize and structure the curriculum, the best methods to deliver course information and the tools to use to engage their learners for optimal learning outcomes. In particular, the distillation of data for human judgment technique provides an opportunity for educators to benefit from EDM because it enables educators to quickly identify behavioral patterns, which can support their teaching methods during the duration of the course or to improve future courses. Educators can determine indicators that show student satisfaction and engagement of course material, and also monitor learning progress.

- Researchers – Researchers focus on the development and the evaluation of data mining techniques for effectiveness. A yearly international conference for researchers began in 2008, followed by the establishment of the Journal of Educational Data Mining in 2009. The wide range of topics in EDM ranges from using data mining to improve institutional effectiveness to student performance.

- Administrators – Administrators are responsible for allocating the resources for implementation in institutions. As institutions are increasingly held responsible for student success, the administering of EDM applications are becoming more common in educational settings. Faculty and advisors are becoming more proactive in identifying and addressing at-risk students. However, it is sometimes a challenge to get the information to the decision makers to administer the application in a timely and efficient manner.

Phases

As research in the field of educational data mining has continued to grow, a myriad of data mining techniques have been applied to a variety of educational contexts. In each case, the goal is to translate raw data into meaningful information about the learning process in order to make better decisions about the design and trajectory of a learning environment. Thus, EDM generally consists of four phases:

- The first phase of the EDM process (not counting pre-processing) is discovering relationships in data. This involves searching through a repository of data from an educational environment with the goal of finding consistent relationships between variables. Several algorithms for identifying such relationships have been utilized, including classification, regression, clustering, factor analysis, social network analysis, association rule mining, and sequential pattern mining.

- Discovered relationships must then be validated in order to avoid overfitting.

- Validated relationships are applied to make predictions about future events in the learning environment.

- Predictions are used to support decision-making processes and policy decisions.

During phases 3 and 4, data is often visualized or in some other way distilled for human judgment. A large amount of research has been conducted in best practices for visualizing data.

Main Approaches

Of the general categories of methods mentioned, prediction, clustering and relationship mining are considered universal methods across all types of data mining; however, Discovery with Models and Distillation of Data for Human Judgment are considered more prominent approaches within educational data mining.

Discovery with Models

In the Discovery with Model method, a model is developed via prediction, clustering or by human reasoning knowledge engineering and then used as a component in another analysis, namely in prediction and relationship mining. In the prediction method use, the created model's predictions are used to predict a new variable. For the use of relationship mining, the created model enables the analysis between new predictions and additional variables in the study. In many cases, discovery with models uses validated prediction models that have proven generalizability across contexts.

Key applications of this method include discovering relationships between student behaviors, characteristics and contextual variables in the learning environment. Further discovery of broad and specific research questions across a wide range of contexts can also be explored using this method.

Distillation of Data for Human Judgment

Humans can make inferences about data that may be beyond the scope in which an automated data mining method provides. For the use of education data mining, data is distilled for human judgment for two key purposes, identification and classification.

For the purpose of identification, data is distilled to enable humans to identify well-known patterns, which may otherwise be difficult to interpret. For example, the learning curve, classic to educational studies, is a pattern that clearly reflects the relationship between learning and experience over time.

Data is also distilled for the purposes of classifying features of data, which for educational data mining, is used to support the development of the prediction model. Classification helps expedite the development of the prediction model, tremendously.

The goal of this method is to summarize and present the information in a useful, interactive and visually appealing way in order to understand the large amounts of education data and to support decision making. In particular, this method is beneficial to educators in understanding usage information and effectiveness in course activities. Key applications for the distillation of data for human judgment include identifying patterns in student learning, behavior, opportunities for collaboration and labeling data for future uses in prediction models.

Applications

A list of the primary applications of EDM is provided by Cristobal Romero and Sebastian Ventura. In their taxonomy, the areas of EDM application are:

- Analysis and visualization of data.

- Providing feedback for supporting instructors.

- Recommendations for students.

- Predicting student performance.

- Student modeling.

- Detecting undesirable student behaviors.

- Grouping students.

- Social network analysis.

- Developing concept maps.

- Constructing courseware – EDM can be applied to course management systems such as open source Moodle. Moodle contains usage data that includes various activities by users such as test results, amount of readings completed and participation in discussion forums. Data mining tools can be used to customize learning activities for each user and adapt the pace in which the student completes the course. This is in particularly beneficial for online courses with varying levels of competency.

- Planning and scheduling.

New research on mobile learning environments also suggests that data mining can be useful. Data mining can be used to help provide personalized content to mobile users, despite the differences in managing content between mobile devices and standard PCs and web browsers.

New EDM applications will focus on allowing non-technical users use and engage in data mining tools and activities, making data collection and processing more accessible for all users of EDM. Examples include statistical and visualization tools that analyzes social networks and their influence on learning outcomes and productivity.

Costs and Challenges

Along with technological advancements are costs and challenges associated with implementing

EDM applications. These include the costs to store logged data and the cost associated with hiring staff dedicated to managing data systems. Moreover, data systems may not always integrate seamlessly with one another and even with the support of statistical and visualization tools, creating one simplified version of the data can be difficult. Furthermore, choosing which data to mine and analyze can also be challenging, making the initial stages very time consuming and labor-intensive. From beginning to end, the EDM strategy and implementation requires one to uphold privacy and ethics for all stakeholders involved.

Criticisms

- Generalizability – Research in EDM may be specific to the particular educational setting and time in which the research was conducted, and as such, may not be generalizable to other institutions. Research also indicates that the field of educational data mining is concentrated in North America and western cultures and subsequently, other countries and cultures may not be represented in the research and findings. Development of future models should consider applications across multiple contexts.

- Privacy – Individual privacy is a continued concern for the application of data mining tools. With free, accessible and user-friendly tools in the market, students and their families may be at risk from the information that learners provide to the learning system, in hopes to receive feedback that will benefit their future performance. As users become savvy in their understanding of online privacy, administrators of educational data mining tools need to be proactive in protecting the privacy of their users and be transparent about how and with whom the information will be used and shared. Development of EDM tools should consider protecting individual privacy while still advancing the research in this field.

- Plagiarism – Plagiarism detection is an ongoing challenge for educators and faculty whether in the classroom or online. However, due to the complexities associated with detecting and preventing digital plagiarism in particular, educational data mining tools are not currently sophisticated enough to accurately address this issue. Thus, the development of predictive capability in plagiarism-related issues should be an area of focus in future research.

- Adoption – It is unknown how widespread the adoption of EDM is and the extent to which institutions have applied and considered implementing an EDM strategy. As such, it is unclear whether there are any barriers that prevent users from adopting EDM in their educational settings.

Data Mining in Agriculture

Data mining in agriculture is a very recent research topic. It consists in the application of data mining techniques to agriculture. Recent technologies are nowadays able to provide a lot of information on agricultural-related activities, which can then be analyzed in order to find important information. A related, but not equivalent term is precision agriculture.

Applications

Relationship between Sprays and Fruit Defects

Fruit defects are often recorded (for a multitude of reasons, sometimes for insurance reasons when exporting fruit overseas). It may be done manually or through computer vision (detecting surface defects when grading fruit). Spray diaries are a legal requirement in many countries and at the very least record the date of spray and the product name. It is known that spraying can have affect different fruit defects for different fruit. Fungicidal sprays are often used to prevent rots from being expressed on fruit. It is also known that some sprays can cause russeting on apples. Currently much of this knowledge comes anecdotally, however some efforts have been in regards to the use of data mining in horticulture.

Prediction of Problematic Wine Fermentations

Wine is widely produced all around the world. The fermentation process of the wine is very important, because it can impact the productivity of wine-related industries and also the quality of wine. If the fermentation could be categorized and predicted at the early stages of the process, it could be altered in order to guarantee a regular and smooth fermentation. Fermentations are nowadays studied by using different techniques, such as, for example, the k-means algorithm, and a technique for classification based on the concept of biclustering. Note that these works are different from the ones where a classification of different kinds of wine is performed.

Predicting Metabolizable Energy of Poultry Feed using GMDH-type Network

A group method of data handling-type neural network (GMDH-type network) with an evolutionary method of genetic algorithm was used to predict the metabolizable energy of feather meal and poultry offal meal based on their protein, fat, and ash content. Published data samples were collected from literature and used to train a GMDH-type network model. The novel modeling of GMDH-type network with an evolutionary method of genetic algorithm can be used to predict the metabolizable energy of poltry feed samples based on their chemical content. It is also reported that the GMDH-type network may be used to accurately estimate the poultry performance from their dietary nutrients such as dietary metabolizable energy, protein and amino acids.

Detection of Diseases from Sounds Issued by Animals

The detection of animal's diseases in farms can impact positively the productivity of the farm, because sick animals can cause contaminations. Moreover, the early detection of the diseases can allow the farmer to cure the animal as soon as the disease appears. Sounds issued by pigs can be analyzed for the detection of diseases. In particular, their coughs can be studied, because they indicate their sickness. A computational system is under development which is able to monitor pig sounds by microphones installed in the farm, and which is also able to discriminate among the different sounds that can be detected.

Growth of Sheep from Genes Polymorphism using Artificial Intelligence

Polymerase chain reaction-single strand conformation polymorphism (PCR-SSCP) method was used to determine the growth hormone (GH), leptin, calpain, and calpastatin polymorphism in Iranian Baluchi male sheep. An artificial neural network (ANN) model was developed to describe average daily gain (ADG) in lambs from input parameters of GH, leptin, calpain, and calpastatin polymorphism, birth weight, and birth type. The results revealed that the ANN-model is an appropriate tool to recognize the patterns of data to predict lamb growth in terms of ADG given specific genes polymorphism, birth weight, and birth type. The platform of PCR-SSCP approach and ANN-based model analyses may be used in molecular marker-assisted selection and breeding programs to design a scheme in enhancing the efficacy of sheep production.

Sorting Apples by Watercores

Before going to market, apples are checked and the ones showing some defects are removed. However, there are also invisible defects, that can spoil the apple flavor and look. An example of invisible defect is the watercore. This is an internal apple disorder that can affect the longevity of the fruit. Apples with slight or mild watercores are sweeter, but apples with moderate to severe degree of watercore cannot be stored for any length of time. Moreover, a few fruits with severe watercore could spoil a whole batch of apples. For this reason, a computational system is under study which takes X-ray photographs of the fruit while they run on conveyor belts, and which is also able to analyse (by data mining techniques) the taken pictures and estimate the probability that the fruit contains watercores.

Optimizing Pesticide use by Data Mining

Recent studies by agriculture researchers in Pakistan (one of the top four cotton producers of the world) showed that attempts of cotton crop yield maximization through pro-pesticide state policies have led to a dangerously high pesticide use. These studies have reported a negative correlation between pesticide use and crop yield in Pakistan. Hence excessive use (or abuse) of pesticides is harming the farmers with adverse financial, environmental and social impacts. By data mining the cotton Pest Scouting data along with the meteorological recordings it was shown that how pesticide use can be optimized (reduced). Clustering of data revealed interesting patterns of farmer practices along with pesticide use dynamics and hence help identify the reasons for this pesticide abuse.

Explaining Pesticide Abuse by Data Mining

To monitor cotton growth, different government departments and agencies in Pakistan have been recording pest scouting, agriculture and metrological data for decades. Coarse estimates of just the cotton pest scouting data recorded stands at around 1.5 million records, and growing. The primary agro-met data recorded has never been digitized, integrated or standardized to give a complete picture, and hence cannot support decision making, thus requiring an Agriculture Data Warehouse. Creating a novel Pilot Agriculture Extension Data Warehouse followed by analysis through querying and data mining some interesting discoveries were made, such as pesticides sprayed at the wrong time, wrong pesticides used for the right reasons and temporal relationship between pesticide usage and day of the week.

Analyzing Chicken Performance Data by Neural Network Models

A platform of artificial neural network-based models with sensitivity analysis and optimization algorithms was used successfully to integrate published data on the responses of broiler chickens to threonine. Analyses of the artificial neural network models for weight gain and feed efficiency from a compiled data set suggested that the dietary protein concentration was more important than the threonine concentration. The results revealed that a diet containing 18.69% protein and 0.73% threonine may lead to producing optimal weight gain, whereas the optimal feed efficiency may be achieved with a diet containing 18.71% protein and 0.75% threonine.

Data Analysis Techniques for Fraud Detection

Fraud is a billion-dollar business and it is increasing every year. The PwC global economic crime survey of 2018 found that half (49 percent) of the 7,200 companies they surveyed had experienced fraud of some kind.

Fraud possibilities co-evolve with technology, information technology, business reengineering, re-organization or downsizing may weaken or eliminate control, while new information systems may present additional opportunities to commit fraud.

Traditional methods of data analysis have long been used to detect fraud. They require complex and time-consuming investigations that deal with different domains of knowledge like financial, economics, business practices and law. Fraud often consists of many instances or incidents involving repeated transgressions using the same method. Fraud instances can be similar in content and appearance but usually are not identical.

The first industries to use data analysis techniques to prevent fraud were the telephone companies, the insurance companies and the banks. One early example of successful implementation of data analysis techniques in the banking industry is the FICO Falcon fraud assessment system, which is based on a neural network shell.

Retail industries also suffer from fraud at POS. Some supermarkets have started to make use of digitized closed-circuit television (CCTV) together with POS data of most susceptible transactions to fraud.

Fraud that involves cell phones, insurance claims, tax return claims, credit card transactions etc. represent significant problems for governments and businesses, but yet detecting and preventing fraud is not a simple task. Fraud is an adaptive crime, so it needs special methods of intelligent data analysis to detect and prevent it. These methods exist in the areas of Knowledge Discovery in Databases (KDD), Data Mining, Machine Learning and Statistics. They offer applicable and successful solutions in different areas of fraud crimes.

In general, the primary reason to use data analytics techniques is to tackle fraud since many internal control systems have serious weaknesses. In order to effectively test, detect, validate, correct error and monitor control systems against fraudulent activities, businesses entities and organizations rely on specialized data analytics techniques such as data mining, data matching, sounds like function, Regression analysis, Clustering analysis and Gap. Techniques used for fraud detection fall into two primary classes: statistical techniques and artificial intelligence. Examples of statistical data analysis techniques are:

- Data preprocessing techniques for detection, validation, error correction, and filling up of missing or incorrect data.

- Calculation of various statistical parameters such as averages, quantiles, performance metrics, probability distributions, and so on. For example, the averages may include average length of call, average number of calls per month and average delays in bill payment.

- Models and probability distributions of various business activities either in terms of various parameters or probability distributions.

- Computing user profiles.

- Time-series analysis of time-dependent data.

- Clustering and classification to find patterns and associations among groups of data.

- Data matching is used to compare two sets of collected data. The process can be performed based on algorithms or programmed loops. Trying to match sets of data against each other or comparing complex data types. Data matching is used to remove duplicate records and identify links between two data sets for marketing, security or other uses.

- Sounds like Function is used to find values that sound similar. The Phonetic similarity is one way to locate possible duplicate values, or inconsistent spelling in manually entered data. The 'sounds like' function converts the comparison strings to four-character American Soundex codes, which are based on the first letter, and the first three consonants after the first letter, in each string.

- Regression analysis allows you to examine the relationship between two or more variables of interest. Regression analysis estimates relationships between independent variables and a dependent variable. This method can be used to help understand and identify relationships among variables and predict actual results.

- Gap analysis is used to determine whether business requirements are being met, if not, what are the steps that should be taken to meet successfully. gap refers to the space between "where we are" (the present state) and "where we want to be" (the target state).

- Matching algorithms to detect anomalies in the behavior of transactions or users as compared to previously known models and profiles. Techniques are also needed to eliminate false alarms, estimate risks, and predict future of current transactions or users.

Some forensic accountants specialize in forensic analytics which is the procurement and analysis of electronic data to reconstruct, detect, or otherwise support a claim of financial fraud. The main steps in forensic analytics are: (a) data collection, (b) data preparation, (c) data analysis, and (d) reporting. For example, forensic analytics may be used to review an employee's purchasing card activity to assess whether any of the purchases were diverted or divertible for personal use. Forensic analytics might be used to review the invoicing activity for a vendor to identify fictitious vendors, and these techniques might also be used by a franchisor to detect fraudulent or erroneous sales reports by the franchisee in a franchising environment.

Fraud detection is a knowledge-intensive activity. The main AI techniques used for fraud detection include:

- Data mining to classify, cluster, and segment the data and automatically find associations and rules in the data that may signify interesting patterns, including those related to fraud.

- Expert systems to encode expertise for detecting fraud in the form of rules.

- Pattern recognition to detect approximate classes, clusters, or patterns of suspicious behavior either automatically (unsupervised) or to match given inputs.

- Machine learning techniques to automatically identify characteristics of fraud.

- Neural networks that can learn suspicious patterns from samples and used later to detect them.

Other techniques such as link analysis, Bayesian networks, decision theory, and sequence matching are also used for fraud detection. A new and novel technique called System properties approach has also been employed where ever rank data is available.

Statistical analysis of research data is the most comprehensive method for determining if data fraud exists. Data fraud as defined by the Office of Research Integrity (ORI) includes fabrication, falsification and plagiarism. The statistical work was performed by Drs. Mark S. Kaiser and Alicia L. Carriquiry of Iowa State University and Dr. Gordon M Harrington of the University of Northern Iowa, where they showed that data thought to be fabricated [HI data] was in fact real, while another set of data [Hansen data] was reported to the statisticians as being fabricated was in fact falsified and plagiarized from the HI data set.

Machine Learning and Data Mining

Early data analysis techniques were oriented toward extracting quantitative and statistical data characteristics. These techniques facilitate useful data interpretations and can help to get better insights into the processes behind the data. Although the traditional data analysis techniques can indirectly lead us to knowledge, it is still created by human analysts.

To go beyond, a data analysis system has to be equipped with a substantial amount of background knowledge, and be able to perform reasoning tasks involving that knowledge and the data provided. In effort to meet this goal, researchers have turned to ideas from the machine learning field. This is a natural source of ideas, since the machine learning task can be described as turning background knowledge and examples (input) into knowledge (output).

If data mining results in discovering meaningful patterns, data turns into information. Information or patterns that are novel, valid and potentially useful are not merely information, but knowledge. One speaks of discovering knowledge, before hidden in the huge amount of data, but now revealed.

The machine learning and artificial intelligence solutions may be classified into two categories: 'supervised' and 'unsupervised' learning. These methods seek for accounts, customers, suppliers, etc. that behave 'unusually' in order to output suspicion scores, rules or visual anomalies, depending on the method.

Whether supervised or unsupervised methods are used, note that the output gives us only an indication of fraud likelihood. No stand alone statistical analysis can assure that a particular object is a fraudulent one, but they can identify them with very high degrees of accuracy.

Supervised Learning

In supervised learning, a random sub-sample of all records is taken and manually classified as either 'fraudulent' or 'non-fraudulent'. Relatively rare events such as fraud may need to be over sampled to get a big enough sample size. These manually classified records are then used to train a supervised machine learning algorithm. After building a model using this training data, the algorithm should be able to classify new records as either fraudulent or non-fraudulent.

Supervised neural networks, fuzzy neural nets, and combinations of neural nets and rules, have been extensively explored and used for detecting fraud in mobile phone networks and financial statement fraud.

Bayesian learning neural network is implemented for credit card fraud detection, telecommunications fraud, auto claim fraud detection, and medical insurance fraud.

Hybrid knowledge/statistical-based systems, where expert knowledge is integrated with statistical power, use a series of data mining techniques for the purpose of detecting cellular clone fraud. Specifically, a rule-learning program to uncover indicators of fraudulent behavior from a large database of customer transactions is implemented.

Cahill et al. design a fraud signature, based on data of fraudulent calls, to detect telecommunications fraud. For scoring a call for fraud its probability under the account signature is compared to its probability under a fraud signature. The fraud signature is updated sequentially, enabling event-driven fraud detection.

Link analysis comprehends a different approach. It relates known fraudsters to other individuals, using record linkage and social network methods.

This type of detection is only able to detect frauds similar to those which have occurred previously and been classified by a human. To detect a novel type of fraud may require the use of an unsupervised machine learning algorithm.

Unsupervised Learning

In contrast, unsupervised methods don't make use of labelled records. Some important studies with unsupervised learning with respect to fraud detection should be mentioned. For example, Bolton and Hand use Peer Group Analysis and Break Point Analysis applied on spending behavior in credit card accounts. Peer Group Analysis detects individual objects that begin to behave in a way different from objects to which they had previously been similar. Another tool Bolton and Hand develop for behavioral fraud detection is Break Point Analysis. Unlike Peer Group Analysis, Break Point Analysis operates on the account level. A break point is an observation where anomalous behavior for a particular account is detected. Both the tools are applied on spending behavior in credit card accounts.

Also, Murad and Pinkas focus on behavioral changes for the purpose of fraud detection and present three-level-profiling. Three-level-profiling method operates at the account level and points to any significant deviation from an account's normal behavior as a potential fraud. In order to do this, 'normal' profiles are created based on data without fraudulent records (semi supervised). In the same field, also Burge and Shawe-Taylor use behavior profiling for the purpose of fraud detection. However, using a recurrent neural network for prototyping calling behavior, unsupervised learning is applied.

Cox et al. combines human pattern recognition skills with automated data algorithms. In their work, information is presented visually by domain-specific interfaces, combining human pattern recognition skills with automated data algorithms.

Data Mining Applications in Healthcare Sector

The purpose of data mining is to extract useful information from large databases or data warehouses. Data mining applications are used for commercial and scientific sides. This study mainly discusses the Data Mining applications in the scientific side. Scientific data mining distinguishes itself in the sense that the nature of the datasets is often very different from traditional market driven data mining applications. In this work, a detailed survey is carried out on data mining applications in the healthcare sector, types of data used and details of the information extracted. Data mining algorithms applied in healthcare industry play a significant role in prediction and diagnosis of the diseases. There are a large number of data mining applications are found in the medical related areas such as Medical device industry, Pharmaceutical Industry and Hospital Management. To find the useful and hidden knowledge from the database is the purpose behind the application of data mining. Popularly data mining called knowledge discovery from the data. The knowledge discovery is an interactive process, consisting by developing an understanding of the application domain, selecting and creating a data set, preprocessing, data transformation. Data Mining has been used in a variety of applications such as marketing, customer relationship management, engineering, and medicine analysis, expert prediction, web mining and mobile and mobile computing.

In health care institutions leak the appropriate information systems to produce reliable reports with respect to other information in purely financial and volume related statements. Data mining tools to answer the question that traditionally was a time consuming and too complex to resolve. They prepare databases for finding predictive information. Data mining tasks are Association Rule, Patterns, Classification and Prediction, Clustering. Most common modeling objectives are classification and prediction. The reason that attracted a great deal of attention in information technology for the discovery of useful information from large collections is due to the perception that we are data rich but information poor. Some the sample data mining applications are:

- Developing models to detect fraudulent phone or credit-card activity.

- Predicting good and poor sales prospectus.

- Redicting whether a heart attack is likely to recur among those with cardiac disease.

- Identifying factors that lead to defects in a manufacturing process.

Expanding the health coverage to as many people as possible, and providing financial assistance to help those with lower incomes purchase coverage. Eliminating current health disparities would decrease the costs associated with the increased disease burden borne by certain population groups.Health administration or healthcare administration is the field relating to leadership, management, and administration of hospitals, hospital networks, and health care systems. In the Healthcare sector Government spends more money.

- Proposal in draft NHP 2001 is timely that State health expenditures be raised to 7% by 2015 and to 8% of State budgets thereafter.

- Health spending in India at 6% of GDP is among the highest levels estimated for developing countries.

- Public spending on health in India has itself declined after liberalization from 1.3% of GDP in 1990 to 0.9% in 1999. Central budget allocations for health have stagnated at 1.3% of the total Central budget. In the States it has declined from7.0% to 5.5% of the State health budget.

Healthcare industry today generates large amounts of complex data about patients, hospital resources, disease diagnosis, electronic patient records, medical devices etc. Larger amounts of data are a key resource to be processed and analyzed for knowledge extraction that enables support for cost-savings and decision making. Data mining applications in healthcare can be grouped as the evaluation into broad categories.

Treatment Effectiveness

Data mining applications can develop to evaluate the effectiveness of medical treatments. Data mining can deliver an analysis of which course of action proves effective by comparing and contrasting causes, symptoms, and courses of treatments.

Healthcare Management

Data mining applications can be developed to better identify and track chronic disease states and high-risk patients, design appropriate interventions, and reduce the number of hospital admissions and claims to aid healthcare management. Data mining used to analyze massive volumes of data and statistics to search for patterns that might indicate an attack by bio-terrorists.

Customer Relationship Management

Customer relationship management is a core approach to managing interactions between commercial organizations typically banks and retailers-and their customers, it is no less important in a healthcare context. Customer interactions may occur through call centers, physicians' offices, billing departments, inpatient settings, and ambulatory care settings.

Fraud and Abuse

Detect fraud and abuses establish norms and then identify unusual or abnormal patterns of claims by physicians, clinics, or others attempt in data mining applications. Data mining applications fraud and abuse applications can highlight inappropriate prescriptions or referrals and fraudulent insurance and medical claims.

Medical Device Industry

Healthcare system's one important point is medical device. For best communication work this one is mostly used. Mobile communications and low-cost of wireless biosensors have paved the way for development of mobile healthcare applications that supply a convenient, safe and constant way of monitoring of vital signs of patients. Ubiquitous Data Stream Mining (UDM) techniques such as light weight, one-pass data stream mining algorithms can perform real-time analysis on-board small/mobile devices while considering available resources such as battery charge and available memory.

Pharmaceutical Industry

The technology is being used to help the pharmaceutical firms manage their inventories and to develop new product and services. A deep understanding of the knowledge hidden in the Pharma data is vital to a firm's competitive position and organizational decision-making.

Hospital Management

Organizations including modern hospitals are capable of generating and collecting a huge amount of data. Application of data mining to data stored in a hospital information system in which temporal behavior of global hospital activities is visualized. Three layers of hospital management:

- Services for hospital management.

- Services for medical staff.

- Services for patients.

System Biology

Biological databases contain a wide variety of data types, often with rich relational structure. Consequently multirelational data mining techniques are frequently applied to biological data. Systems biology is at least as demanding as, and perhaps more demanding than, the genomic challenge that has fired international science and gained public attention.

Mainly data mining tools are used to predict the successful results from the data recorded on healthcare problems. Different data mining tools are used to predict the accuracy level in different healthcare problems. In this study, the following list of medical problems has been analyzed and evaluated.

- Heart Disease,
- Diabetes Mellitus,
- Cancer,
- Kidney dialysis,
- HIV/AIDS,
- Dengue,
- Brain Cancer,
- IVF,
- Tuberculosis,
- Hepatitis C.

In the table, the most important healthcare problems specifically in disease side and research results have been illustrated. The diseases are the most critical problems in human. To analyze the effectiveness of the data mining applications for diagnosing the disease, the traditional methods of mathematical/statistical applications are also given and compared. Listed eleven problems are taken for comparison with this work.

Table: Data mining applications in healthcare.

S. No.	Type of disease	Data mining tool	Technique	Algorithm	Traditional method	Accuracy level (%) from dm application
1	Heart disease	ODND NCC2	Classification	Naive	Probability	60
2	Cancer	WEKA	Classification	Rules. Decision Table		97.77
3	HIV/AIDS	WEKA 3.6	Classification. Association Rule Mining	J48	Statistics	81.8
4	Blood Bank Sector	WEKA	Classification	J48		89.9
5	Brain Cancer	K-means Clustering	Clustering	MAFIA		85
6	Tuberculosis	WEKA	Naive Bayes Classifier	KNN	Probability, Statistics	78
7	Diabetes Mellitus	ANN	Classification	C4.5 algorithm	Neural Network	82.6
8	Kidney dialysis	RST	Classification	Decision Making	Statistics	75.97
9	Dengue	SPSS Modeler		C5.0	Statistics	80
10	IVF	ANN, RST	Classification			91
11	Hepatitis C	SNP	Information Gain	Decision rule		73.20

Graph chart formed by using this table with the values of health care problems, Data Mining tools and Accuracy Level is as illustrated in figure. In this chart, the prediction accuracy level of different data mining applications has been compared.

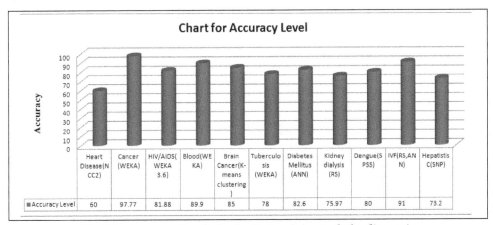

Chart for Accuracy Level of using Data mining tools for diagnosis.

Comparative Study of IVF Success Rate Prediction

The section deals with the comparative study of three different data mining application for predicting the success rate of IVF treatment. The process of data mining applications, its advantages and results obtained are compared. The detailed study of selected works gives a broad idea about the application of data mining techniques. This study mainly compares the three different data mining applications carried out on the prediction of the IVF treatment success rate.

Application of Rough Set Theory for Medical Informatics Data Analysis

The data reduction process has been done using rough set theory reduction algorithm. Rough set is mainly used to reduce the attributes without compromising its knowledge of the original. To analyze the fertilization data, ROSETTA tool kit reduction algorithm is used in this work to produce the optimal reduct set without affecting the original knowledge. The treatment success rate is predicted and tabulated as depicted in table.

Table: IVF success rate predicted by rough set.

		Paredicted		
		Success	Unsuccess	
Actual	Success	17	4	0.80952
	Unsuccess	26	10	0.27777
		0.395349	0.714286	0.47368

The actual and desired outputs are compared with each other. It also depicts that the success rate obtained after reducing the number of attributes is 47%.

Artificial Neural Network in Classification and Prediction

The artificial neural network is constructed with multi-layer perception and back-propagation training algorithm, and constructed network is trained, tested and validated using patients' sample IVF data. This work finally compares the success rate between desired output which is field recorded data and actual output which is predicted output of neural network. In the table, the comparison between desired and actual output of the neural network is illustrated.

Table: IVF success rate predicted by ANN.

Performance	Desired Output	Actual Network Output
MSE	0.209522132	0.212860733
NMSE	1.164459543	1.18301446
MAE	0.23114814	0.25780224
Min Abs Error	9.90854E-07	6.66044E-06
Max Abs Error	1.015785003	0.998857054
R	0.498099362	0.498099362
Percent Correct	73.07692308	75

This work finds the actual output using patients' IVF data by applying Artificial Neural Network. By comparing success rate, desired and actual output, the result obtained has a prediction accuracy of 73%.

Analyzing Medical Data by Neural Networks Modeling and Rough Sets

Two kinds of rules Deterministic and Non-deterministic are effected in the application of Rough set tool. For the rough set application, the software tool Neuro solution is used to predict the result. The performance of the combined technique of Artificial neural network and rough set theory is described in the table.

Table: Performance of IVF success rate prediction using hybrid technique.

Performance	Unsuccess of treatment	Success of treatment
MSE	0.092835478	0.110601021
NMSE	0.378803726	0.451293836
MAE	0.14313612	0.191653959
Min Abs Error	0.002563409	0.005851654
Min Abs Error	1.055555499	1.055555556
R	0.789058201	0.789058201
Percent Correct	89.23076923	91.83673469

The prediction accuracy of this hybrid approach of combined use of ANN and RST is around 90%. These comparison results of three different data mining applications for predicting the success rate of IVF treatments are shown in table and figure.

Table: Comparison between three different data mining applications.

	Rough Set	ANN	Rough Set and ANN (Hybrid)
Perscentage of Accuracy in Estimating Success	47	73	90

The application of combined Rough Set and Artificial Neural Network yields better result when compared with other techniques. It is observed that the hybrid technique of combined use of two or more machine learning tool yields better results than the use of a single technique for mining information from the database.

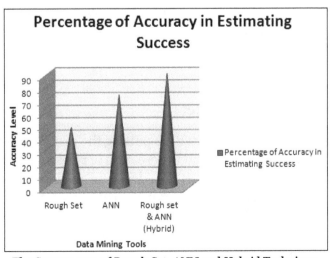

The Success rate of Rough Set, ANN and Hybrid Technique.

Data Mining and Marketing Intelligence

The streamlining of a marketing campaign, the creation of new products or services, the set-up of new branches, the design of a cross-selling activity are generally issues tackled by using the experience in the market as well as mistakes made in the past. By contrast, the technological advance has made possible to create Data Bases designed for the Marketing Intelligence, so the availability of large information raises a few questions, examples:

- Which are the guidelines that enable us to carry out effectively quantitative analyses focused on business matters?

- Which are the characteristics and what is the expertise needed to infer relevant information from the large company Data Bases?

- In what way can an appropriate methodology, supported by an adequate "tool box", give rise to remarkable economic benefits?

Data Mining, the process of selection, research and modeling of large amounts of data aimed to find out unknown business relationships in order to achieve a business edge, is a satisfactory answer to the above issues.

Query, Reporting and Data Mining

In recent years, the expression Data Mining has been sometimes used for other types of analyses, like Data Retrieval or OLAP. These analyses, however, are different both for their implementation and their purposes. The Data Retrieval is a simple query activity that enables to get detailed answers with regard to detailed requests: who and how many are, for instance, the clients between 40 and 50 years of age who have subscribed the XY policy in the first quarter of 2005. The Data Mining activity, on the other hand has the objective to discover unknown relationships aimed to access information like, for instance, who are the customers more likely to purchase the XY policy. We could say that the Data Mining activity has a searching approach in the data analysis: discover new relationships without an "a priori" hypotheses on the subject. The Data Retrieval has, instead, a simply assess-approach. In addition, the Data Mining activity cannot be confused with the multi-dimensional reporting. As a matter of fact, Data Mining enables to go well beyond the visualization of simple statistics provided by OLAP applications, by carrying out statistical models consistent with business activity.

Implementing a Data Mining Project

An element that typifies the Data Mining activity is putting the results into production: on the one hand the business expertise, on the other hand the creation of rules and their application in the operational systems are the necessary tools to set up a decision-making engine. The results achieved through the activity of analysis, therefore, are not just written reports on specific issues; but they are operative regulations designed to select a specific target which may be used by a marketing campaign manager or they can be rules used to compute the insolvency score of a bank loan or the churn rate of a telephone contact.

Such rules are the outputs of projects aimed at business activities. Let's now have a look at the main issues which we may come across in the implementation of these projects. Specifically, we are going to address the following issues:

- Settlement of the business problem;

- Modeling of Data Bases;

- Choice of the instruments;

- Line-up of the work team.

Settlement of the Business Problem

The good outcome of a Data Mining project consists of turning a business matter into an issue of quantitative analysis. For instance, one of the most common requests in marketing field is choosing the best recipients of a commercial promotion. The choice of such recipients cannot always be carried out by using a simple query led by experience or by product knowledge. The application of Data Retrieval criteria sometimes brings about the choice of too large a number of targets in considering the budget available for the campaign, especially if the contact with each client turns out to be quite expensive. In such cases, it is necessary to sort out the clients so as to identify subsets with different degree of likelihood to join a commercial activity or to purchase specific products or services. Such a classification is implemented through a Scoring Model giving each client the probability to accept the commercial promotion or not, to buy the product-service or not. Therefore it is possible to sort out the population of potential recipients of a marketing campaign based on estimated degree of likelihood.

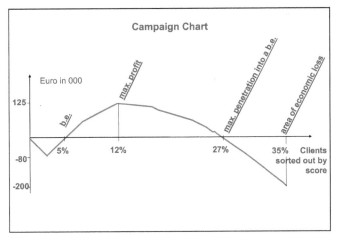

Campaign Chart.

Once the population is classified, the problem arising is about how many clients should be contacted. The choice of an exact number of recipients is crucial to the objectives of the marketing campaign which may be the revenue maximization, the achievement of the break even point, as well as the maximization of profitable contacts. In order to make such a choice we need to take into consideration also the economic data such as:

- The costs sustained in relation to the campaign structure,

- The costs for each client contacted,

- The revenues expected from the product-service sold in the campaign.

By so doing we can simulate the outcome of the campaign and build up the "Campaign Chart": the line which matches the expected revenue with the number of the recipients to be contacted. Above we show an example of Campaign Chart in which the 12% of clients with the highest degree of purchase likelihood ensures the highest possible profit, the extension of the campaign to the 27% of the population would enable to reach the break even point, while a further extension of the 35% of population would lead us into an area of expected economic loss.

Modeling of Data Bases

Those who have experienced Data Mining projects are well aware of how crucial it is to have a data environment focused on the activity of quantitative analysis. In particular, the set-up and use of a Customer Database (CDB), regularly updated with information regarding customers and prospects, plays a major role in order to successfully carry out the Data Mining activity. The CDB is the place where the clients are identified and where the significant data for the next stages of the analysis are stored. In other words the CDB is the necessary tool to count and assess the basic indicators which are put into the analysis processes of the Data Mining.

The logical and conceptual design of the CDB must reflect the complexity of the customers-company relationship. To make it simple, a CDB structure may be represented in two levels:

- Level 1: Subject oriented detail tables (facts for dimensions) with the highest possible amount of information. The Query-Report tools can refer to these detail tables in order to select and visualize information multidimensionally. In addition, the processes of creation and updating of the customer tables refer to the detail tables, too.

- Level 2: Subject oriented table sorted out by customers (customer table: one record for each customer), which enable to measure all the dimensions relevant for the quantitative analyses. In other words they are the matrix of basic data used in the Data Mining processes.

The shift from the Detail tables to the Customer Table involves taking decisions on how to sum up the detailed data, and this is a highly significant aspect for the effectiveness of the forthcoming analyses.

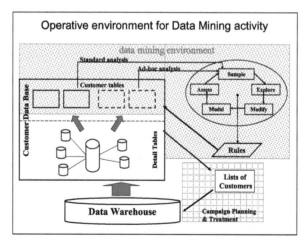

Operative Environment for Data Mining Activity.

Choice of the Instruments

An instrument of Data Mining must meet specific requirements for its use:

- Power of calculation: It must be an instrument capable of operating on multiplatformed environments, with a client/server frame, to be able to quickly solve algorithms of calculus and implement patterns of analysis;

- Exploring analysis: It must enable the analyst to achieve descriptive statistics on the variables of analysis (i.e. mean, median, mode, quantiles of the distribution, frequency distribution, contingency tables) so as to find out in advance potential relationships and outliers in the data;

- Preparation of data: Tools must be present for the calculation of new variables, for the replacement of the missing values, for the identification and possible treatment of the outliers to enable the analyst to build up the final data base on which the modeling should be carried out;

- Variety of techniques: It must enable the analyst to have a wide range of analysis instruments in order to choose the best solution both in terms of statistical performances and in terms of fulfilling the company objectives;

- Comparison: It must provide assessment indexes suitable for the different models created in order to enable the analyst to carry out a quick comparison of the various performances; it is especially useful to compare graphically the performances through lift chart, response threshold chart, roc chart;

- Generalization: The build-up of the models must be carried out according to validation approaches of the results such to ensure the generalization capacity of the models;

- Production environments: It must be capable of interacting with the company CDB and must enable the transfer of decisional rules in a production environment conducive to the implementation of the whole process time and again.

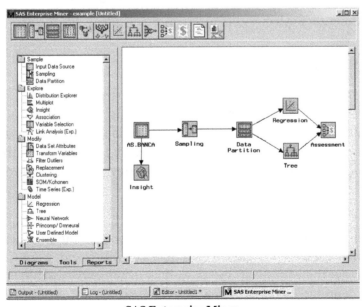

SAS Enterprise Miner.

The software solutions nowadays in the market can meet the above mentioned features. In particular, the most effective solutions are the ones provided by SPSS with Clementine and by SAS with SAS Enterprise Miner.

Line-up of the Work Team

A good outcome of the project implies the set-up of a work team made of people working in different areas which involves the following aspects:

- Sponsor of the project;

- Business expert;

- Data environment expert;

- Data analysis techniques expert.

The sponsor of the project must be of high standards. A Data Mining project may affect different areas of the company and may also have a significant impact on its strategies. Therefore the company sponsorship is needed to achieve the objective.

The other members of the team have a more operative task which can be described as follows:

- A proper use both of the IT instruments supporting the project and of the implementation of those rules produced by data analysis;

- Set-up of the statistical models;

- Interpretation of these models and their application to the business;

- Marketing campaign planning;

- Set-up of the operative processes to carry out the campaigns;

- Set-up of the operative processes to assess the campaigns' outcome.

Data Mining Applications

We have described Data Mining as a process in which several statistical techniques may be used to produce through the data information supporting the business activity: the choice of which techniques during the analysis essentially depends on the nature of the problem being handled (dependence analysis – interdependence analysis) as well as on the type of data available for the analysis (quantitative data – qualitative data). Among the most common applications are:

- Customer Profiling (Segmentation): application of clustering techniques in order to identify homogeneous groups in terms of behavior and social demographical features. The identification of the various typologies of customers enable to carry out direct marketing campaigns and assess their implications as well as to achieve valuable information as to how to modify the commercial offer. This will make it possible to monitor the evolution of one's customers in time and the possible presence of new typologies.

- Market Basket Analysis (Affinity Analysis): application of statistical techniques to sales data in order to know which products are purchased along with others. This type of information allows to improve the offer of the products (shelf layout) as well as to increase the sales of some products through specific offers on other products related to them.

- Scoring System (Predictive Modeling): integrated system of procedures aimed to set up a model which may link features of target population (list of prospects) with an objective variable. Such variable measures the acceptance of a commercial offer, while the explanatory variables measure the behavior of target population individuals with regard to similar initiatives in the past. The purpose of such technique is to be able to give a score to each individual of the target population. This score will be related to how likely the individual is to accept the commercial offer. By so doing we can sort out the customers based on their score and eventually select those who have turned out to be the most likely to accept the initiative.

- Text Mining (Segmentation): Application of clustering techniques in order to identify homogeneous groups of documents and papers related to the words/subjects found in them. This application enables to quickly assess the chosen subjects and identify possible links with others.

It is common wisdom that Data Mining uses statistical techniques related only to large numbers: this phrase is way too vague if you think that the above techniques have been developed in psychology, medicine and biology; in those fields the width of sample surveyed is in the order of some dozens or at most some hundreds. Therefore even though Data Mining is being widely used nowadays in those business sectors where companies have a large number of customers like the telecoms and big bank and insurance groups, this does not mean that the analyses carried out on some geographical areas being potentially more interested in what is offered could be quite helpful even for those companies of a smaller size.

We can again emphasize that Data Mining has a wide range of applications and that the development of the software instruments and the increasingly big availability of data will further expand the applications in potentially new business areas.

Application of Data Mining in Bioinformatics

In recent years, rapid developments in genomics and proteomics have generated a large amount of biological data. Drawing conclusions from these data requires sophisticated computational analyses. Bioinformatics, or computational biology, is the interdisciplinary science of interpreting biological data using information technology and computer science. The importance of this new field of inquiry will grow as we continue to generate and integrate large quantities of genomic, proteomic, and other data.

A particular active area of research in bioinformatics is the application and development of data mining techniques to solve biological problems. Analyzing large biological data sets requires making sense of the data by inferring structure or generalizations from the data. Examples of this type of analysis include protein structure prediction, gene classification, cancer classification based on microarray data, clustering of gene expression data, statistical modeling of protein-protein interaction, etc. Therefore, we see a great potential to increase the interaction between data mining and bioinformatics.

Data Mining Tasks

The two "high-level" primary goals of data mining, in practice, are prediction and description. The main tasks wellsuited for data mining, all of which involves mining meaningful new patterns from the data, are:

- Classification: Classification is learning a function that maps (classifies) a data item into one of several predefined classes.

- Estimation: Given some input data, coming up with a value for some unknown continuous variable.

- Prediction: Same as classification & estimation except that the records are classified according to some future behavior or estimated future value).

- Association rules: Determining which things go together, also called dependency modeling.

- Clustering: Segmenting a population into a number of subgroups or clusters.

- Description and visualization: Representing the data using visualization techniques.

Learning from data falls into two categories: directed ("supervised") and undirected ("unsupervised") learning. The first three tasks – classification, estimation and prediction – are examples of supervised learning. The next three tasks – association rules, clustering and description & visualization – are examples of unsupervised learning. In unsupervised learning, no variable is singled out as the target; the goal is to establish some relationship among all the variables. Unsupervised learning attempts to find patterns without the use of a particular target field.

The development of new data mining and knowledge discovery tools is a subject of active research. One motivation behind the development of these tools is their potential application in modern biology.

Applications of data mining to bioinformatics include gene finding, protein function domain detection, function motif detection, protein function inference, disease diagnosis, disease prognosis, disease treatment optimization, protein and gene interaction network reconstruction, data cleansing, and protein sub-cellular location prediction. For example, microarray technologies are used to predict a patient's outcome. On the basis of patients' genotypic microarray data, their survival time and risk of tumor metastasis or recurrence can be estimated. Machine learning can be used for peptide identification through mass spectroscopy. Correlation among fragment ions in a tandem mass spectrum is crucial in reducing stochastic mismatches for peptide identification by database searching. An efficient scoring algorithm that considers the correlative information in a tunable and comprehensive manner is highly desirable.

Bioinformatics and data mining are developing as interdisciplinary science. Data mining approaches seem ideally suited for bioinformatics, since bioinformatics is data-rich but lacks a comprehensive theory of life's organization at the molecular level.

However, data mining in bioinformatics is hampered by many facets of biological databases, including their size, number, diversity and the lack of a standard ontology to aid the querying of them as well as the heterogeneous data of the quality and provenance information they contain. Another problem is the range of levels the domains of expertise present amongst potential users, so it can be difficult for the database curators to provide access mechanism appropriate to all. The integration of biological databases is also a problem. Data mining and bioinformatics are fast growing research area today. It is important to examine what are the important research issues in bioinformatics and develop new data mining methods for scalable and effective analysis.

References

- "Assessing the Economic Impact of Copyright Reform in the Area of Technology-Enhanced Learning". Industry Canada. Archived from the original on 13 April 2014. Retrieved 6 April 2014

- Useful-applications-of-data-mining: bigdata-madesimple.com, Retrieved 19 May, 2019

- Baker, R.S.; Yacef, K (2009). "The state of educational data mining in 2009: A review and future visions". JEDM-Journal of Educational Data Mining. 1 (1): 2017

- Urtubia, A.; Perez-Correa, J.R.; Meurens, M.; Agosin, E. (2004). "Monitoring Large Scale Wine Fermentations with Infrared Spectroscopy". Talanta. 64 (3): 778–784. Doi:10.1016/j.talanta.2004.04.005. PMID 18969672

- Nigrini, Mark (June 2011). "Forensic Analytics: Methods and Techniques for Forensic Accounting Investigations". Hoboken, NJ: John Wiley & Sons Inc. ISBN 978-0-470-89046-2

6

Data Mining Softwares

There are many popular data mining tools and software which assist in data preparation, modeling, evaluation and deployment. A few such software are rapid miner, KNIME, SPSS Modeler, etc. The topics elaborated in this chapter will help in gaining a better perspective about these data mining software.

Data mining and proprietary software helps companies depict common patterns and correlations in large data volumes, and transform those into actionable information. For the purpose, best data mining software suites use specific algorithms, artificial intelligence, machine learning, and database statistics. Certain systems will also offer advanced functionalities such as data warehouses and customizable KDD processes, which often have the last say on which application you should choose.

Sisense

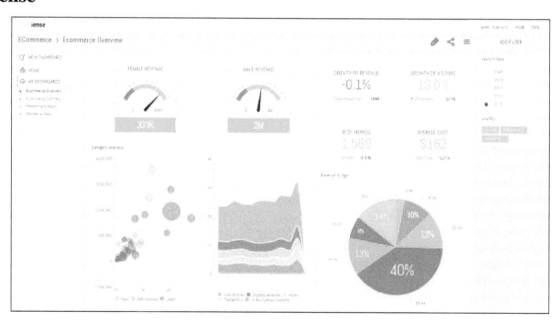

Sisense allows companies of any size and industry to mash up data sets from various sources and build a repository of rich reports that are shared across departments. If you want to test the software the vendor offers a great free demo plan.

Designed for non technical users with drag-and-drop ease and widget simplicity, this business intelligence software boasts of a proprietary in-chip technology that powers its engine. It's built on a 64-bit computer using multi-core CPUs for optimal parallelization capabilities. Generating highly visual reports culled from myriad prepared sources is fast. Users can present reports in different ways by selecting from a plate of visualization widgets to create pie charts, bar graphs, line charts, tabular formats, whatever best suits the purpose. From bird's eye-view, reports can be clicked to drill down to details for accuracy and a more comprehensive data outlook.

Microsoft SharePoint

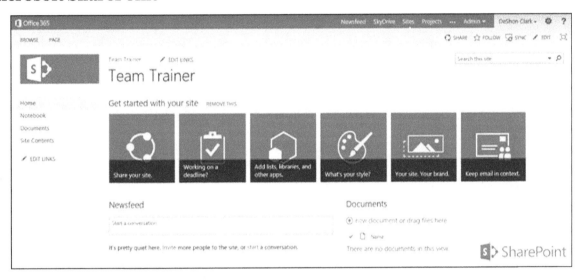

Microsoft SharePoint is everyone's first association when speaking of data management, and there is a good reason for that. The system has simply imposed itself with simplified intelligence ever since Microsoft entered the BI market, and is still considered as one of the smartest analytical options for corporate and non-commercial users. The application is web-based, and fully integrated with all Microsoft Office products. While it may not be the most powerful analyzer you can find, SharePoint certainly is the simplest information tool beginners should consider.

SharePoint offers an array of custom development capabilities used to accelerate prototyping of web and line-of-business applications. Developers can integrate it with their data sources and corporate directories using standards like oData, oAuth, and REST. The tool is also packed with information management tools and security considerations, and provides access to multiple development scenarios.

IBM Cognos

Cognos is IBM's business intelligence suite used for reporting and data analytics, with several customizable components that make it applicable in all niches and industries: Cognos Connection (the web portal that gathers data and summarizes it in scoreboards and reports), the Query Studio (provides self-service queries used to format data, and create diagrams that answer core business questions), the Report Studio (used to generate accurate management reports via professional or express authoring mode); the Analysis Studio (the part that processes large data sources, understand anomalies, and identify trends); the Event Studio (a notification module that keeps users in line with enterprise events); and Workspace Advanced (the user-friendly interface where you can create all types of personalized documents).

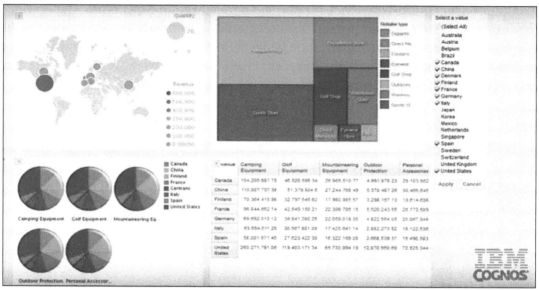

You can also extend IBM Congnos's functionality with several add-ons, including Go Office that provides access to metadata and diagrams; Go Search that conducts a full-text search for content in all documents and reports; and Go Dashboard where you can find external data sources and use those as additional reporting objects.

Dundas BI

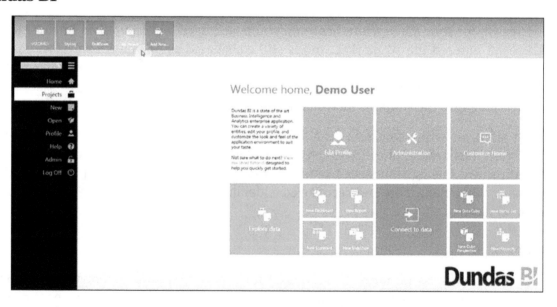

Dundas BI is another top rated data analytics platform known by its superb integrations and fast insights. The system brings together several analytic tools to allow unlimited transformation of industry data, and enriches standard reporting with appealing tables, graphs, and charts. Another thing you will appreciate about it is the gap-free protection of your documents, as well as the possibility to access data from literally any device.

Dundas does more than simply analyzing your data: it structures all pieces in a selective way to make processing easier for you, and links your charts and tables to help you understand what that data means. Thanks to its relational methods, you can perform multidimensional analyses in the blink of an eye, and focus easily on matters that are critical for your business. To make matters even better, Dundas BI helps reduce corporate costs, as it generates reliable reports, and eliminates all need to use additional software.

Board

Board is an intelligence management toolkit recommended to all companies looking to improve decision making. The platform combines business intelligence and performance management in a single package, collects data from literally any available source, and streamlines reporting letting you extract documents in all preferred formats. The first encounter with the system is likable, to say at least, as Board has one of the most appealing and comprehensive interfaces you will ever see in the BI software industry.

How can Board benefit your business? The system leverages HBMP in-memory technology, which means each of its components works with full steam to boost your performance. Board helps you perform multidimensional analyses with unparalleled simplicity, while it is also able to manage and track all performance planning and control workflows including budgeting, planning and forecasting to profitability analysis. Among other features, Board offers Marketing, HR, and Supply Chain Management solutions.

Orange

Orange is a tool that gives dull business analytics the fun vibe they need, which explains why users are fascinated by it. This open source data visualization and machine learning system certainly knows how to streamline widget programming, and help you make smarter decisions without spending hours comparing and analyzing numbers. With Orange, all incoming data is immediately prepared and put in the right format, and then moved where needed with simple widget flips.

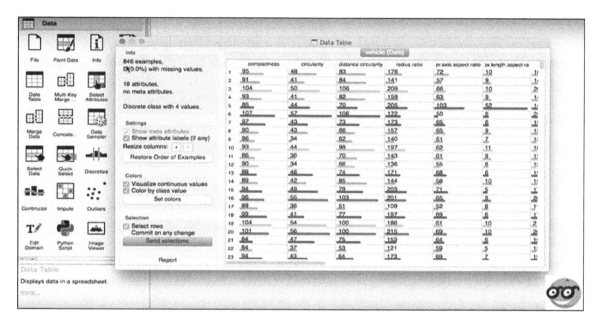

Orange is perfect for data visualization – with it, you will understand all box and scatter plots, and statistical distributions, and examine the details of your MDS, heatmaps, hierarchies and linear projections. You can do the same even with multidimensional data, using the tool's intelligent selections and attribute rankings. Visual Programming is also enabled, and offers fast prototyping, rapid qualitative analysis with clean visualizations, and configurable data connections.

SAP Business Objects

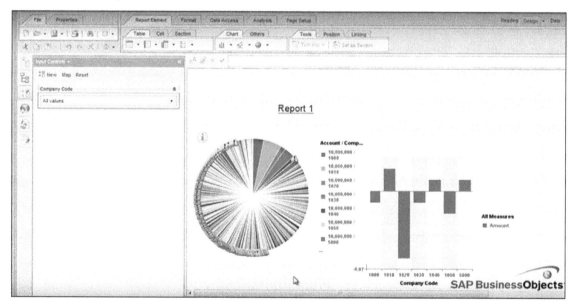

As SAP experts like to put it, Business Objects is the system that can empower your organization's IQ with around-the-clock access to outstanding BI functionality. Having tested SAP's quality service ourselves, we see where they're coming from, and absolutely recommend the tool to all users in need of informed decisions. The system is available both on premise and in cloud, and fully optimized for mobile usage to put information into users' hands anywhere and anytime.

Why choosing SAP to cater to your BI needs? This flexible and easily scalable platform leverages latest technologies and unites all meaningful data sources, and generates some of the best data visualizations available in the BI industry. You can also use it to depict troubles and opportunities, and captivate audiences with engaging data stories. Its interactive data dashboards, on the other hand tell a story of their own, making it possible for inexperienced users to understand numbers at a glance. Meaningful reports for the company, customers, and partners are also included in the package, and so are handy integrations used to connect SAP to third-party systems.

Salesforce Analytics Cloud

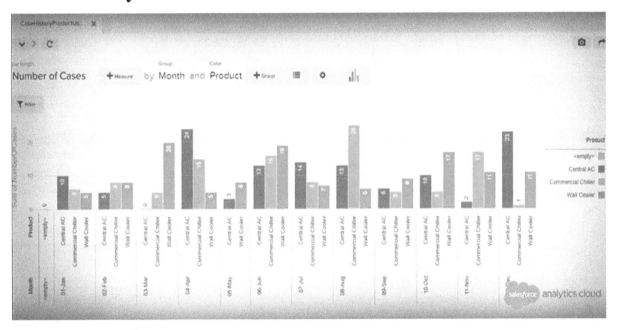

Salesforce Analytics Cloud is a reputed intelligence product created to help medium-sized businesses to large enterprises implement fast, iterative exploration of data, with results displayed via layers of dynamic visualization over underlying data sets. Keeping in line with recent developments, Salesforce Analytics offers full mobile functionality, an affordable pricing scheme with options suitable for small businesses, and flexible deployment options.

How is Salesforce Analytics Cloud better than similar data mining systems? The answer is simple. The system doesn't only identify trends and anomalies, but detects immediately when and why such happened. It is highly recommended to companies working with sensitive and complex numerical data, as their information will be encrypted and regularly backed up to stop intrusions from causing permanent damage to your business.

DOMO

There is little chance you've researched the BI market and didn't get acquainted with DOMO, as the company's innovative policy is praised across all review platforms making competing developers sweat. DOMO is exactly what each data-driven business needs: a single system that derives actionable insights from all data sources, and which you get to use without training.

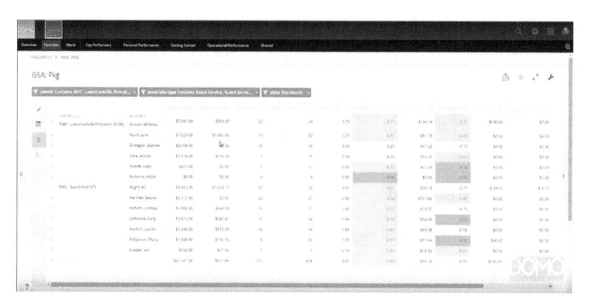

DOMO offers some of the widest data set and connector support among the tools you will discover on the market, and delivers a unique set of social collaboration features as well. The system makes it possible to combine various data sets with standard SQLs, or to develop personalized model cases combining cloud and local data. For instance, you can easily connect your page view numbers coming from Google Analytics with specific products, and measure its influence. This makes Domo ideal for specific businesses and creative teams, as large as they may be. You should also have in mind the numerous integrations that make DOMO usable in any software ecosystem.

SPSS Modeler

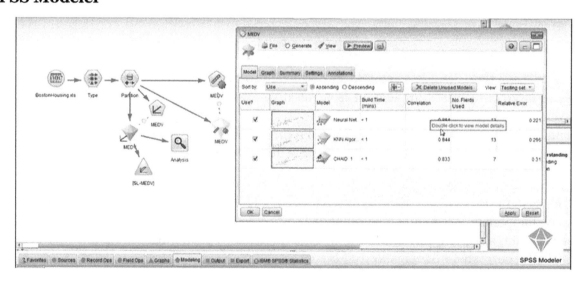

SPSS Modeler is IBM's prominent predictive analysis and data mining solution that helps companies build predictive models and leverage statistical algorithms without any programming skills. This means that SPSS Modeler eliminates all unnecessary complications raising from data transformation, simplifying at the same time text, entity, and social network analyses. Users get to choose between the company's Professional and Premium version, depending on whether they need to analyze text in addition to running mainframe data systems and analyzing flat files.

The system integrated spotlessly with Cognos and InfoSphere warehouse to help you maximize the value of your IT investment, as the combination of this three tools help you make accurate future predictions on how the state of your business is going to develop. It also helps improve business outcomes in CRM, marketing, resource planning, risk mitigation, and other areas.

Limestats

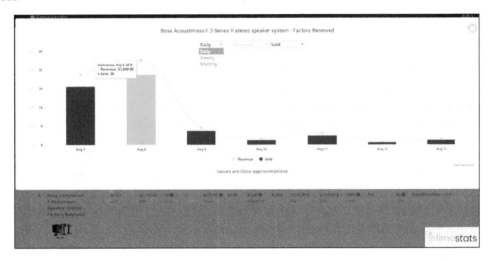

Built to drill down actionable insights from one's competitors in the eBay Marketplace, Limestats utilizes a data-driven approach to provide users with all key metrics needed to gain an advantage against the competition. Simply put, you no longer have to guess how to attract more buyers into purchasing your products.

The software does all the grunt work in gathering product level insights, detailed analytics, best sale price trends, and promotions. With these information on hand you are able to gain a better understanding on how to drive your revenue and gain the lead on eBay.

AtomLynx Insights Engine

AtomLynx Insights Engine provides companies with a 360-degree view of their business by gathering data from various sources and connecting the dots accordingly. Whether the data is located in various business systems or external platforms, this AI-powered business intelligence and data analytics solution will collate all information so you can benefit from smart, data-driven insights and make decisive actions. With all important metrics easily accessible, you are able to significantly reduce the time needed for analyzing and understanding data.

Being an AI-driven solution, AtomLynx Insights Engine can competently identify the right metrics and KPIs relevant to your business. It's user-friendly as well, allowing novice users to easily adapt to the platform. Furthermore, AtomLynx assures utmost data protection as only authorized individuals are able to access your sensitive information thanks to its top-class security.

Data Mining Extensions

Data Mining Extensions (DMX) is a language that you can use to create and work with data mining models in Microsoft SQL Server Analysis Services. You can use DMX to create the structure of new data mining models, to train these models, and to browse, manage, and predict against them. DMX is composed of data definition language (DDL) statements, data manipulation language (DML) statements, and functions and operators.

Microsoft OLE DB for Data Mining Specification

The data mining features in Analysis Services are built to comply with the Microsoft OLE DB for Data Mining specification.

The Microsoft OLE DB for Data Mining specification defines the following:

- A structure to hold the information that defines a data mining model.

- A language for creating and working with data mining models.

The specification defines the basis of data mining as the data mining model virtual object. The data mining model object encapsulates all that is known about a particular mining model. The data mining model object is structured like an SQL table, with columns, data types, and meta information that describe the model. This structure lets you use the DMX language, which is an extension of SQL, to create and work with models.

DMX Statements

You can use DMX statements to create, process, delete, copy, browse, and predict against data mining models. There are two types of statements in DMX: data definition statements and data manipulation statements. You can use each type of statement to perform different kinds of tasks.

The following topics provide more information about working with DMX statements:

- Data Definition Statements.

- Data Manipulation Statements.

- Query Fundamentals.

Data Definition Statements

Use data definition statements in DMX to create and define new mining structures and models, to import and export mining models and mining structures, and to drop existing models from a database. Data definition statements in DMX are part of the data definition language (DDL).

You can perform the following tasks with the data definition statements in DMX:

- Create a mining structure by using the CREATE MINING STRUCTURE statement, and add a mining model to the mining structure by using the ALTER MINING STRUCTURE statement.

- Create a mining model and associated mining structure simultaneously by using the CREATE MINING MODEL statement to build an empty data mining model object.

- Export a mining model and associated mining structure to a file by using the EXPORT statement. Import a mining model and associated mining structure from a file that is created by the EXPORT statement by using the IMPORT statement.

- Copy the structure of an existing mining model into a new model, and train it with the same data, by using the SELECT INTO statement.

- Completely remove a mining model from a database by using the DROP MINING MODEL statement. Completely remove a mining structure and all its associated mining models from the database by using the DROP MINING STRUCTURE statement.

Data Manipulation Statements

Use data manipulation statements in DMX to work with existing mining models, to browse the models and to create predictions against them. Data manipulation statements in DMX are part of the data manipulation language (DML).

You can perform the following tasks with the data manipulation statements in DMX:

- Train a mining model by using the INSERT INTO statement. This does not insert the actual source data into a data mining model object, but instead creates an abstraction that describes the mining model that the algorithm create.

- Extend the SELECT statement to browse the information that is calculated during model training and stored in the data mining model, such as statistics of the source data. Following are the clauses that you can include to extend the power of the SELECT statement:

    ◦ SELECT DISTINCT FROM <model > (DMX).

    ◦ SELECT FROM <model>.CONTENT (DMX).

    ◦ SELECT FROM <model>.CASES (DMX).

    ◦ SELECT FROM <model>.SAMPLE_CASES (DMX)

    ◦ SELECT FROM <model>.DIMENSION_CONTENT (DMX)

- Create predictions that are based on an existing mining model by using the PREDICTION JOIN clause of the SELECT statement.

- Remove all the trained data from a model or a structure by using the DELETE (DMX) statement.

DMX Query Fundamentals

The SELECT statement is the basis for most DMX queries. Depending on the clauses that you use with such statements, you can browse, copy, or predict against mining models. The prediction query uses a form of SELECT to create predictions based on existing mining models. Functions extend your ability to browse and query the mining models beyond the intrinsic capabilities of the data mining model.

You can use DMX functions to obtain information that is discovered during the training of your models, and to calculate new information. You can use these functions for many purposes, including to return statistics that describe the underlying data or the accuracy of a prediction, or to return an expanded explanation of a prediction.

Oracle Data Mining

Oracle Data Mining (ODM) is an option of Oracle Database Enterprise Edition. It contains several data mining and data analysis algorithms for classification, prediction, regression, associations, feature selection, anomaly detection, feature extraction, and specialized analytics. It provides means for the creation, management and operational deployment of data mining models inside the database environment.

Oracle Corporation has implemented a variety of data mining algorithms inside its Oracle Database relational database product. These implementations integrate directly with the Oracle database kernel and operate natively on data stored in the relational database tables. This eliminates the need for extraction or transfer of data into standalone mining/analytic servers. The relational database platform is leveraged to securely manage models and to efficiently execute SQL queries on large volumes of data. The system is organized around a few generic operations providing a general unified interface for data-mining functions. These operations include functions to create, apply, test, and manipulate data-mining models. Models are created and stored as database objects, and their management is done within the database - similar to tables, views, indexes and other database objects.

In data mining, the process of using a model to derive predictions or descriptions of behavior that is yet to occur is called "scoring". In traditional analytic workbenches, a model built in the analytic engine has to be deployed in a mission-critical system to score new data, or the data is moved from relational tables into the analytical workbench – most workbenches offer proprietary scoring interfaces. ODM simplifies model deployment by offering Oracle SQL functions to score data stored right in the database. This way, the user/application-developer can leverage the full power of Oracle SQL – in terms of the ability to pipeline and manipulate the results over several levels, and in terms of parallelizing and partitioning data access for performance.

Models can be created and managed by one of several means. Oracle Data Miner provides a graphical user interface that steps the user through the process of creating, testing, and applying models (e.g. along the lines of the CRISP-DM methodology). Application- and tools-developers can embed predictive and descriptive mining capabilities using PL/SQL or Java APIs. Business analysts can quickly experiment with, or demonstrate the power of, predictive analytics using Oracle Spreadsheet Add-In for Predictive Analytics, a dedicated Microsoft Excel adaptor interface. ODM offers a choice of well-known machine learning approaches such as Decision Trees, Naive Bayes, Support vector machines, Generalized linear model (GLM) for predictive mining, Association rules, K-means and Orthogonal Partitioning Clustering, and Non-negative matrix factorization for descriptive mining. A minimum description length based technique to grade the relative importance of input mining attributes for a given problem is also provided. Most Oracle Data Mining functions also allow text mining by accepting text (unstructured data) attributes as input. Users do not need to configure text-mining options - the Database_options database option handles this behind the scenes.

Oracle Data Mining was first introduced in 2002 and its releases are named according to the corresponding Oracle database release:

- Oracle Data Mining 9iR2 (9.2.0.1.0 - May 2002).

- Oracle Data Mining 10gR1 (10.1.0.2.0 - February 2004).

- Oracle Data Mining 10gR2 (10.2.0.1.0 - July 2005).

- Oracle Data Mining 11gR1 (11.1 - September 2007).

- Oracle Data Mining 11gR2 (11.2 - September 2009).

Oracle Data Mining is a logical successor of the Darwin data mining toolset developed by Thinking Machines Corporation in the mid-1990s and later distributed by Oracle after its acquisition of Thinking Machines in 1999. However, the product itself is a complete redesign and rewrite from ground-up - while Darwin was a classic GUI-based analytical workbench, ODM offers a data mining development/deployment platform integrated into the Oracle database, along with the Oracle Data Miner GUI.

The Oracle Data Miner 11gR2 New Workflow GUI was previewed at Oracle Open World 2009. An updated Oracle Data Miner GUI was released in 2012. It is free, and is available as an extension to Oracle SQL Developer 3.1 .

Functionality

As of release 11gR1 Oracle Data Mining contains the following data mining functions:

- Data transformation and model analysis:

  ○ Data sampling, binning, discretization, and other data transformations.

  ○ Model exploration, evaluation and analysis.

- Feature selection (Attribute Importance):

  ○ Minimum description length (MDL).

- Classification:
  - ○ Naive Bayes (NB).
  - ○ Generalized linear model (GLM) for Logistic regression.
  - ○ Support Vector Machine (SVM).
  - ○ Decision Trees (DT).
- Anomaly detection:
  - ○ One-class Support Vector Machine (SVM).
- Regression:
  - ○ Support Vector Machine (SVM).
  - ○ Generalized linear model (GLM) for Multiple regression
- Clustering:
  - ○ Enhanced k-means (EKM).
  - ○ Orthogonal Partitioning Clustering (O-Cluster).
- Association rule learning:
  - ○ Itemsets and association rules (AM).
- Feature extraction:
  - ○ On-negative matrix factorization (NMF).
- Text and spatial mining:
  - ○ Combined text and non-text columns of input data.
  - ○ Spatial/GIS data.

Input Sources and Data Preparation

Most Oracle Data Mining functions accept as input one relational table or view. Flat data can be combined with transactional data through the use of nested columns, enabling mining of data involving one-to-many relationships (e.g. a star schema). The full functionality of SQL can be used when preparing data for data mining, including dates and spatial data.

Oracle Data Mining distinguishes numerical, categorical, and unstructured (text) attributes. The product also provides utilities for data preparation steps prior to model building such as outlier treatment, discretization, normalization and binning (sorting in general speak).

Graphical User Interface: Oracle Data Miner

Users can access Oracle Data Mining through Oracle Data Miner, a GUI client application that provides access to the data mining functions and structured templates (called Mining Activities) that automatically prescribe the order of operations, perform required data transformations, and set model parameters. The user interface also allows the automated generation of Java and SQL code associated with the data-mining activities. The Java Code Generator is an extension to Oracle JDeveloper. An independent interface also exists: the Spreadsheet Add-In for Predictive Analytics which enables access to the Oracle Data Mining Predictive Analytics PL/SQL package from Microsoft Excel.

PL/SQL and Java Interfaces

Oracle Data Mining provides a native PL/SQL package (DBMS_DATA_MINING) to create, destroy, describe, apply, test, export and import models. The code below illustrates a typical call to build a classification model:

```
BEGIN
  DBMS_DATA_MINING.CREATE_MODEL (
    model_name           => 'credit_risk_model',
    function             => DBMS_DATA_MINING.classification,
    data_table_name      => 'credit_card_data',
    case_id_column_name  => 'customer_id',
    target_column_name   => 'credit_risk',
    settings_table_name  => 'credit_risk_model_settings');
END;
```

where 'credit_risk_model' is the model name, built for the express purpose of classifying future customers' 'credit_risk', based on training data provided in the table 'credit_card_data', each case distinguished by a unique 'customer_id', with the rest of the model parameters specified through the table 'credit_risk_model_settings'.

Oracle Data Mining also supports a Java API consistent with the Java Data Mining (JDM) standard for data mining (JSR-73) for enabling integration with web and Java EE applications and to facilitate portability across platforms.

SQL Scoring Functions

As of release 10gR2, Oracle Data Mining contains built-in SQL functions for scoring data mining models. These single-row functions support classification, regression, anomaly detection, clustering, and feature extraction. The code below illustrates a typical usage of a classification model:

```
SELECT customer_name
  FROM credit_card_data
 WHERE PREDICTION (credit_risk_model USING *) = 'LOW' AND customer_value = 'HIGH';
```

PMML

In Release 11gR2 (11.2.0.2), ODM supports the import of externally created PMML for some of the data mining models. PMML is an XML-based standard for representing data mining models.

Predictive Analytics MS Excel Add-In

The PL/SQL package DBMS_PREDICTIVE_ANALYTICS automates the data mining process including data preprocessing, model building and evaluation, and scoring of new data. The PREDICT operation is used for predicting target values classification or regression while EXPLAIN ranks attributes in order of influence in explaining a target column feature selection. The new 11g feature PROFILE finds customer segments and their profiles, given a target attribute. These operations can be used as part of an operational pipeline providing actionable results or displayed for interpretation by end users.

RapidMiner

RapidMiner is a data science software platform developed by the company of the same name that provides an integrated environment for data preparation, machine learning, deep learning, text mining, and predictive analytics. It is used for business and commercial applications as well as for research, education, training, rapid prototyping, and application development and supports all steps of the machine learning process including data preparation, results visualization, model validation and optimization. RapidMiner is developed on an open core model. The RapidMiner Studio Free Edition, which is limited to 1 logical processor and 10,000 data rows is available under the AGPL license, by depending on various non-opensource components. Commercial pricing starts at $5,000 and is available from the developer.

RapidMiner uses a client/server model with the server offered either on-premises or in public or private cloud infrastructures.

According to Bloor Research, RapidMiner provides 99% of an advanced analytical solution through template-based frameworks that speed delivery and reduce errors by nearly eliminating the need to write code. RapidMiner provides data mining and machine learning procedures including: data loading and transformation (ETL), data preprocessing and visualization, predictive analytics and statistical modeling, evaluation, and deployment. RapidMiner is written in the Java programming language. RapidMiner provides a GUI to design and execute analytical workflows. Those workflows are called "Processes" in RapidMiner and they consist of multiple "Operators". Each operator performs a single task within the process, and the output of each operator forms the input of the next one. Alternatively, the engine can be called from other programs or used as an API. Individual functions can be called from the command line. RapidMiner provides learning schemes, models and algorithms and can be extended using R and Python scripts.

RapidMiner functionality can be extended with additional plugins which are made available via RapidMiner Marketplace. The RapidMiner Marketplace provides a platform for developers to create data analysis algorithms and publish them to the community.

Products

- RapidMiner Studio.
- RapidMiner Auto Model.

- RapidMiner Turbo Prep.

- RapidMiner Server.

- RapidMiner Radoop.

Adoption

In 2019, Gartner placed RapidMiner in the leader quadrant of its Magic Quadrant for Data Science & Machine Learning Platforms for the sixth year in a row. The report noted that RapidMiner provides deep and broad modeling capabilities for automated end-to-end model development. In the 2018 annual software poll, KDnuggets readers voted RapidMiner as one of the most popular data analytics software with the poll's respondents citing the software package as the tool they use. RapidMiner has received millions of total downloads and has over 400,000 users including BMW, Intel, Cisco, GE, and Samsung as paying customers. RapidMiner claims to be the market leader in the software for data science platforms against competitors such as SAS and IBM.

Developer

About 50 developers worldwide participate in the development of the open source RapidMiner with the majority of the contributors being employees of RapidMiner. The company that develops RapidMiner received a $16 million Series C funding with participation from venture capital firms Nokia Growth Partners, Ascent Venture Partners, Longworth Venture Partners, Earlybird Venture Capital and OpenOcean. OpenOcean partner Michael "Monty" Widenius is a founder of MySQL.

IBM Cognos Analytics

IBM Cognos Business Intelligence is a web-based integrated business intelligence suite by IBM. It provides a toolset for reporting, analytics, scorecarding, and monitoring of events and metrics. The software consists of several components designed to meet the different information requirements in a company. IBM Cognos has components such as IBM Cognos Framework Manager, IBM Cognos Cube Designer, IBM Cognos Transformer.

Basic Components

The elements described below are web-based components that can be accessed from most popular browsers (IBM Cognos specifically supports Mozilla Firefox, Google Chrome and Internet Explorer).

Cognos Connection

Cognos Connection is the Web portal for IBM Cognos BI. It is the starting point for access to all functions provided with the suite. Using this portal, content can be searched in the form of reports, scorecards and agents, it can be managed, structured and displayed. In addition, the portal is used for multiple functions, for example to schedule and distribute reports, for creating tasks, administering the server and the access permissions to content available to different users. You can also create shortcuts, URLs and pages.

Query Studio

Query Studio allows simple queries and self-service reports to answer basic business questions. The report layout can be customized and data can be filtered and sorted. Formatting and creation of diagrams is also supported.

Report Studio

The Report Studio is used to create management reports. It offers two different modes: the professional authoring mode enables users to access the full range of Report Studio functionality. In this mode, users can create any type of report, including charts, maps, lists, and repeat functions. In professional authoring mode all types of Data (relational or multidimensional) can be used, but dynamic data can not be displayed.

The express authoring mode has a more simple user interface, designed for non-technical users. It enables them to create traditional financial or management reports in a more focused user interface. In contrast to the professional authoring mode, the express authoring mode allows the use of dynamic data.

Analysis Studio

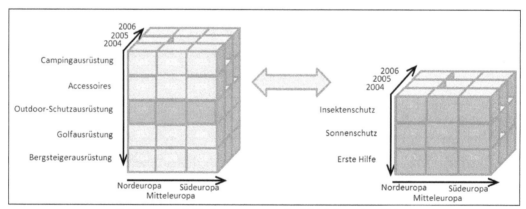

Drill-up and drill-down as example OLAP-functionalities.

Users can create analyses of large data sources and search for background information about an event or action. Multidimensional analysis allows identifying trends and understanding of anomalies or deviations, which are not obvious in other types of reports. Drag-and-drop features, elements and key performance indicators can be included in the analysis, rows and columns can be switched, OLAP-functionalities like drill-up and drill-down can be used to get a deeper understanding about the sources of the information used in the analysis.

Event Studio

The Event Studio is a notification tool that informs about events within the enterprise in real time. Therefore, agents can be created to detect the occurrence of business events or exceptional circumstances, based on the change of specified event or data conditions. A notification may be served by sending an e-mail, its publication in the portal, or by triggering reports. This can be used to handle failure with notification. It is very robust in nature.

Workspace

IBM Cognos Workspace (formerly introduced in version 10.1 as IBM Cognos Business Insight and renamed in version 10.2.0) is a web-based interface that allows business users to use existing IBM Cognos content (report objects) to build interactive workspaces for insight and collaboration.

Workspace Advanced

IBM Cognos Workspace Advanced (formerly introduced in version 10.1 as IBM Cognos Business Insight Advanced and renamed in version 10.2.0) is a web-based interface that allows business users to author/create reports and analyze information.

Windows-based Components

- IBM Cognos Framework Manager.

- IBM Cognos Cube Designer.

- IBM Cognos Transformer.

- IBM Cognos Lifecycle Manager.

- IBM Cognos Map Manager.

Additional Components

Go! Office

The Go! Office component lets users work with IBM Cognos content in their familiar Microsoft Office environment. The component provides access to all IBM Cognos Report contents, including data, metadata, headers and footers, and diagrams. Users can use predefined reports or create new content with Query Studio, Analysis Studio or Report Studio. By importing content into Microsoft Excel users can use the formatting, calculation and presentation features. The created documents can then be imported using Cognos Connection, published and made available for other users.

Go! Search

In Cognos Connection, you can do a full-text search for content contained in reports, analyses, dashboards, metric information and events. When searching, an index of the prompts, titles, headings, column names, row names, data elements and other important fields is used as base. The full text search in IBM Cognos Go! Search is related to the search in regular search engines such as Google. Users can search operators such as +, - or use "" (quotation marks) to change the default behavior of search queries with multiple words. Search terms are not case sensitive, word and spelling variants are included in the results. You can also search for a specific type of entry, such as an agent. The search results are sorted in descending order, the entry with the greatest amount of relevant metadata is displayed at the top of the list. In Analysis Studio, Query Studio and IBM Cognos Viewer, you can either perform a full text search, as also search for content related to the data of the current view.

Go! Dashboards

With IBM Cognos Go! Dashboard, interactive dashboards containing IBM Cognos content and external data sources can be created to fit the information needs of an individual user.

The following items can be added to a dashboard:

Report objects, they are displayed in a Cognos Viewer portlet. Report parts such as lists, crosstabs, and charts are displayed in interactive portlets. Lists or crosstabs can be displayed as a chart and vice versa. Content can be shown or hidden dynamically by the use of sliders and checkboxes. The Cognos Search portlet allows searching for published content. In addition, Web links, Web pages, RSS feeds, and images can be displayed on the dashboard.

The user interface has two modes: In the interactive mode, existing dashboards are viewed and interacted with, creating and editing of dashboards can be done in assembly mode.

Business Applications

According to an IBM publication from 2006, the NYPD uses Cognos systems for the "Real Time Crime Center" to provide real time visualizations of CompStat crime data.

SPSS Modeler

IBM SPSS Modeler is a data mining and text analytics software application from IBM. It is used to build predictive models and conduct other analytic tasks. It has a visual interface which allows users to leverage statistical and data mining algorithms without programming. One of its main aims from the outset was to get rid of unnecessary complexity in data transformations, and to make complex predictive models very easy to use. The first version incorporated decision trees (ID3), and neural networks (backprop), which could both be trained without underlying knowledge of how those techniques worked.

IBM SPSS Modeler was originally named Clementine by its creators, Integral Solutions Limited. This name continued for a while after SPSS's acquisition of the product. SPSS later changed the name to SPSS Clementine, and then later to PASW Modeler. Following IBM's 2009 acquisition of SPSS, the product was renamed IBM SPSS Modeler, its current name.

Early versions of the software were called Clementine and were Unix-based. The first version was released on Jun 9th 1994, after Beta testing at 6 customer sites. Clementine was originally developed by a UK company named Integral Solutions Limited (ISL), in Collaboration with Artificial Intelligence researchers at Sussex University. The original Clementine was implemented in Poplog, which ISL marketed for Sussex University. Clementine mainly used the Poplog languages, Pop11, with some parts written in C for speed (such as the neural network engine), along with additional tools provided as part of Solaris, VMS and various versions of Unix. The tool quickly garnered the attention of the data mining community (at that time in its infancy). In order to reach a larger market, ISL then Ported Poplog to Microsoft Windows using the NutCracker package, later named MKS Toolkit to provide the Unix graphical facilities. Original in many respects, Clementine was the first data mining tool to use an icon based Graphical user interface rather than requiring users to write in a Programming language, though that option remained available for expert users.

In 1998 ISL was acquired by SPSS Inc., who saw the potential for extended development as a commercial data mining tool. In early 2000 the software was developed into a client/server architecture, and shortly afterward the client front-end interface component was completely re-written and replaced with a new Java front-end, which allowed deeper integration with the other tools provided by SPSS.

SPSS Clementine version 7.0: The client front-end runs under Windows. The server back-end Unix variants (Sun, HP-UX, AIX), Linux, and Windows. The graphical user interface is written in Java.

IBM SPSS Modeler 14.0 was the first release of Modeler by IBM.

IBM SPSS Modeler 15, released in June 2012, introduced significant new functionality for Social Network Analysis and Entity Analytics.

Applications

SPSS Modeler has been used in these and other industries:

- Customer analytics and Customer relationship management (CRM)
- Fraud detection and prevention
- Optimizing insurance claims
- Risk management
- Manufacturing quality improvement
- Healthcare quality improvement
- Forecasting demand or sales
- Law enforcement and border security
- Education
- Telecommunications
- Entertainment: e.g., predicting movie box office receipts

Editions

IBM sells the current version of SPSS Modeler (version 18.2.1) in two separate bundles of features. These two bundles are called "editions" by IBM:

- SPSS Modeler Professional: Used for structured data, such as databases, mainframe data systems, flat files or BI systems.
- SPSS Modeler Premium: Includes all the features of Modeler Professional, with the addition of:
  - Text analytics.

Both editions are available in desktop and server configurations.

In addition to the traditional IBM SPSS Modeler desktop installations, IBM now offers the SPSS Modeler interface as an option in the Watson Studio product line which includes Watson Studio (cloud), Watson Studio Local, and Watson Studio Desktop.

KNIME

KNIME the Konstanz Information Miner, is a free and open-source data analytics, reporting and integration platform. KNIME integrates various components for machine learning and data mining through its modular data pipelining concept. A graphical user interface and use of JDBC allows assembly of nodes blending different data sources, including preprocessing (ETL: Extraction, Transformation, Loading), for modeling, data analysis and visualization without, or with only minimal, programming.

Since 2006, KNIME has been used in pharmaceutical research, it also used in other areas like CRM customer data analysis, business intelligence and financial data analysis. KNIME's headquarters are based in Zurich, with additional offices in Konstanz, Berlin, and Austin.

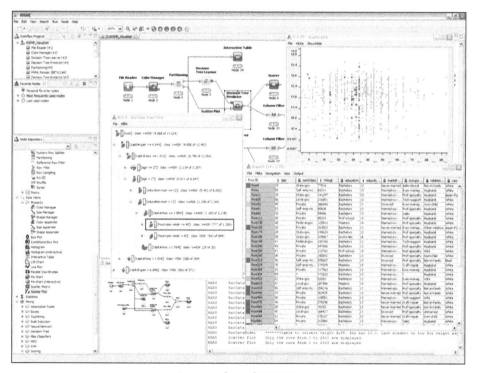

A screenshot of KNIME.

The Development of KNIME was started January 2004 by a team of software engineers at University of Konstanz as a proprietary product. The original developer team headed by Michael Berthold came from a company in Silicon Valley providing software for the pharmaceutical industry. The initial goal was to create a modular, highly scalable and open data processing platform which allowed for the easy integration of different data loading, processing, transformation, analysis and visual exploration modules without the focus on any particular application area. The platform was intended to be a collaboration and research platform and should also serve as an integration platform for various other data analysis projects.

In 2006, the first version of KNIME was released and several pharmaceutical companies started using KNIME and a number of life science software vendors began integrating their tools into KNIME. As of 2012, KNIME is in use by over 15,000 actual users (i.e. not counting downloads but users regularly retrieving updates when they become available) not only in the life sciences but also at banks, publishers, car manufacturer, telcos, consulting firms, and various other industries but also at a large number of research groups worldwide. Latest updates to KNIME Server and KNIME Big Data Extensions, provide support for Apache Spark 2.3, Parquet and HDFS-type storage.

For the sixth year in a row, KNIME has been placed as a leader for Data Science and Machine Learning Platforms in Gartner's Magic Quadrant.

Internals

KNIME allows users to visually create data flows (or pipelines), selectively execute some or all analysis steps, and later inspect the results, models, and interactive views. KNIME is written in Java and based on Eclipse and makes use of its extension mechanism to add plugins providing additional functionality. The core version already includes hundreds of modules for data integration (file I/O, database nodes supporting all common database management systems through JDBC or native connectors: SQLite, SQL Server, MySQL, PostgreSQL, Vertica and H2), data transformation (filter, converter, splitter, combiner, joiner) as well as the commonly used methods of statistics, data mining, analysis and text analytics. Visualization supports with the free Report Designer extension. KNIME workflows can be used as data sets to create report templates that can be exported to document formats like doc, ppt, xls, pdf and others. Other capabilities of KNIME are:

- KNIMEs core-architecture allows processing of large data volumes that are only limited by the available hard disk space (not limited to the available RAM). E.g. KNIME allows analysis of 300 million customer addresses, 20 million cell images and 10 million molecular structures.

- Additional plugins allows the integration of methods for text mining, Image mining, as well as time series analysis.

- KNIME integrates various other open-source projects, e.g. machine learning algorithms from Weka, H2O, Spark, the R project and LIBSVM; but also plotly, JFreeChart, ImageJ, and the Chemistry Development Kit.

KNIME is implemented in Java but also allows for wrappers calling other code in addition to providing nodes that allow to run Java, Python, Perl and other code fragments.

License

As of version 2.1, KNIME is released under GPLv3 with an exception that allows others to use the well defined node API to add proprietary extensions. This allows also commercial SW vendors to add wrappers calling their tools from KNIME.

SharePoint

Microsoft SharePoint is a document management and collaboration platform that helps companies manage archives, documents, reports and other content that is vital to the business process. Industries in all sectors use SharePoint, but the platform focuses on enterprise content management. SharePoint use cases can be found in any department within an organization.

SharePoint is configured using a web browser and it provides most of its capabilities via a web UI and web applications. It can be used to manipulate content and site structure, create and delete sites, enable or disable product features, configure basic workflows, and manage analytics.

New and Updated SharePoint 2016 Features

SharePoint 2016 is delivered via Microsoft's Azure Cloud, but Microsoft also offers an on-premises version for organizations that prefer to keep their data in-house for compliance or security reasons.

Like SharePoint 2013, SharePoint 2016 is part of the Office 365 suite, where it is known as SharePoint Online. The on-premises version is known as SharePoint Server 2016.

Notable features in Microsoft SharePoint 2016 include:

- Access services: Users can support Office 365 apps or download Excel features to pivot Microsoft Access database tables. Microsoft also improved related item control so users can add new items.

- Compliance features: The In-place Hold Policy Center and the Compliance Center enable administrators to build policies and apply them in their SharePoint environment. The updated features allow users to delete documents from their OneDrive for Business sites.

- Document library accessibility: Users can use landmarks on a page to make it easier to navigate, use keyboard shortcuts to document tasks, use announcements for upload progress, use improved callout readings and use updates for help documentation.

- Expanded file names: Support for file names with special characters, leading with dots and longer than 128 characters will no longer be blocked.

- Hybrid: Better integration with Office 365 tools and services, including Delve, Sway and Office Graph.

- Information rights management: A subset of digital rights management that uses technology to protect sensitive information or intellectual property from unauthorized access.

- Large file support: Users can now exceed the previous 2 GB limit for files. Though there's no real limit, Microsoft recommends a 10 GB maximum.

- MinRole: Administrators can now install only the roles they want on SharePoint servers.

- Mobile experience: Touch-friendly mobile interface. Users can also switch from mobile view to PC view.

- Open document format (ODF): This enables users to create files in a document library and save files in ODF to edit later with a program of the user's choosing.

- Project server: Project managers can request resources from other resource managers and use a heat map functionality to see where resources spend time. They can also create multiple timelines. The project server also has improved backup and restoration capabilities.

- SharePoint business intelligence: Users have added access to business intelligence, including Power Pivot Gallery, scheduled data research, workbooks as a data source, the Power Pivot management dashboard, Power View reports, Power View subscriptions and report alerts.

- Improvements to sharing features: Users can see who is sharing a folder and can invite and approve or deny access requests easily.

- Sites page pinning: Users can pin sites to follow them when on premises and through Office 365.

More recently, Microsoft added the ability to create SharePoint team sites via Office 365 to provide a location where teams can work on projects and share information from anywhere. A team site includes a group of related web pages, as well as a default document library for files, lists for data management and web parts that are customizable.

Microsoft's focus on artificial intelligence and virtual reality will shape future versions of SharePoint. One example is the 2018 launch of SharePoint spaces, where users wear virtual reality headsets to interact with content from every angle to visualize and manipulate data and product models.

Depreciated Microsoft SharePoint Features

SharePoint 2016 is focused on traditional document management. Microsoft has stripped away the collaboration, social media and enterprise search functions that are included in other Office 365 offerings such as:

- Delve: A data visualization and discovery tool that incorporates elements of social networking and machine learning with the search capabilities of the Office 365 suite.

- Office Graph: A back-end tool in the Office 365 Suite that facilitates search across integrated applications and applies machine learning to organizational interactions and content use.

- Sway: A presentation tool in the Office suite.

- Teams: A work collaboration tool that allows employees to interact on a working document wherever they are.

- Yammer: A private microblogging and collaboration platform for enterprise social networking.

While Microsoft is focusing the lion's share of its development roadmap on SharePoint Online, it will continue to release an on-premises version of SharePoint, as customers may have compliance requirements that require certain data be kept on premises or because they cannot migrate all their data to the cloud.

The following features that have been removed from the SharePoint 2016 server:

- SharePoint Foundation: SharePoint Foundation is a free edition that provides a secure, web-based collaboration platform. It is not available in SharePoint Server 2016, but is still available in SharePoint 2013.

- Stand-alone install mode: This feature is no longer available on SharePoint 2016. It has been replaced by the MinRole farm topology.

- Forefront identity manager client (FIM): FIM synchronizes between Active Directory and SharePoint. SharePoint 2016 does not use FIM, but instead uses Microsoft Identity Manager 2016 or another third-party tool.

- Excel services: Excel capabilities are no longer hosted on SharePoint Server. Instead, it is part of Excel Online in Office Online Server.

- SharePoint BI capabilities: Power Pivot and Power View for BI solutions are not deployed in SharePoint 2016. Power Pivot for SharePoint and Power View for SharePoint add-ins can only be deployed with SharePoint 2016 when using SQL Server 2016.

- Tags and notes: Users can still create new tags and access any existing ones, but Microsoft discourages using the feature, as it will be removed in the next release of SharePoint.

- Work management service application: This application has been removed from Share-Point 2016, including My Tasks and other associated Exchange Task Sync features.

SharePoint 2016 Architecture Changes and Options

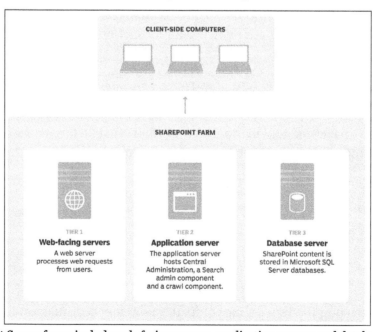

SharePoint Server farms include web-facing servers, application servers and database servers.

Because SharePoint Server 2016 has the same code as SharePoint Online, on-premises customers have the same benefits of support and performance for their SharePoint server farms thanks to a few architecture changes.

SharePoint 2013 and its previous editions relied on service deployments to patch problem servers. SharePoint 2016 has MinRole, a streamlined topology that has a server in a SharePoint farm that runs an explicit set of services based on its role, and which has no other services turned on. This allows for more flexibility, easy fixes and quick updates to each server resulting in faster and more reliable service.

There are four architectural models for SharePoint 2016:

- SharePoint Online: SharePoint is delivered using a software-as-a-service subscription model. Microsoft provides updates automatically, but the customer is responsible for SharePoint management.

- SharePoint hybrid: The combination of a SharePoint Online subscription with an on-premises version of SharePoint. With this approach, customers can meld SharePoint Online services into their overall SharePoint environment while creating a bridge to ultimately migrate SharePoint sites and apps to the cloud.

- SharePoint in Azure: Customers can extend their on-premises SharePoint farms to Microsoft's Azure infrastructure as a service cloud for production, disaster recovery and testing SharePoint Server 2016 environments.

- SharePoint on premises: Customers maintain control over all the planning, deployments, maintenance and customizations of their SharePoint environments within their own data centers.

References

- Boriana L. Milenova and Marcos M. Campos (2002); O-Cluster: Scalable Clustering of Large High Dimensional Data Sets, ICDM '02 Proceedings of the 2002 IEEE International Conference on Data Mining, pages 290-297, ISBN 0-7695-1754-4

- Data-mining-software-systems: financesonline.com, Retrieved 20 June, 2019

- "Python eats away at R: Top Software for Analytics, Data Science, Machine Learning in 2018: Trends and Analysis". Www.kdnuggets.com. Retrieved 2018-10-05

- Nisbet, Robert; Elder, John; Miner, Gary (2009). Handbook of Statistical Analysis and Data Mining Applications. Elsevier. Pp. 391–415. ISBN 978-0-12-374765-5

- Tiwari, Abhishek; Sekhar, Arvind K.T. (October 2007). "Workflow based framework for life science informatics". Computational Biology and Chemistry. 31 (5–6): 305–319. Doi:10.1016/j.compbiolchem.2007.08.009

Permissions

We would like to thank the editorial team for lending their expertise to make the book truly unique. They have played a crucial role in the development of this book. Without their invaluable contributions this book wouldn't have been possible. They have made vital efforts to compile up to date information on the varied aspects of this subject to make this book a valuable addition to the collection of many professionals and students.

This book was conceptualized with the vision of imparting up-to-date and integrated information in this field. To ensure the same, a matchless editorial board was set up. Every individual on the board went through rigorous rounds of assessment to prove their worth. After which they invested a large part of their time researching and compiling the most relevant data for our readers.

The editorial board has been involved in producing this book since its inception. They have spent rigorous hours researching and exploring the diverse topics which have resulted in the successful publishing of this book. They have passed on their knowledge of decades through this book. To expedite this challenging task, the publisher supported the team at every step. A small team of assistant editors was also appointed to further simplify the editing procedure and attain best results for the readers.

Apart from the editorial board, the designing team has also invested a significant amount of their time in understanding the subject and creating the most relevant covers. They scrutinized every image to scout for the most suitable representation of the subject and create an appropriate cover for the book.

The publishing team has been an ardent support to the editorial, designing and production team. Their endless efforts to recruit the best for this project, has resulted in the accomplishment of this book. They are a veteran in the field of academics and their pool of knowledge is as vast as their experience in printing. Their expertise and guidance has proved useful at every step. Their uncompromising quality standards have made this book an exceptional effort. Their encouragement from time to time has been an inspiration for everyone.

The publisher and the editorial board hope that this book will prove to be a valuable piece of knowledge for students, practitioners and scholars across the globe.

Index

Printed in the USA
CPSIA information can be obtained
at www.ICGtesting.com
JSHW051415221024
72173JS00006B/1365